ACHIEVING OUR HUMANITY

ACHIEVING OUR HUMANITY

THE IDEA OF THE POSTRACIAL FUTURE

Emmanuel Chukwudi Eze

ROUTLEDGE

NEW YORK AND LONDON

Published in 2001 by
Routledge
29 West 35th Street
New York, NY 10001

Published in Great Britain by
Routledge
11 New Fetter Lane
London EC4P 4EE

Routledge is an imprint of the Taylor & Francis Group.

Design and layout by Lisa Vaughn, Two of Cups Design Studio, Inc.

Library of Congress Cataloging-in-Publication Data
Eze, Emmanuel Chukwudi.
    Achieving our humanity : the idea of the postracial future / Emmanuel Chukwudi Eze.
    p. cm.
    Includes bibliographical references and index.
    ISBN – 0-415-92940-7 (alk. paper) – ISBN 0-415-92941-5 (pbk.: alk. paper)
    1. Race relations. 2. Racism. I. Title.

HT1521.E94   2001
305.8—dc21   00-068965

Printed on acid-free, 250-year-life paper.
Manufactured in the United States of America.
10 9 8 7 6 5 4 3 2 1

For Udoka, Ada, and Nnamdi
Ifé di oku ga-emecha jie oyi

and for their mother, Katherine

Contents

*beyond the idea
of race w/o denying the fact [of racism]
that racial identitys [are more important aspects]
of modern experience*

How would an African or a black person anywhere think about the world—the global modern world which thinks of "blacks" as a race—beyond the idea of race but without denying the fact that racial identities and racism are important aspects of the modern experience? In what ways could one transcend the race-conscious traditions of both modern European and African thought which sustain ideologies of race and racism while recognizing that there are in these intellectual traditions powerful tools against racialism and racism? *transcend race conscious traditions which support race + racism while recognizing tools when against racism*

Must we always have racial identities? If one answers "yes," then, is *a racial* there a way to racialize oneself or others without at the same time becoming racist—or directly encouraging racism? What would racial identities look like if there were no intrinsic or extrinsic racisms to sustain them?[1] If one answers "no" to the original question, then how does one explain and remedy the racist consequences of current scientific, philosophical, and juridical racialism? Of course, the cause-and-effect relationship between racialism and racism is not obvious; the relationship may be indirect or even tenuous. But it is unimaginable to think that this relationship does not at all exist, or that it is insignificant. This is why it is of interest, I think, to explore to what extent modern philosophical thought has contributed to the formation and maintenance of ideologies of racialism and, indirectly, racism—in academic discourse as in general culture. To notice, for example, that philosophy is not indifferent or irrelevant to modern race discourse is also to ask if the discipline could reform itself in ways that preclude a covert or overt, conscious or unconscious theoretical and institutional support of racism.

I acknowledge that it is quite unfamiliar to many in my audience to think of modern philosophy as having, for example, a "racial unconscious." Following Hegel, we have accustomed ourselves to thinking that philosophy itself is consciousness come into its own existence. I presume, however, that modern philosophy, as it manifests itself in texts and institutions in Europe, Africa, and the United States, has a racial unconscious. To transcend both the racialism and racism implicit in these philosophic traditions would require—from no other than these philosophy traditions themselves—a new mode of self-enlightenment: an ethnographic critique.

The prospect or even substance of a postracial philosophy does not suggest a break with the modern traditions (this is not an unreflective assertion of another aspect of a popular if little understood "postmodernity"), but it requires a recognition that modern philosophy's pretension to universality and cross-cultural values has often been just that: a pretense. The virtue of an ethnographic critique of modern traditions of philosophy is that while maintaining the strength of modern philosophy's universal achievements, it also contextualizes these achievements in the racial and ethnic attitudes that limit them—in view of calling on philosophy to further transcend these limits. The project of a postracial philosophy is, as it were, an effort to enlighten further modern philosophy's projects of enlightenment.

The idea of a critical and progressive self-enlightenment of philosophy is not alien to the histories of philosophy in Africa or Europe. Husserl speaks of this in his understanding of philosophical criticism in *The Idea of Philosophy*. An ethnographic critique is also compatible with the idea of critique as advocated or practiced by Descartes, Hume, or Kant, or Adotevi, Hountondji, or Appiah in African philosophy. The virtue of philosophy's radical autocriticism is taken for granted in the quip "In philosophy 'attack' is the highest form of flattery." Autocriticism is necessary and healthy for philosophy because, as the more distinctively African proverb puts it, a tussle does not kill a robust child.

A most useful way to initiate an ethnographic critique of modern philosophy is, I think, to recognize philosophy's debts to ethnography and anthropology.[2] We can also start in the conjunction of philosophy and ethnography (the so-called ethnophilosophy) at one of anthropology's most favorable hunting grounds: Africa. In what ways does the idea of Africa and the historical experiences of Africans as blacks figure in the modern philosophical imagination? In what ways does "Africa"—or more strictly what Toni Morrison calls "Africanism"[3]—structure the modernity of (or the "whiteness" often claimed for) modern philosophy? How does the prefiguration of the African as "black" negatively and positively structure modern philosophy's ideas of reason, culture, and humanity?

One of course would speak of Africa and Africans with reference to a geographical continent, but the extravagant concept of Africanism refers to a more dynamic and imaginary process: the process that constitutes the African as "wild," archaic, or static—a suitable opposite to an idea of "the Modern." In contrast to Africanism, Chinua Achebe noted that the identity of the African is always in the making; "there isn't a final identity that is African," even if one also acknowledges that the word African has acquired established, stable meanings in modern times.[4] It is from such stable meanings, for example, that one assumes that "real" Africans are a race—a race of blacks.

Sociologists say that in most languages, to be assigned the label "black," racially or otherwise, is to be asked to negotiate a label that, a priori, is morally partisan. In *Rituals of Blood: The Consequences of Slavery in Two American Centuries*, Orlando Patterson enumerates the following coded meanings under the entry "black" from a casual search of *Webster's New Twentieth Century Dictionary*:

> 1. figuratively, dismal, gloomy, sullen, forbidding, or the like; destitute of moral light or goodness; mournful; calamitous; evil; wicked; atrocious; thus Shakespeare speaks of black deeds, thoughts, envy, tidings, despair, etc. 2. soiled; dirty. 3. disgraceful. 4. without hope, as a black future. 5. inveterate, confirmed, deep-dyed, as a black villain. 6. humorous or satirical in a morbid, cynical or savage way, as black comedy.

On the other hand, in the same dictionary the entry "white" carries moral meanings exactly opposite to "black":

> 1. having the color of pure snow and milk . . . opposite of black. 2. morally and spiritually pure; spotless; innocent. 3. free from evil

intent; harmless; as white magic; a white lie. 4. happy; fortunate; auspicious. 5. (a) having light colored skin; Caucasian; (b) of or controlled by the white race; as *white* supremacy; (c) [from notions of racial superiority.] [Slang.] honest; honorable; fair; dependable. 6. favorite.

Patterson concludes, "It is preposterous to assume that when Americans call each other 'white' and 'black' they are somehow able to mentally bracket these historically and culturally ingrained and dictionary sanctioned meanings."[5]

The stability of the binary investments of moral meanings in otherwise everyday words that refer primarily to nonhuman colors is not invalidated by counterexamples in which "black" may be valued more than "white"—for example, a "black horse" or "black leather." It is obvious that these classical and popular ideas of black as strong, virile, exotic, even dangerous, ambiguous, and liminal are derived from the original binary constructions, so that the preference for black may be a desire for the unusual, the special, the different—a desire for a power perceived as out of the ordinary and therefore to be reckoned with, an assertion of the counternormal as countercultural. Modern philosophic traditions—and those of other professions—have used the ideas of blackness and whiteness as morality-regulating principles.

Speaking about the English language, Winthrop Jordan noted that long before there were actual "black" Africans in England, the language had already sanctioned the word "black" for describing those experiences the English found morally objectionable. What is the source of this original identification of blackness with moral evil or unacceptable state of being? Jordan's historical approach is inadequate to provide an answer.

In the philosophic tradition, one could appeal to Kant, the *Critique of Judgment* in particular. Here Kant tries to reconstruct the infrastructures of the transcendental faculty of the imagination, a faculty whose dialectical, reality-constituting operations he explains in the language of "pleasure" and "unpleasure."[6] As aesthetic principles, pleasure and unpleasure are the "subjective side of a representation which is *in*capable of becoming [itself] an element of cognition." The "representation" is imaginary precisely because, though dynamic in the operations of the mind, it nevertheless lacks cognitive grounding; though not a component of cognition, it is a "final" regulative principle of cognition. Kant explains: "The finality of a thing, so far as represented in our perception of it, is in no way a quality of the object itself (for a quality of this kind is not one that can be perceived), although it can be inferred from a cognition of things." He also adds: "In the finality . . . which is prior to the cognition of an object . . . we have the subjective quality belonging to it that is incapable of becoming a constituent of knowledge."[7] Following Kant, one could suggest that racial "blackness" and "whiteness" are indeed original and primal qualities attendant to acts of perception: the "black" person need not be actually black—as the "white" person need not be white. The African or African-descended person is deemed black not necessarily because the skin color is black, just as the white European is white not by virtue of his or her skin color. It seems that beyond what is given in cognitive or rational apprehension, the modern mind, through known processes of the constitution of its aesthetic experience, sees "black" and "white" of peoples or individuals. Philosophically, this interpretation is hardly revolutionary, for what we have is no more than evidence for an argument popularized (in philosophy of language) by Wittgenstein, namely, that seeing is seeing as.[8] The problem posed by this epistemological condition is, however, as Kant also enoted, that "terror" and "madness" easily originate from the same zone of mind that allows humans to see this as that.[9]

Richard Rorty, quite familiar with the racial terrain in the United States, writes in a recent book about the "sadistic pleasure" derived by racists in attaching a "stigma [to their] victim[s] of socially accepted sadism."[10] For Rorty, it is unfortunate that it was only in the 1960s that most radical and progressive intellectuals in his country, philosophers included, realized that the "sadistic humiliation of black Americans" had origins beyond poverty—or even ignorance. He explains:

> One of the good things which happened in the Sixties was that the American Left began to realize that its economic determinism had been too simplistic. Sadism was recognized as having deeper roots than economic insecurity. The delicious pleasure to be had from creating a class of putative inferiors and then humiliating individual members of that class was seen as Freud saw it—as something which would be relished even if everybody were rich.[11]

Before Freud, Kant—and before Kant, Hume, in his theories of sensual impressions and the role of these impressions in the constitution of the states of what we call "mind"—had laid out the basis of a theoretical understanding of humans that Freud would later mold into an autonomous field of psychological and psychoanalytic research. It is therefore not extravagant on our part to seek to return to Hume and Kant as starting points for an understanding of the philosophical and political significance of the modern constitution of Africans and Afros (African—descended peoples) as a "race" of blacks.

It is easy to show that prominent modern European philosophers were eager to rationalize their cultural assumptions by arguing that white and black racial labels describe actual superior and inferior moral characters; some of them in fact produced theories arguing that the racial labels described the true "nature" of those who bore the labels. If the English dictionary got the meanings it attributes to the words "black" and "white" from everyday speech, philosophers were ready to provide the words and their unreflective everyday usages with sophisticated epistemological and transcendental justifications.

Along with the general—and some would say, boring—discussions of the anthropological backgrounds to modern philosophy in chapter 1, I hope that the technical discussions of Hume and Kant in chapters 2 and 3 open up a debate about whether or not "black" and "white," as social-conceptual categories, are indeed morally *a priori* ideas. Are the ideas of racial blackness and whiteness indeed natural, as Hume makes them out to be, or transcendental, as Kant argues? At the same time, Africans and African-descended theorists such as Léopold Sédar Senghor, W. E. B. Du Bois, and Aimé Césaire argued about what it means to be "black," a notion which they have now invested with more positive moral content, with palpable longings for racial freedom and equality. The impact of these moral arguments and debates among black leaders of opinion, in the uses of the revalued ideas of blackness in the formation of black and the critique of white ideologies of identities, are discernible in the processes of evolution of contemporary black consciousness. Today, throughout the world, in labels such as "Afro-Caribbean," "Afro-British," "Afro-American" or "African American," the transformations in self-naming—from "Negroes" to "blacks" to "Afros," in these examples—do not unambiguously reflect an end to earlier racist "white" thinking. Modern Africans, it seems, name themselves in awareness of a racial imperative: the imperative of whiteness as a normative idea which, even today, seems to operate to consign diverse Afros in diverse nations to a "race" of inferiors.

Are there present realities and theoretical dispositions that could allow us to think about future identities of Africans and African-descended peoples as national and transnational social and cultural formations without the racial principle, or its white imperative? I would like to think that this is possible. Historical evidence suggests that it is not just having a common geographical origin in Africa but more palpably the experience of having been "blackened" in the modern world that sustains, for many individuals and groups, the various identifications with Africa.[12] To the extent therefore that modern Afros can recognize themselves in a common anguished and ecstatic historical encounter with self-whitened Europeans and in the transforming experiences of modernity itself, to the extent that blacks can mutually recognize themselves in the vitality of immensely mobile and transatlantically shared cultural values and survival skills—including those fashioned in the crucibles of slavery, colonialism, and racial degradation—and, finally, to the extent that "race" continues to be valued as a means of recognition or apportionment of worth, the social identity "black" raises questions not only about "the future of the race" but also about the future of race itself—anyone's race. Perhaps only the future can address these questions, but I see no harm in reading the present for signs of this future.

Unlike those who wish to prove that races are illusions, this book should invite one to ask, rather: What are we allowed to think about the future existence of races? Specifically, should philosophy continue to provide arguments to promote definitions of human beings according to race—especially in those countries which traditionally assumed race to be an inalienable human quality? It may well occur to both professional philosophers and non-philosophers to retort: Are philosophers part of the best groups of thinkers to which one should address questions about race? It has always been difficult, it seems, for modern philosophy to think of itself as race conscious or as contributing to social and cultural race consciousness, in national and global polities. But we are not bound to understand modern philosophy—whether in Africa, Europe, or America—only in those ways that philosophy explains itself to itself.

Modern philosophy anywhere may not see itself as "racial" because of two forms of cultivated ignorance. First, the initiates often are ready to deny that the very idea of philosophy has something to do with race, whether in the constitution of the idea or in its social applications. Philosophy, for the practitioners of this first form of historical denial, concerns itself only with pure and universal questions about whether humans—any humans anywhere—have souls, the nature of the mind, the relationship between mind and body, the *a priori* conditions of knowledge, the nature of beauty, justice, and other such sublime topics. To suggest to someone who thinks about modern philosophy only in this restricted manner that the philosophical questions just enumerated have had core racial assumptions appears to be a scandalous enterprise. But would it help to show that major past philosophers—even those idolized as "pure" thinkers—also thought and wrote about race in serious ways? Or would the mere reference to dated and often racist works produced by the pure philosophers only collude with the interests of the one who already wishes to discredit our questions, without a hearing, as sensationalism?

To think that modern philosophy is immune from the intellectual processes that fashioned and consolidated the modern idea of race, or from the modern national and international social contestations carried out in the name of race, is to overlook the existence of large bodies of significant work done in the area, especially in the seventeenth and eighteenth centuries. Second, modern philosophy's role in formulating our racial concepts and categories of thought is easily overlooked by those who claim that, whatever this role might have been during the High Modern period of the seventeenth and eighteenth centuries, philosophy today no longer has anything to do with race because the sciences, especially genetics and population biology, have taken over and advanced the territory beyond anything philosophy could currently contribute. The proponents of this view point to the fact that postmodern philosophical literature is not wedded to the idea of humans as rational beings constituted by "essences," racial or otherwise. Hence, to continue to associate philosophy with race would equal the error that, it is assumed, the modern philosophers made when they wrote about race.

There is a simple and effective objection to this brand of postracial postmodernism: there exist not only relationships of discontinuities but also of continuities between modern and postmodern traditions of philosophy, so that our "postmodern" thought hardly connotes a total break with key experiences and themes in the modern. Like most, I would be pleased to hear that that race has indeed been postmodernly transcended; but the contemporary reality of social experiences instructs otherwise. If a postmodern neutrality on race is dogmatically asserted by the opponent, we must not hesitate to enumerate our evidence: the everyday life-and-death events of racism.[13]

NOTES

1. The notions of "intrinsic" and "extrinsic" racism were explored in *The Anatomy of Racism*, ed. David T. Goldberg (Minneapolis: University of Minnesota Press, 1990), in particular in the essay "Racisms," by Kwame Anthony Appiah.

2. See, for example, Clifford Geertz, *Available Lights: Anthropological Reflections on Philosophical Topics*, Princeton, NJ: Princeton University Press, 2000.

3. Toni Morrison, *Playing in the Dark: Whiteness and the Literary Imagination*, Cambridge, MA: Harvard University Press, 1992.

4. Chinua Achebe, quoted in Kwame Anthony Appiah, *In My Father's House: Africa in the Philosophy of Culture*, New York: Oxford University Press, 1992, p. 173.

5. Orlando Patterson, *Rituals of Blood: Consequences of Slavery in Two American Centuries*, Washington, D.C.: Civitas/Counterpoint, 1998, p. xxi.

6. Immanuel Kant, *The Critique of Judgment*, London: William Benton, 1952.

7. Ibid., p. 471.

8. Ludwig Wittgenstein, *Philosophical Investigations*, Oxford: Blackwell, 198?.

9. Immanuel Kant, in *Anthropology from a Pragmatic Point of View* (trans. Mary J. Gregor, The Hague: Martinus Nijhoff, 1974); see Book One, "On the Cognitive Powers," particularly pp. 14–15.

10. Richard Rorty, *Achieving Our Country: Leftist Thought in Twentieth-Century America*, Cambridge, MA: Harvard University Press, 1998, p. 80. The emphasis is mine.

11. Ibid., p. 76. My emphasis.

12. See, for the example of one—but a paradigmatic—man, Du Bois's personal reflections in "On the Conservation of Races," as reprinted in Emmanuel Chukwudi Eze, *African Philosophy: An Anthology* (Oxford: Blackwell, 1998), chapter 32.

13. In a remarkable coincidence—remarkable since it could look like a god decided to attack the country on all fronts with pestilence—the hottest topic in the 2001 British political cycle, after foot-and-mouth disease, is the pervasive anxiety that post imperial Britain has become a "mongrel" race. On May 11, 2001, in Germany, the appropriately named, charity-infused, Christian Democratic Party adopted a campaign platform that explicitly too the position that Germany "is not a . . . country for immigration." The racial scenes

on the streets of the cities and sometimes little town in these countries echo the racism that drive the political debates: a Romani, a Sinti, or an African immigrant murdered, beaten, or robbed her and there—sometimes by the police. Bruce Springsteen's "American Skin (41 Shots)" could have been inspired by incidents in Berlin or London. And in a recent study of the 2000 U.S. Census, blacks and non-blacks are residentially more segregated than they were fifteen years ago. An international newspaper ran the story with a quote from a prominent African-American professor at Harvard University who said he moved his family from one city to another because he felt "uncomfortable" by the racial attitudes of his first neighbors. This was a piece of news I found interesting, for when I taught at a university in Pennsylvania and lived only a few blocks from the campus, I woke up every fourth of July to racial slurs scrawled graffiti-style on the outside walls of my house.

ACHIEVING OUR HUMANITY

PART I

ARGUING WITH THE PAST

CHAPTER 1

THE MODERN INVENTION OF RACE

THE COGITO

How did the origins of modern philosophy and the science of anthropology provide theoretical grounds for the formation of race as a modern idea? The choice of philosophical figures included in the following discussion—Descartes, Hume, and Kant—is not arbitrary, although they represent an intellectual lineage that takes only indirect interest in, for example, the romantic tendencies represented by Pascal, Rousseau, or Herder. The discussion therefore makes no claims to exhausting all that could be said about philosophy and race in modern philosophy; it hopes to illustrate only the dominant patterns of thought that account for the nineteenth and twentieth centuries' beliefs about the varieties of humans, beliefs that underlie many of our present racial practices.

The modern masters of philosophy tenaciously, and extravagantly, investigated the nature of "man." In 1637, Descartes, in *Discourse on Method*, established the question concerning *l'homme* as one whose resolution should determine the foundation, the "first principle," on the basis of which all of philosophy and science should be reconstructed. In asking "Who am I?" Descartes thought, I am inquiring not only ontologically about what I am constituted of but also epistemologically about what can I know. The metaphysical reflections on the nature of the soul, in the *Discourse* as in the *Meditations*, are therefore anthropologico-philosophical exercises, guided by the need to establish, with certainty, the rational essence of the human.

In a carefully composed letter about the *Meditations* to the faculty of theology in Paris ("those most learned and most illustrious men, the Dean and Doctors of the Sacred Faculty of Theology of Paris"), Descartes pleaded:

> Gentlemen: My reason for offering you this work is so logical, and after you have learned its plan you will also, I am sure, have so logical a reason to take it under your protection, that I believe nothing will recommend it to you more than a brief statement of what I herein propose to do. I have always thought that the two questions, of God and the soul, were the principal questions among those that should be demonstrated by rational philosophy rather than theology.[1]

The requirement that "rational philosophy" demonstrate the principal question of the soul contextualizes the famous "cogito" passage: "I noticed that, during the time I wanted to think that everything was false, it was necessary that I, who thought thus, be something. And noticing that this truth—*I think, therefore I am*—was so firm and so certain that the most extravagant suppositions of the skeptics were unable to shake it, I judged that I could accept it without scruple as the first principle of the philosophy I was seeking."[2] From here onward the question becomes "Who is this 'I'?," a question that Descartes discussed with equal gusto:

> Examining with attention what I was, I saw that I could pretend that I had no body and that there was no world nor any place where I was, but that I could not pretend, on that account, that I did not exist; and that, on the contrary, from the very fact that I thought about doubting the truth of other things, it followed very evidently and very certainly that I existed. On the other hand, had I simply stopped thinking, even if all the rest of what I have ever imagined is true, I would have no reason to believe that I existed. From this I knew that *I was a substance the whole essence or nature of which was merely to think.*[3]

The essence of the human, then, is the capacity to think. Although many of Descartes's views about other things (including his proof of God's existence) have been defeated by subsequent thinkers, his essential definition of "man" as a being whose reason for being is "merely to think" has remained acceptable. Even Pascal, a contemporary and dedicated opponent, conceded that one "can easily conceive of a man without hands, feet, head. . . . But I cannot conceive of man without thought."[4] In our century, Paul Ricoeur writes that Descartes's "I think, therefore I am" is "the reflective foundation of every proposition concerning man."[5] From Pascal to Ricoeur, the validity of Descartes's assertion, in its original form or with subsequent qualifications in response to criticism from figures like Nietzsche, continues to generate conversations that dominate modern and postmodern philosophy.

In Germany, Kant's *Logic* reformulated Descartes's anthropological thesis. Although Kant took more seriously the consideration that cultures may differ in their conception of human subjectivity, so that "I think, therefore I am" is not the only interesting thing that could be said about human nature, in the *Logic* the question of determining the rational nature of man remained the major focus. Unchanged was the conviction that the most important work for philosophy was the accurate description of the interior and exterior structures of humanity, and how to conserve and improve it. When he classified the field of philosophy into four categories: 1. What can I know? 2. What ought I to do? 3. What may I hope? and 4. What is man? Kant remarked that the first question belongs to metaphysics, the second to morality, the third to religion, but all could be reckoned to the fourth, anthropology, because "at bottom . . . the first three questions relate to the last."[6]

In *Anthropology from a Pragmatic Point of View*, Kant expressed the view that "the aim of every step in the cultural progress which is man's education is to assign this knowledge and skill he has acquired to the world's use. But *the most important object in the world to which he can apply them is man*."[7] The *Anthropology* was, accordingly, intended to explain the internal and external nature of the "earthly being endowed with reason"; it would be a "systematic treatise comprising our knowledge of man."[8]

Some have argued that the preoccupation with "man" in the *Logic* and *Anthropology* is unrelated to the epistemological, moral, and aesthetic issues that were the focus of the three critical works: the *Critique of Pure Reason*, *Critique of Practical Reason*, and *Critique of Judgment* (see chapter 4). But the anthropological and epistemological aspects of Kant's oeuvre are thematically not unconnected. Compare, for example, these passages from the *Anthropology* and the *Critique of Pure Reason*—passages that address the central issue of the transcendental unity of human consciousness.

> The fact that man can have the idea "I" raises him infinitely above all the other beings living on earth. By this he is a *person*; and by virtue of his unity of consciousness through all the changes he may undergo, he is one and the same person—that is, a being altogether different in rank and dignity from *things*, such as irrational animals, which we can dispose of as we please. This holds even if he cannot yet say "I"; for he still has it in mind. So any language must *think* "I" when it speaks in the first person, even if it has no special word to express it. For this power (the ability to think) is *understanding*.[9] (*Anthropology*)

> The thought that the representations given in intuition one and all belong to me, is . . . equivalent to the thought that I unite them in one self-consciousness, or can at least so unite them. . . . In other words, only in so far as I can grasp the manifold of the representations in one consciousness, do I call them one and all *mine*. For otherwise I should have as many-coloured and diverse a self as I have representations of which I am conscious to myself . . . this principle of the necessary unity of apperception is itself, indeed, an identical, and therefore analytic, proposition [because] through the "I," as simple representation, nothing manifold is given. . . . An understanding in which through self-consciousness all the manifold would *eo ipso* be given would be *intuitive*; our understanding can only *think*.[10] (*Critique of Pure Reason*)

The two passages address, respectively, the nature and the function of the "I" within the human frame. The anthropological definition of "Man's Inner Self" (*Anthropology*) is cognitivist; and the epistemological definition of the transcendental consciousness (*Critique of Pure Reason*) is also anthropological.

For another example: consider the longer passage in the section "On Distinctness and Indistinctness in Consciousness of Our Ideas," in the *Anthropology*:

> When we can *distinguish* one object from another in our ideas, we have CLEAR consciousness of them. But if the *composition* of our ideas is also clear, our consciousness of them is DISTINCT. Only when our ideas are distinct does a collection of them become *knowledge*. Knowledge, then, implies an ordering in the manifold, since any composition involving consciousness presupposes unity of consciousness and so a rule for the composition. The opposite of a distinct idea is not a *confused* one but merely an *indistinct* one. Only composite things can be confused, for in simple things there is neither order nor confusion. So confusion *causes* indistinctness but does not *define* it. In any *complex* idea— and knowledge is always complex (since both intuition and concept are essential to it)—the basis of its distinctness is the *order* according to which the partial ideas are put together [*zusammengesetzt werden*], and these give rise to either a *mere logical* division (once concerned only with the form) into higher and subordinate ideas, or a real division into principal and accessory ideas. It is by this order that knowledge becomes clear. We readily see that, if the power of *knowledge* in general is to be called understanding (in the most general sense of the term), understanding must include: 1) *the power of apprehending* given ideas to produce an intuition (*attentio*); 2) *the power of abstracting* what is common to several of these to produce a concept (*abstractio*); and 3) the power of recollecting to produce *knowledge* of the object (*reflexio*). If a man has these powers in a pre-eminent degree, he is called a *brain*; if he has a very limited share of them, a *donkey* (since he always needs someone else to lead him); but if he possesses *originality* in using these powers (so that he brings forth from himself what must normally be learned under others' direction), he is called a *genius*.[11]

Without the curiosity represented in the last sentence, Kant's argument, in

substance and schema, is no different from the crucial passages on apperception in the *Critique of Pure Reason* (B233 and following). In both places
distinctions are made between "apprehension," "abstraction," and "recollec-
tion"; and "apprehension" is treated in the same manner as "perception,"
involving imagination, which in turn is different from thought.[12]

Regardless of what one thinks about the thematic unity of Kant's
works, what is of interest to us at the moment is to establish the continuities in the tradition of modern European philosophical reflections on
"man." Though there is a difference between Descartes's formalistic "I
think, therefore I am" and Kant's "synthetic" version of the doctrine of the
subject (this, certainly, is one way to read Kant's stipulations: the "I" reveals
"the necessity of a synthesis of the manifold given in intuition, without
which the thoroughgoing identity of self-consciousness cannot be thought";
and "To know anything . . . I must . . . synthetically bring into being a determinate combination of the given manifold, so that the unity of this act is at
the same time the unity of consciousness");[13] but the similarities between
the privileges accorded by both thinkers to the faculty of *understanding* is
quite striking. Whether "thin" and formalistic as in Descartes or "thick" and
synthetic as in Kant, the faculty of understanding is advanced by both as the
bearer of anthropological identity, as in the assertion: "I am human."
Succinctly, Kant explains:

> Man is one of the appearances of the sensible world, and in so far
> one of the natural causes the causality of which must stand under
> empirical laws. . . . Man, however, who knows all the rest of
> nature solely through the senses, knows himself also through *pure*
> apperception; and this indeed, in acts and inner determinations
> which he cannot regard as impressions of the senses. He is thus to
> himself, on the one hand, phenomenon, and on the other hand, in
> respect of certain faculties the action of which cannot be ascribed
> to the receptivity of sensibility, a purely intelligible object. We
> entitle these faculties understanding and reason.[14]

In Kant as in Descartes, and therefore in this stream of modern thought, the
position assigned to reason, the position of the subject, is one in which

"man" on its own (1) constitutes itself and through this self-act (2) stabilizes otherwise dispersed and contradictory states of reality. The details of the theories formulating these anthropological and epistemological revolutions represent what the philosophers understood as philosophy of culture. The theories, as we shall see, left openings through which a racialization of both man and culture was possible.

David Hume was probably more radical than either Descartes or Kant on the question of the role of racial/national customs in the formation of the modern self. Hume's *Treatise of Human Nature* works out, as the title indicates, a rigorous "science of man."[15] In an abstract of the *Treatise* he explains: "It may be safely affirmed that almost all the sciences are comprehended in the science of human nature, and are dependent on it."[16] The task then was to lay the groundwork for an important science, a science that would "regard human nature as a subject of speculation, and with a narrow scrutiny examine it in order to find those principles which regulate our understanding, excite our sentiments, and make us approve or blame any particular object, action or behavior."[17] The entailment of thought ("understanding") and custom, the moral self and culture are in full display. Hume's philosophy of human nature encompassed anthropology, a philosophy of (the scientific) method, and morality.

A closer examination of Hume's project in relation to Descartes and Kant shows that a programmatic continuity could be established on the basis of their modern studies of "man." Kant's position on the relationship between the branches of philosophy, in the *Logic*, was clearly foreshadowed by Hume in the *Treatise*: " 'Tis evident," Hume wrote, "that all the sciences have a relation, greater or less, to human nature; and that however wide any of them seem to run from it, they will return back by some passage or another." He was convinced that even "Mathematics, Natural Philosophy, and Natural Religion, are in some measure dependent on the science of Man."[18] And like Descartes, Hume hoped to "contribute a little to the advancement of knowledge, by giving in some particulars a different turn to the speculations of philosophers, and pointing out to them more distinctively those subjects, where alone they can expect assurance and conviction." While Descartes made the study of man ("soul") the basis of all sciences, Hume would more emphatically declare: "Human nature is the only [necessary] science."[19]

Questions: Why was the task of giving a definition to man so central to philosophy during this period? What explains the urgency with which the major philosophers approached the issue? Among historians of philosophy, the search for answers is always directed at a series of revolutions in science and culture, revolutions collectively referred to as the Renaissance, between 1300 and 1500. According to Vincent Potter: "As a result of the rebirth of culture [the Renaissance], which took place mainly in Italy through the rediscovery of Classical civilization, man and things human became the center of attention."[20] In this sense philosophy, for example, was interested in determining the nature of the human mind in order to establish and advance the projects of modern science. In this context, too, Descartes's conception of man as "a substance whose whole essence . . . was merely to think" would be not simply an attempt at description but also in praise of "the competence of human reason for handling human affairs and for solving human problems."[21] The ideology and the achievements of the Renaissance in Italy, given this understanding of history, constituted the roots of later scientific and cultural movements in England, France, and Germany, the Enlightenment movements, in the seventeenth and eighteenth centuries.

Now we must supplement this standard account by exploring wider sources of information that have been neglected, among them the histories of the encounters between the races, or what the philosophers at that time called "varieties of men." The challenge of understanding the meaning and significance of racial varieties was a major factor motivating the interest in determining the "essential" nature of a human person—as opposed to a person's accidental qualities. The philosophers were certainly influenced by the Renaissance discovery of the Greek cultures, but they also made another discovery: the discovery of the savage.

The "savage" of the Renaissance and, subsequently, of the Enlightenment is a category parallel to, but quite different from that of the "barbarian" or the "Gentile" prevalent in the preceding medieval centuries.

The barbarian or the Gentile was, indeed, the Other against which, respectively, the medieval Latin or the Christian civilization defined itself. The title of Thomas Aquinas's *Summa Contra Gentiles*, a book influential throughout the twelfth and the thirteenth centuries, testifies to this. Barbarians, on the other hand, were so because they lived outside the Latin culture. As a commentator put it, "their languages sounded so much *bar-bar* to the Latin ears."[22] For the medieval Latin or Christian, however, there was little historical content to this category of the Other, and lack of travel and knowledge left ample room for imaginative speculation restrained only by the requirements of church biblical teachings.[23] This medieval background helps us to understand the worldview within which the "strangeness" of the African, and other non-Europeans, would emerge in the modern philosophic and cultural imagination.

The fabulous stories about unknown races which populated the medieval imaginings of the world beyond known Christendom—for example, in the works composed between 1209 and 1218 by Gervase of Tilbury—do not command historical authority because they do not pretend to be other than fables. But there were more serious speculations about humans who were different from those in the known Christendom, categorized under the general term *monstrosities*. Monstrosities were believed to be abnormal beings that populated faraway lands. However, as John Block Friedman explains in *The Monstrous Races in Medieval Art and Thought*, those called by that name "were not monstrous at all. They simply differed in physical appearance and social practices from the person describing them." Furthermore: "The monstrous races were always far away, in India, Ethiopia, Albania, or Cathay, places whose outlines were vague to the medieval mind but whose names evoked mystery. As geographical knowledge grew, and the existence of many of these races began to appear unlikely, they were shifted to regions less well known—the Far North and ultimately the New World."[24]

The faraway places and peoples gripped writers' attention because the stories fascinated and, terrified; they challenged the Christian's or Westerner's understanding; and revealed a fragility in the traditional conceptions of man. Although Friedman argues that the earlier medieval (early

Renaissance) conception of man was more fragile and threatened by contact with "different" humans,[25] this is doubtful. The opposite could have been the case (and the greater portion of Friedman's own findings contradict his conclusions): there is evidence that theologians in the medieval world explain away what they considered "irregularities" in nature, whether these supposed irregularities were found among humans or other animal or plant species. The work of the thirteenth-century Dominican Vincent Beauvais is a case in point: following an Augustinean framework, Beauvais explained that monstrosities and irregularities in nature were acts of God; he classified them in the same category as miracles. In monstrosities as in miracles, God, from the time of creation, left Himself the liberty to intervene in His creation at will, in order to confound or edify the faithful. "If God," writes Beauvais, "had chosen to set the nature of each creation at the first moment of its creation so that it would persist unchangeably in its order, nature would have come to direct herself and the works and power of God would be forgotten by man. That Nature often turns from her usual [i.e., the Christian, "normal" or "regular"] order, however, continually reminds men that God is the artisan of all natures and that He acted not once only, but does so each day."[26] This is perhaps not vastly different from the theological perspective within which, in our time, Mahatma Gandhi referred to the Dalits, those at the bottom of India's caste systems, dark-skinned Indians— the "untouchables"—as "the children of God." It was a convenient way to explain various kinds of difference, geographical and cultural, and it remained an accepted formula throughout the Middle Ages. While it did not remove the anxiety aroused by *monstra* and *miracula*, the theological story rendered them intellectually and morally acceptable, and therefore tolerable, as deep and impenetrable but respected acts of God.

During the Renaissance, however, what constituted acceptable forms of explanation of nature radically altered. Although theological arguments never completely disappeared (as evident in Descartes), there was a shift among scholars to the scientific and the secular paradigm. Greater reliance on experiments and empirical observations produced more need for travel and exploration, leading to an increasingly less baroque attitude to knowing the world. Recall, for example, that for Saint Augustine, in A.D. 500, the

Bible was unquestionably the ultimate judge of what was rational and irrational. The Bible was the ultimate source of knowledge not just in theological matters relating to salvation but also in regard to matters of science, from cosmology to geography to ethnology. In a typical argument, Augustine wrote:

> As to the fable that there are Antipodes, that is to say, men on the opposite side of the earth, where the sun rises when it sets to us, men who walk with their feet opposite ours, that is on no ground credible. And, indeed, it is not affirmed that this has been learned by historical knowledge, but by scientific conjecture, on the ground that the earth is suspended within the concavity of the sky, and that it has as much room on the one side of it as on the other; hence they say that the part which is beneath must also be inhabited. But they do not remark that, although it be supposed or scientifically demonstrated that the world is of a round and spherical form yet it does not follow that the other side of the earth is bare of water; nor even, though it be bare, does it immediately follow that it is peopled.

The authority appealed to in these geographical and human evolutionary questions was the Bible: "Scripture, which proves the truth of its historical statements by the accomplishment of its prophecies, gives no false information; and it is too absurd to say, that some men might have taken ship and traversed the whole wide ocean, and crossed from this side of the world to the other, and that thus even the inhabitants of that distant region were descended from one first man."[27]

By the Renaissance, with increased travels and the emerging humanistic secular framework, the medieval worldview had come to an end. Augustine's unknown "opposite side" of the earth, his ideas about the descent of man, and the conditions of knowledge were disintegrated. By the end of the twelfth century, explorers had indeed "taken ship and traversed the whole wide ocean," and from then on, rather than Scripture and its prophecies as the authoritative sources of knowledge, new sciences of geography and ethnography, grounded upon a new cosmology, assumed this position, including the power to account for the origins and the varieties of the species.

Evidence of the new regimes of truth and the processes through which they displaced the old order can be found in numerous familiar and unfamiliar places. In Christopher Columbus's reports from the Americas to Europe, he was concerned to reassure his audience that he had yet to meet the "monsters" that were supposed to populate the continent. In his "Letter to the Sovereigns," Columbus described the inhabitants of Guyana, saying, "In this Island I have so far found no human monstrosities, as many expected; on the contrary, among all these people good looks are esteemed." He concluded: "I have found neither monsters nor have heard report of any."[28]

Renaissance transformations in geographical and anthropological knowledge arose, therefore, not just from the rediscovery of the Greeks. In addition to Columbus, others who made this transformation possible included Marco Polo (c. 1254–1324), who visited China; Henry the Navigator (1394–1460), whose ships sailed southward along the West African coast in search of India and gold; and Bartolomeu Dias (c. 1450–1500), who had reached the Cape of Good Hope and circled Africa by 1485. Ethnographic knowledge produced by these voyages of discovery (of peoples of China, sub-Saharan Africa, and America) provided modern philosophers new questions and a new horizon. By interrupting the medieval idea of "man," the discoveries of peoples and cultures different from the familiar was a source of social and cultural anxiety. The philosophers, cultural workers that they are, assumed the task of generating new theories and new ideological paradigms to reestablish a sense of order and normality. In the new world order, instead of the medieval opposition between the Latin and the barbarian, the morally relevant opposition would be articulated as the civilized and the savage, the historical and the primitive. Travel and ethnography paved the way for a new philosophy of history, conditions of truth, and in light of the discovery of peoples and cultures different and, apparently inferior, raised new questions about the destiny of "man."

In *Race: The History of an Idea, 1760–1850*, H. F. Augstein writes that race discourse "evolved without interruption from the 1750s to the 1850s."[29] The sources of the discourse on race, which dominated the human sciences by the 1750s, had however been gathering steam from as far back as the Renaissance humanistic transformations in science and culture. In the introduction to *The Travels of Marco Polo*, R. E. Latham informs us that the classic was introduced to the reading public at the end of the thirteenth century as a "Description of the World." It was, in fact, a description of an amazingly large part of the world: Java, Zanzibar, Japan, and other countries. Latham warns that "the book can be enjoyed by the modern reader . . . as a vivid description of a fantastic world so remote from his own experience that it scarcely matters whether he thinks of it as fact or as fiction," but his opinion is in accord with Polo's on a crucial point: the work represents a new *historical* development in "human intercourse and knowledge."[30] And Giambattista Vico's *Scienza Nuova*, a work clearly in the "profane" historical modes that would only intensify in the social and cultural research programs of the Enlightenment, was already published by 1725; in fact, an outline of the major arguments of the book had been published as a conclusion to an earlier volume, *De constantia Jurisprudentia*, in 1721. In 1735 Linnaeus, who wished to be considered the "Luther of science,"[31] published the acclaimed *Systema Naturae*.

In the formation of several modern and Enlightenment philosophical projects, the cultures and peoples considered savage are thought of as a surrounding darkness,[32] out of which the light of Europe's reason would be delineated. The historian John Burcke writes about "the surprise of the explorers in encountering savages and *in determining whether they were indeed fellow humans*." The question was relevant because some

> Greek and Roman chroniclers, such as Diodorus Siculus and Pliny the Elder, had passed on tales of headless men whose eyes and mouths were located in their breasts; men with one, three, or four eyes; men with such large ears that they slept wrapped in them; men with feet growing from the backs instead of the fronts of their legs; men with feet shaped like those of geese; men with no mouths who survived solely by smell; and men with hairy bodies and dogs' faces. These fictions were recorded and illustrated in various encyclopedia and compendiums . . . of the Middle Ages and the Renaissance, and they had wide appeal.[33]

Although travels and explorations removed the shrouds and paved the way for stricter scientific interest in "foreigners," the question whether these were truly humans derived from an anxiety: Who are *we*? And for the philosophers: What does it mean to be human? It is my argument that the philosophers answered these questions with ethnocentric flair and racial chauvinism.

Speaking of the historical and cultural sources of Descartes's doubts, Hannah Arendt, in *The Human Condition*, explained:

> Descartes's philosophy is haunted by two nightmares which in a sense became the nightmares of the whole modern age, not because the age was so deeply influenced by Cartesian philosophy but because their emergence was almost inescapable once the true implications of the modern world were understood. These nightmares are very simple and very well known. In the one, the reality of the world as well as of human life, is doubted; if neither common sense nor reason can be trusted, then it may well be that all we take for reality is only a dream. The other concerns the general human condition as it was revealed by the new discoveries. . . . [U]nder these circumstances it seems, indeed, much more likely that an evil spirit, a *dieu trompeur*, willfully and spitefully betrays man than that God is the ruler of the universe.[34]

The cogito, transformed in various ways by Hume and Kant, amounts to a new project for philosophy in an age of modern science. It signaled the demise of one worldview and the pain of the birth of another. It pointed, above all, to both the possibility and the impossibility of man—the modern man—"to trust his sense and reason."[35] Descartes's doubt, expressed in the *Meditations* and evident in questions asked by both Hume and Kant, is inflected with anxiety about other racialized human beings.[36]

I am convinced that the Renaissance idea of "Africa" and the modern idea of the African "race" was forged by a concentration of powers of economic, political, and cultural activities that oriented Europe's Age of Discovery. Léopold Sédar Senghor had pointed out that "the latest colonization, that of Europe over the world, was the work of the Renaissance."[37]

There is room to question, following tracks I shall indicate, the ways in which the racialization of the African was instrumental to Europe's understanding of itself as "white"; how the conception of the African continent as dark simultaneously made it possible for Europe to articulate its own spaces as enlightened; and how the African and the "black" responded to these constructions of both European and African racial identities. Edward Said's sprawling *Orientalism*, very Renaissance and omnivorously urbane, is a model in this area of study; but by anchoring my effort to a discipline, even one as currently marginal as philosophy, and to a period, in this case the Enlightenment, I may be able to gain in depth what may be lost in breadth.

The field is wide open. As V. Y. Mudimbe acknowledged in *The Invention of Africa*, while criticizing Christoher Miller's *Theories of Africans* (1985),

> No one has yet made a detailed study of Greek and Latin writers' influence on the European invention of Africa. Miller's synthesis . . . of the ambivalence about blackness in antiquity is too brief and, as such, a bit controversial. It refers to Snowden's thesis [in *Blacks in Antiquity*, 1970], according to which Greeks and Romans were only culturally biased and distinguishing the civilized from the *barbaros*, independently of race. [38]

Snowden's thesis was what I assumed in the all-too-brief introduction to *Race and the Enlightenment*.[39] It is consistent with my current position, to the effect that whereas for the Latin or medieval Christian the difference between oneself and the "barbarian" or "Gentile" remained far more cultural and religious than an issue of "race," the situation radically changed with the advent of commercial, diplomatic/military, and scientific and missionary travels that increasingly linked modern Europe to a world wider than that imagined prior to the transformations made possible by the Renaissance worldview and the technologies of travel. With regard to Saint Augustine and his world of Roman Africa, for example, there is room to think that the race of the African was far less important to his Catholic brethren in Rome than his proper conversion to Christianity. As Orlando Patterson notes, the Romans "were essentially inclusive and antiethnic in their bestowal of

Roman citizenship. They were, in fact, the first Indo-European people to have transcended tribalism fully and to have created a truly cosmopolitan world order in which all men were potentially members."[40] Likewise,

> The medieval world order was . . . a peculiarly nonethnic system. With the collapse of the Roman empire in the West and the emergence of that strange process of cultural metamorphosis we have come to call feudalism, only two types of allegiances were possible. The most important was allegiance to the local manor-ial domain existing within the framework of the fragile feudal state, the other to the universal world order of Christendom. The local branch of the Catholic church was the only intermediary between the two. The average medieval individual lived through a daily routine circumscribed by the village with its economic base in land. It was essentially a rural civilization.[41]

These arguments find supporting echoes in J. Huizinga's *The Waning of the Middle Ages*, which, although dealing principally with the fourteenth and fifteenth centuries, argues that "the common feature of the various mani-festations of civilization" during this time contains none of the racialist ele-ments that characterized the late Renaissance and the modern period, when Europeans had vastly greater contacts with peoples different in religion *and* looks.[42]

In any event, my arguments from here onward do not depend upon a final resolution of the issues surrounding the existing notion of race in the ancient or medieval world.[43] I think of the spirit of the Age of Enlighten-ment and the modern period not as a prolongation of the past but as pri-marily an embodiment of revolutionary ideals and techniques representative of the emergence of new and truly global intellectual and commercial forms, and therefore an inauguration of new forms of acquisition and circulation of knowledge, power, and wealth. It is to the examination of the objective bod-ies of knowledge from this period, and their relationships to the practices that produced both the civilized and the savage, the colonizer and the colonized, the white and the black, that I shall now turn.

PHILOSOPHY'S "VARIETIES OF MEN"

To fruitfully think the history of modern philosophy in conjunction with the history of "savage" peoples, and to press this philosophy to yield, so to speak, the savage structures through which it framed its most intimate questions about man, require, some new ways of looking at old things. We would certainly have to overcome the disciplinary prejudice that separates cultural studies and philosophy; the distinction between the two was not always as clear as we imagine. The need for philosophy to see itself as "pure" and concerned with only questions about knowledge in itself may lead one to neglect the fact that accomplished works in philosophy were produced as works in cultural anthropology, for example.[44] Hume wrote essays "Of National Characters," "Of Some Remarkable Customs," "Of Love betwixt the Sexes," "Of Love and Marriage," "Of Chastity and Modesty," "Of the Effects of Custom," and so forth.[45] Kant wrote "On the Different Human Races," "Conjectures on the Beginning of Human History," *Anthropology from a Pragmatic Point of View*, and the lectures that are collected in *Physical Geography*.[46] These works contain observations and theories about physical attributes, moral character, and customs of Europeans, Africans, Americans, Chinese, Hindus, and Jews. They seek to establish, through comparison, a unitary idea of "man." What are the images of the non-European and the nonwhite that emerge from these studies? How do philosophers responded to these works and to the identities we inherit from them?

There is a curious turn to psychological defensiveness by most modern African intellectuals when they encounter anti-African prejudices in the works of canonical European thinkers. Appiah, for example, writes: "Few contemporary readers are likely to be undisturbed when they discover the moments when Africa is banished from Hegel's supposedly universal history and when David Hume declares, in the essay on 'National Characters,' that blacks are incapable of eminence in action or speculation."[47] Kwasi Wiredu offers: "an African needs a certain level-headedness to touch [these books]."[48] He explains:

> The African philosopher cannot . . . take the sort of cultural
> pride in the philosophical achievement of Aristotle or Hume or

Kant or Frege or Husserl of which the Western student of philosophy may permit himself. Indeed an African needs a certain
level-headedness to touch some of these thinkers at all. Hume,
for example, had absolutely no respect for black men. Nor was
Marx, for another instance, particularly progressive in this
respect. Thus, any partiality the African philosopher may develop
for these thinkers must rest mostly on considerations of truth-
value.[49]

Lurking beyond these psychological uneasinesses are, however, serious historical questions: What is the critical significance of the role of non-
Europeans in both the formation and resolution of the modern
philosophical questions about man?

What does it mean to say that the African cannot take "cultural pride"
in Western philosophy? Is this a "cultural geneticism" —the doctrine that,
as Appiah puts it, "you earn rights to culture that is marked with the mark
of your race"?[50] What would be a "level-headed" position on the question of
the relationships that exist or should not exist between modern philosophy
and race, racialism, or racism?

In the book *T. S. Eliot, Anti-Semitism, and Literary Form*, Anthony
Julius asked if there were intrinsic connections between Eliot's "literary
form" and his "anti-Semitism." According to Julius, anti-Semitism is internal to Eliot's aesthetics. He cautions that "indifference to the offense given
by [racist] poems is, among other things, a failure of interpretation" because
"to ignore these insults is to misread the poems."[51]

But Julius also thinks—more controversially—that "If the work, or
some notable part of it, is anti-Semitic, it is the work of an anti-Semite."[52]
Could this be accepted as a principle of interpretation? To ask whether an
author, in person, is anti-Semitic and racist because a part of his or her work
may be anti-Semitic or antiblack is not the same as asking if *a piece of work*
is anti-Semitic and racist. Could we always deduce an author's racial intentions from the work, without getting bogged down in issues of authorial
intentions? In these days when the "death of the author" is proclaimed,
could the author be known? Determining whether or not a piece of work is
racist, on the other hand, with a focus on a body of work or scholarship,

does not require investigations into the subjectivity of the author; a text or a theory would be examined, interpreted, and judged regarding its implicit or explicit relation, if any, to a range of issues of concern, such as racism.

Historical periods are defined by interlocking systems of cultural, scientific, and literary discourses, which generate highly specific vocabularies deployed by artists and scholars whose awareness of the provenance of their vocabularies varies greatly. In the same way that children are unable to choose a first language or first languages, yet go on to use these languages at different levels of competence and creativity, depending on talent and skill, so are artists and scholars educated into cultural, literary, and scientific vocabularies. Each works with this inheritance at varying degrees of awareness. It could be argued that only a few have the talent to transform received vocabulary into new forms. If thinkers not only use language but are also used by it, we can imagine situations where a scientist, poet, or philosopher appropriates and even makes productive use of words, images, and received definitions without a comparable level of a critical grasp of all their cultural and historical significance, as may be available to subsequent generation of critics. The problem of a racist thinker could not therefore be separated from the contexts of his or her time.

By locating the problem of race in modern thought at the level of the language of the works and the intellectual and cultural environment (the Enlightenment, for example), it is easier to understand when a universe of discourse is race conscious. I ask, then, not if Hume or Kant, as individual, was racist. It is more philosophically interesting, I believe, to inquire about the ways modern philosophy articulated and used the idea of race, and to what ends. If Hume and Kant were philosophers in the modern time and bearers of the Enlightenment projects in particular, could their philosophical writings be considered ethnocentric and racialist? Are there indeed philosophical relationships between the light and reason of the Enlightenment and the darkness and irrationality of the Savages? If so, what remains of the "universal" theories of knowledge, ethics, and politics advocated by these authors? These questions are interesting, I think, because they offer insights into the historical dimensions of modern philosophy, showing the conflicted manner in which the tradition aspired to universality and cross-cultural significance.

If Wiredu is correct to suggest that not only Hume and Kant but also authors as diverse as Aristotle and Marx and Husserl and Frege made remarks and wrote theories that suggest they "had absolutely no respect" for the black person,[53] it is appropriate to raise the race question in modern philosophy to a systemic and general level. In 1754, David Hume stated:

> I am apt to suspect the Negroes and in general all other species of men (for there are four or five different kinds) to be naturally inferior to the whites. There never was a civilized nation of any other complexion than white, nor even any individual eminent either in action or speculation. No ingenious manufacturers amongst them, no arts, no sciences. On the other hand, the most rude and barbarous of the whites, such as the ancient GERMANS, the present TARTARS, have still something eminent about them, in their valour, form of government, or some other particular. Such a uniform and constant difference could not happen, in so many countries and ages, if nature had not made an original distinction betwixt these breeds of men. Not to mention our colonies, there are NEGROE slaves dispersed all over EUROPE, of which none ever discovered any symptoms of ingenuity; tho' low people, without education, will start up amongst us, and distinguish themselves in every profession. In JAMAICA, indeed, they talk of one negroe as a man of parts and learning; but 'tis likely he is admired for very slender accomplishments, like a parrot, who speaks a few words plainly.[54]

In 1761, Immanuel Kant wrote:

> In the hot countries the human being matures in all aspects earlier, but does not, however, reach the perfection of those in the temperate zones. Humanity is at its greatest perfection in the race of the whites. The yellow Indians do have a meager talent. The Negroes are far below them and at the lowest point are a part of the American peoples.
>
> The Moors and the other peoples between the tropics of Cancer and Capricorn can run quite astonishingly. They as well

as other savages have more strength than the other civilized peoples, which stems from the free movement allowed them in their childhood. The Hottentots can perceive a ship with the naked eye at the same distance as a European can with a telescope. The women in the hottest parts of the world produce children already at the age of nine or ten and finish before they are twenty-five years old.

Don Ulloa remarks that in Cartagena in America and in the surrounding areas people become clever very early but they do not continue to grow in intelligence at the same rate. All inhabitants of the hottest zones are exceptionally lethargic. With some this laziness is somewhat mitigated by rule and force.

When an Indian sees a European going somewhere, he thinks, he has something to accomplish. When he comes back, he thinks, he has already taken care of his business, but if he sees him going out a third time he thinks, he has lost his mind, as the European is going for a walk for pleasure, which no Indian does or about which he is only capable of imagining. Indians are also indecisive, and both traits belong to the nations that live very far north. The weakening of their limbs is supposedly caused by brandy, tobacco, opium and other strong things. From their timidity comes superstition, particularly in regard to magic, and the same with jealousy. Their timidity makes them into slavish underlings when they have kings and evokes an idolatrous reverence in them, just as their laziness moves them to rather run around in the forest and suffer need than to be held to their labors by the orders of their masters.

Montesquieu is correct in his judgment that the weak-heartedness that makes death so terrifying to the Indian or the Negro also makes him fear many things other than death that the European can withstand. The Negro slave from Guinea drowns himself if he is to be forced into slavery. The Indian women burn themselves. The Carib commits suicide at the slightest provocation. The Peruvian trembles in the face of an enemy, and when he is led to death, he is ambivalent, as though it means nothing.

His awakened imagination, however, also makes him dare to do something, but the heat of the moment is soon past and timidity resumes its old place again. . . .

The inhabitant of the temperate parts of the world, above all the central part, has a more beautiful body, works harder, is more jocular, more controlled in his passions, more intelligent than any other race of people in the world. That is why at all points in time these peoples have educated the others and controlled them with weapons.[55]

And in 1822, G. W. F. Hegel said:

Africa proper . . . is the land of childhood, removed from the light of self-conscious history and wrapped in the dark mantle of night. . . . There is no subjectivity, but merely a series of subjects who destroy one another. . . . The consciousness of the inhabitants has not yet reached an awareness of any substantial and objective existence. Under the heading of substantial objectivity, we must include God, the eternal, justice, nature. . . . But the Africans have not yet attained this recognition of the universal; their nature is as yet compressed within itself: and what we call religion, the state . . . all this is not yet present to them.

All our observations of African man shows him as living in a state of savagery and barbarism, and he remains in this state to the present day. The negro is an example of animal man in all its savagery and lawlessness, and if we wish to understand him at all, we must put aside all our European attitudes. We must not think of a spiritual God or of moral laws; to comprehend him correctly, we must abstract from all reverence and morality, and from everything which we call feeling. All this is foreign to man in his immediate existence, and nothing consonant with humanity is to be found in his character. . . . We cannot properly feel ourselves into his nature, no more than into a dog.[56]

Should we, as Hannah Arendt argues, dismiss these and similar anthropological works as "noncritical" or "of no philosophical significance"?[57] Can we learn anything about the history of philosophy from them? Should we consider them part of the "tradition"? If not, why not? Should modern African thinkers ignore them—and pretend that the attitudes reflected toward Africans in these works belong only to the past?

Instead of avoiding the more ethnic aspects of modern philosophy, should one ask what these aspects might reveal about philosophy's more abstract and rarefied doctrines in metaphysics or epistemology? We could use three more general questions as guides: (1) What logical interconnections exist between modern "critical" philosophical and "noncritical" anthropological (or political) works? (2) When we study Hume's "science of man" project or Kant's "critique of pure reason" with inadequate appreciation of the broader anthropological tradition, are we distorting our sense of the significance of these works? (3) While paying attention to the controlling ideas of "human nature," "man," and "race" in Hume and Kant, for example, what survives of the usual view of these thinkers as, respectively, a "skeptic" and "purist"?

THE MODERN IDEA OF RACE: A SHORT HISTORY

A critic might ask, Why isolate race, among many other social or identity categories, as a superior factor on which the structuration of modern philosophy might be questioned? Aren't class and gender, individually or in combination, more profound and therefore more enlightening as sites for a critical history of modern philosophy? An answer: I consider race neither "prior" nor "superior" to the many markers of various forms of inclusions and exclusions organized by philosophy. In fact, when philosophy has been turned—or turned itself—to racist ends, the race issues are inseparable from wider economic, political, and cultural conditions. To study philosophy *and* race, with this understanding, is only one way to reexamine the relationships between modern philosophy and the social and cultural worlds that made it possible, if not necessary.

For example, if Augstein is correct in the suggestion that "the origins of nineteenth-century racial theory can be grasped only through an understanding of the eighteenth-century view of mankind,"[58] it should be equally said that the Enlightenment racial theories are more fully understood by taking into account the conceptual resources inherited by this period from Renaissance geography and ethnography. We know, for instance, that the English word "race" originated from the French *race* and referred in the medieval ages to, simply, a royal lineage. By the eighteenth century, however, it had acquired not only the Latin meanings of *gens* and *genus*, but had expanded to encompass "stock," "tribe," and "nation." The novelty in these expanded usages is that, because of the new interests in secular history, social change, and new methods of empirical descriptions, "race" took over the function of distinguishing, within Europe, "nation" (considered as a historical political unit, "people") from the biological descent of individuals and groups ("stock"). The new concept of race functioned within new research spaces categorized as *social* and *natural* history, and both sciences constituted a "science of man."

By the time that the conceptual and practical transitions were complete, the word "race," according to Michael Banton, had acquired at least these meanings: "the notion that mankind is divisible into a certain number of 'races' whose characteristics are fixed and defy the modifying influences of external circumstances; . . . the idea that intellectual and moral capacities may be unevenly spread within the various human races; . . . and the notion that mental endowments are bound up with certain physiognomical specificities which, being defined as racial characteristics, are considered to reveal the inward nature of the individual or the population in question."[59] Attending the contemporary "natural" science of race or the art of racial classification is therefore the moral question of whether a particular race lived according to instinct, custom, or reason.

This is why Banton's claim that "the theory of racial typology" was indeed "the beginning of the study of race relations" is fabulously accurate. No clearer example of this confusion of domains—of the nature of the races and the rules that must govern race relations—is more evident that in Thomas Jefferson's arguments in *Notes on the State of Virginia*, where he wrote that the "natural" differences between whites and blacks required them to be segregated, "beyond reach of mixture."[60] Jefferson explained: "Whether the black of the negro resides in the reticular membrane between the skin and scarf-skin, or in the scarf-skin itself; whether it proceeds from the colour of the blood, the colour of the bile, or from that of some other secretion, the difference is fixed in nature, and it is real as if its seat and cause were better known to us. And is this difference of no importance?"[61] The "importance," Jefferson suggested, was to free black slaves and send them back to Africa. And Lincoln the emancipationist shared similar views. At one of a series of visits by black leaders to the White House, Lincoln explained to them:

> You and we are different races. We have between us a broader difference than exists between any other two races. Whether it is right or wrong I need not discuss, but this physical difference is a great disadvantage to us both, as I think your race suffer very greatly, many of them by living among us, while ours suffer from your presence.[62]

It is not easy to distinguish here between the science and the politics of race.

In *The Idea of Race*, Robert Knox (1791–1862) argued that races are naturally and eternally fixed kinds.[63] Others who held this view included J. C. Nott, G. R. Giddon,[64] and Comte de Gorbineau.[65] But their ideas had their origins in Linnaeus. The Swedish naturalist classified racial varieties in a hierarchical table of nature supposedly arranged by God. This quasi-religious order of reality had its origins in medieval cosmology, but Linneaus repositioned it as a "great book of nature," open for science to read. Nature, he wrote, "unfolds herself to him who, with great patience and perseverance, will search into her mysteries." The words and grammar of this book, then,

> comprehends whatever exists; whatever can come to our knowl-edge by the agency of our senses. The Stars, the Elements, and this our Globe. The Stars are bodies remote, lucid, revolving in perpetual motion. They shine either by their own proper light, as the Sun, and the remoter fixed Stars; or are Planets receiving light from stars. Of these the primary planets are solar; Saturn, Jupiter, Mars, the Earth, Venus, Mercury, and Georgium Sidus; the sec-ondary are those subservient to, and rolling around the primary, as the Moon around the Earth. . . . The study of natural history,

is simple, beautiful, and instructive in the collection, arrangement, and exhibition of the various productions of the earth.

Included in the "productions of the earth" is "man." While minerals inhabit the interior parts of the earth in rude and shapeless masses, the vegetables "clothe the surface with verdure, imbibe nourishment through bibulous roots, breathe by quivering leaves, celebrate their nuptials in a genial metamorphosis, and continue their kind by the dispersion of seed within prescribed limits. They are bodies organized, and have life and not sensation." Next are animals, who "adorn the exterior parts of the earth, respire, and generate eggs; are impelled to action by hunger, congeneric affections, and pain; and by preying on other animals and vegetables. . . . They are bodies organized, and have life, sensation, and the power of locomotion." At the summit of the pyramid is man:

> The last and best of created works, formed after the image of his Maker, endowed with a portion of intellectual divinity, the governor and subjugator of all other beings, is, by his wisdom alone, able to form just conclusions from such things as present themselves to his senses, which can only consist of bodies merely natural. Hence the first step of wisdom is to know these bodies; and be able, by those marks imprinted on them by nature, to try to distinguish them from each other, and to affix to every object its proper name.

To give something its proper name is also to declare its proper place in the hierarchy of beings. The name is not just a label but a mirror of nature, "the great alphabet."

Though there is a recognition of as much diversity among humans as among any other species, in Linnaeus's system one racial group—the white—constitutes the ideal representation of man, the norm against which the rest, as variations, are hierarchically classified depending on how near or far they approximate the ideal. The white is "inventive," "gentle," and "governed by laws," but the black, for example, is "indolent," "negligent," and governed by "caprice." The "Copper-colored" Americans are "obstinate," "content," and "regulated by customs"—and share with "monstrosities," at the bottom of the pyramid, the quality of "beardlessness."

Although he declared that "the anatomical, physiological, natural, moral, civil, and social histories of man, are best described by their respective writers,"[66] Linnaeus did provide observations that cover many of these areas. In general, his observations focused on bodily attributes, potency and impotency, and moral discipline and licenses. The attributes thus highlighted manifest what Robert Young would later call a "colonial desire,"[67] with its emphases on the non-European's "immodest dress and sexual license" which, as John Block Friedman noted, were "two traits that had long offended the Christian West in its dealing with Plinian peoples." These were also the two traits assumed to characterize the African and New World savages.[68] Reduced thus to the "natural" aspect (animal sexual vitality) and caricature, Linnaeus set the tone for later anthropological descriptions of the "primitive" races.[69]

What, Then, Is Race?

When population genetics became well established the 1930s, scientists realized that "racial type" should be substituted with "population." They also realized that only statistics, rather than typology, is capable of providing accurate pictures of both intra- and intergroup biological characteristics—the factors previously used to classify the "races." Unlike Linnaeus's racial types with static characters, populations are conceptualized as dynamic, because, as Elazer Barkan wrote in *The Retreat of Scientific Racism*, "their individual members are subjected to the pressures of selection as they adapt themselves to changing environments."[70]

But as the controversy surrounding efforts to appropriate genetic science to defend the fact that there are no biological races has shown, one would not presume that the science of genes has "solved" the social and historical race problem. And there are good reasons for this. If the populations about which the geneticist speaks are geographically distributed, then we must deal with the fact that there are gene pools that display consistent frequencies which result in physical displays that average observers, as if by a rule of thumb, ascribe to "races." Genetic science may not be able to dispel this empirical knowledge deriving from, so to speak, street knowledge; there is therefore a gap between expert science and popular wisdom. If geneticists have shown that "race" is not a useful concept, it may be up to the social scientists to invent new ways of making this development available to the general culture.

As early as the 1920s, the Chicago University sociologist Robert E. Park emphasized that race is about *relationships*—relationships that are formed through quasi-arbitrary regulations of ethnic solidarities and social distances.[71] In "The Nature of Race Relations," he explained:

> Race relations, as that term is defined in use and wont in the United States, are the relations existing between peoples distinguished by marks of racial descent, particularly when these racial differences enter into the consciousness of the individuals and groups so distinguished, and by so doing determine in each case the individual's conception of himself as well as his status in the community. . . . Anything that intensifies race consciousness . . . particularly if it is a permanent physical trait, . . . increases an individual's visibility and by so doing makes more obvious his identity with a particular ethnic unit or genetic group [and] tends to create and maintain the conditions under which race relations, as here defined, may be said to exist. Race consciousness, therefore, is to be regarded as a phenomenon, like class or caste consciousness, that enforces social distances.[72]

This emphasizes the normative, institutional character of race. It refers to "relations which are not now conscious or personal, though they have been; relations which are fixed in and enforced by the custom, convention, and the routine of an expected social order."[73]

The essay "The Negro as Contrast Conception," by Lewis C. Copeland, supports Park's views. The essay traces the logic of the social relationships involved in the making of both "white" and "black" identities in the U.S. South. It explains:

Relations between white and black people in the South have given rise to a distinctive conception of the Negro. As a natural outcome of the juxtaposition of two divergent ethnic groups, white people have sharply distinguished themselves from black people. It is not surprising then to find that there has been a marked tendency to conceive of the Negro in terms of contrast. In fact, one may speak of the Negro as a "contrast conception."[74]

The emphasis on the *ethnic* character of so-called racial identities—an emphasis also present in Patterson and Park—points to race as a social and a practical concept derived from a juxtaposition of ethnicities, the "black" and the "white." Copeland observed that "social opposition" gives rise to

a conceptual dichotomy somewhat analogous to that between God and the devil in popular religion. The devil is a contrast conception set in juxtaposition to God as an antonym to represent the antithesis of Christian values. By this conceptual polarity the values are exalted and made all the more impressive. The contrast introduces a dichotomy which is conceived as running through the whole universe, dividing not only the natural world but the social order, and relegating object and conducts either to the kingdom of God or to the kingdom of devil. The counter-concept likewise forms the basis for the interpretation of human nature and society.[75]

Race, then, operates in a globalizing moral frame, assuming a public outlook that projects the social into the natural world. Within this mythic imagination, the racial-conceptual schemes serve to sanction social values. "Just as the moral virtues are made more tangible and forceful by personalizing them, so are the unacceptable acts made more fearful by attributing them to personal beings. The latter are conceived to be antithetical to the benevolent personages but, nevertheless, are complementary to them and essential to the world view." [76]

This interpretation confirms the findings in Maurice Evans's *Black and White in South East Africa*, a work which explains how Europeans in Africa became white and the Africans black, a division solidified in institutions such as apartheid. Evans thinks that in no other lands ruled by the British, "except, perhaps, in the Far East, certainly in none of the great self-governing colonies with which we rank ourselves, is the position of white man *qua* white man so high, his status so impugnable, as in South East Africa"; and he thinks that the white identity and status was forged in the following manner:

> Differing in much else, the race instinct binds the whites together to demand recognition as a member of the ruling and inviolable caste, even for the poorest, the degraded of their race. And this position connotes freedom from all manual and menial toil; without hesitation the white man demands this freedom, without question the black man accedes and takes up the burden, obeying the race command of one who may be his personal inferior. . . . A white oligarchy, every member of the race is an aristocrat; a black proletariat, every member of the race a server; the line of cleavage is as clear and deep as the colours. The less able and vigorous of our race, thus protected, find here an ease, a comfort, a recognition to which their personal worth would never entitle them in a homogenous white population.[77]

That the race concept is simultaneously a race command shows that race structures thought, language, and behavior in such a way that all the white "master" had to do was *speak* and an entire order of society was instantaneously activated to affirm his or her authority and superiority over the subservient black subject. It is this power of speech, this force of logos, in its easily perverted form in the "racial" command, that is worthy of philosophical attention.

The racial command, the crudely exploitative and therefore unfree speech, under the pretext of differences in skin color, framed and justified a superior caste of Europeans and an inferior caste of Africans, in a relationship that the law endlessly reproduced and cruelly enforced until—in the case of South Africa—1992. No wonder so many were delighted that Mandela's emergence from jail symbolized the emergence of a different speech, a different language, suggesting a more human and universal logic and, they hoped, a freer and a different kind of command by the law.

The rise of Enlightenment race speech is an expansive transition from the racialization of the West to a racialization of the world. This progression represents a transition from, relatively speaking, local "racial" conflicts within Europe to the European replication and intensification of the adaptive practices of racialism in other parts of the world to which Europeans ventured. The local, or "native," European racial conflicts have been well covered in studies by Tzvetan Todorov, Jacques Barzun, and Léon Poliakov.[78] They show how, for example, from the sixteenth century to the eighteenth century, the Teutons and the Latin "races" negotiated power, territory, and cultural claims to superiority. Later world manifestations of race were more cosmic, as "racial" conflicts structured and governed the very ideas of secular history and universal progress. Whereas in earlier cases of race conflicts, European monarchies and royal families struggled to impose themselves on European populations through assertions of pedigrees and "purity of blood," in the global cases of race conflict, similar reasons and processes were reproduced, but this time in the name of "civilization" and the "whiteness" of Europeans.

In comparing British East Africa and British West Africa, specifically Kenya and Nigeria, in the period 1880–1914, H. D. Perraton shows how the idea of Africans as a race—an idea already consolidated in the bodies of Africans transported to Europe and the Americas as slaves—was also imposed upon Africans in Africa, by the British. This stemmed from practical social and political needs of the settlers, rather than genuine observations about forms of social uplift for the administered peoples, or science.[79] In non-British colonies, similar processes of racialization could be detected: Belgian administrators created (or refined into proportions capable of erupting into now-familiar genocidal catastrophes) the idea that the Hutus and the Tutsis are opposite "races." And when the Sanskrit scholar Max Müller advanced the theory of a common Aryan racial origin for both the English and the Bengali, Sir Henry Maine, at the time law member of the government of India, is said to have remarked: "I myself believe that the government of India by the English has been rendered appreciably easier by the discoveries which have brought home to the educated of both races the common Aryan parentage of the Englishman and the Hindoo."[80]

The conceptual transitions required to go from a racialized West to a racialized world could be traced in the Enlightenment intellectual abandonment of the anthropological elements in the earlier medieval polarization of Christians and heathens. Once God has been reconceptualized as a "clock maker" rather than as unknowable dice thrower, the human sciences—and philosophy in its suit—found new modes of existence and new frames of reference. As Augstein explains it:

> Starting from medicine, natural history, and political science, the rising discipline of anthropology stood on three legs: dealing with the individual, Medicine told people how to be legislators of their own bodily constitutions. Cultural and political philosophers, by contrast, treating society, turned towards inquiring into the historical laws according to which civilization grew up. The naturalist, finally, became increasingly interested in trying to devise natural systems which assigned mankind a place among their fellow creatures. Savages were still deemed unfit for historicity. But it was precisely their supposed vicinity to the animal creation which made them, as humans, into an object of study. Being part of the realm of descriptive natural history, they were considered analogous to the animal tribes.[81]

But these shifts in conceptual perspectives were not historically isolated; they were framed in economic, political, and cultural intentions that can only be characterized, from the standpoint of those perceived as belonging to the "animal tribes," as a war of conquest—a conquest of one tribe by another, more powerful tribe.

Europe, it seems, constructed itself as a "white" racial tribe in order to enact, and simultaneously as it enacted, "colored" racial tribes upon others. Every human group that would represent itself as homogenous of necessity constitutes itself by establishing ideas that make the members feel that they are "in." And a group, at a moment that it regards itself as *the* human race, would be threatened to encounter "others" whom it considers heterogeneous, for the encounter would force it to entertain the idea that it is just one among many "varieties of men." The birth of the modern idea of race is therefore inseparable from the dialectic of the Same with Other.

It was in the economically and politically charged modern encounters between the Europeans and the Africans that modern racial ideas of "white" and "black" acquired specific meanings as markers of Otherness. The historical sources of the modern idea of a "black" race could hardly be understood if separated from the encounters between those who invented a parallel "white" identity. These encounters were made possible by new technologies of travel but also, more morally significant, new motives for travel.

So when precisely, you might ask, did the peoples of Africa become "black," in the sense in which modern Europeans applied the term not merely to designate a people or peoples of a geographical area, but also as physical embodiment of the moral idea of blackness?[82] Could one trace the constitution of the African as a morally significant Other in the history of modern European thought? How did this moral idea of the black African feature in Europe's quest to constitute itself as modern and enlightened?

If we may be allowed to speak abstractly, the dialectical nature of the languages of racial consciousness echoes the historical achievement of modernity as a global capitalist civilization. It reveals, I think, the brutalities that this civilization inflicted upon those it considered to be obstacles in the paths of its progress. We know from anthropologists and sociologists that "the words tribesmen have for strange peoples always emphasize their nonhumanness. They are monsters, Cyclops, strange, perverted creatures lying somewhere between humanity and the beasts, between the natural and the supernatural."[83] For Mircea Eliade, who studied tribal religions, the boundaries of a tribal territory, eminently moral, always demarcate "us" from "them," our "cosmos" from their "chaos." While Europe was conceptualized as "inhabited and organized" space ("our world"), Africa, from the xenophobic and ethnocentric perspectives indicated by Eliade, "shares in the fluid and alluvial modality of chaos."[84] Within this "we-and-them" normative framework, the racialized projects of modern economic and political domination of Africans, whether on the continent or in plantation slavery in the New World, must have appeared to be a necessary moral task. This was, in fact, the imperative Hegel assigned to the European enslavement of Africans in the *Philosophy of History*. At popular levels, too, slavery and colonialism were conceptualized and morally justified in Europe in the language of religious self-sacrifice—the "white man's burden," white European Jesuses carrying black African crosses.

Traces of this schizophrenic understanding of not only slavery but also colonization as both acts of aggression and acts of moral uplift, injurious and beneficial, were shared by those who implemented the racialized economic and political relationships that bounded Africa and Europe in a mutual if unequal dependence, as black and white races. During the late 1800s and early 1900s, Fredrick Lugard, a ruthless soldier turned hired hand for private trading companies and later antislavery crusader, was an empire builder for England and a consultant to several European states who occupied or had indirect interests in Africa. In a book highly regarded as "an authoritative justification of Britain's annexation and government of tropical Africa,"[85] Lugard writes, in a characteristic understatement, that it would be naive to believe that Europe ventured into Africa for philanthropic reasons:

> Let it be admitted at the outset that European brains, capital, and energy have not, and never will be, expended in developing the resources of Africa from motives of pure philanthropy; that Europe is in Africa for the mutual benefit of her own industrial classes, and of the native races in their progress to a higher plane; that the benefit can be made reciprocal; and that it is the aim and desire of civilized administration to fulfill this dual mandate.[86]

I suggested that this is understated because a contemporary book, Leonard Woolf's *Empire and Commerce in Africa,* offers a stronger, more critical assessment of British colonialism and its economic motives. Honest people can disagree about how "reciprocal" or mutually beneficial were/are Africa's entanglements with Europe, England, and the United States.

Lugard appears to have been sincere in his wish to reconcile competing European motives at the time: measurable increases in wealth for the white "industrial classes" and an amorphously defined "progress to a higher plane" for the "darker" races, which were suspected both in the scientific as well as in the popular European imaginations to provide the missing link between white humans and apes. It was this dual mandate that Lugard implemented for the British governments in East, West, Central, and Southern Africa.

According to Margery Perham, a turn-of-the-century Oxford University expert on British colonialism, Lugard conscientiously sought to mediate these "seeming opposites" in his practical conquests and organization of Africa. But Lugard's colonial rhetoric of "racial progress" for Africans suggests that such progress was measured in nearly predictable ways—by the level of industrial developments that enhanced cultivation and processing of cash crops and the infrastructures for their export to Europe; in the reorganization of politics, religion, and medicine to serve the new externally oriented social and political economy; and in the levels of obedience and docility of the reorganized populations to the new economic and social order, which guaranteed the effectiveness of the white governor's executive authority over the newly internationalized local population. It is in this spirit that Lugard observes:

> By railways and roads, by reclamation of swamps and irrigation of deserts, and by a system of fair trade and competition, we have added to the prosperity and wealth of these lands, and checked famine and disease. We have put an end to the awful misery of the slave-trade and inter-tribal war, to human sacrifice and the ordeals of the witch-doctor. Where these things survive they are severely suppressed. We are endeavoring to teach the native races to conduct their own affairs with justice and humanity, and to educate them alike in letters and in industry.[87]

A thought experiment: What if a group of Senegalese investors made the decision to attempt to colonize the United States in view of further civilizing it? First they would balance the budget, reform campaign finance laws, and end judicial execution of citizens, sexual depredation of women, persecution of gay men and women, consignment of black brains and bodies to ever-expanding and increasingly privatized, for-profit prisons, and racism that pervades social life. Then, they would win the war on drugs and revitalize urban "war" zones, reform K–12 education, end deadly violence in high schools, and so forth. In exchange for this "progress to a higher plane," however, the Senegalese investors who finance the colonizing army would appoint an executive governor general to run the United States as a colony of Senegal. The governor's mandate would be to restructure and expand the American economy according to the dictates of the Senegalese "industrial class" and the African population.

Although this proposition may sound unlikely, it made perfect sense to Lugard when the colonizing force was England. He concluded his inventory of European achievements in Africa with a blunt statement: "As Roman imperialism laid the foundation of modern civilization, and led the wild barbarians of these islands along the path of progress, so in Africa today we are repaying the debt, and bringing to the dark places of the earth, the abode of barbarism and cruelty, the torch of culture and progress, while ministering to the material needs of our civilization."[88] We can only imagine the statement our hypothetical Senegalese governor general, presiding over the "protectorate" of the United States, might have produced in a similar, self-contented sense of history: "As the ancient Egyptians, thanks to the Nile, brought civilization southwards to us in Senegal and cured us all of our cruelty, so now. . . . "

To be fair, Lugard anticipated that sooner or later the "dark races" would reject imperial domination and through "unrest and desire for independence" further spread the value of liberty and civilization. "Their very discontent," he wrote, "is a measure of their progress."[89] But the gem in this argument is obvious: however you looked at it, British imperialism and colonialism were the *right* way to do things. If the "natives" accommodated themselves to the forces of foreign domination, which they were incapable of repealing, it was because they wished to be taught by the colonizer; on the other hand, if they revolted and successfully overthrew the yoke of foreign domination, it was because they were taught well by the British.

Lugard saw clear benefits in the convenient colonial arrangement between the European state, the colonizing "industrial class," and the "material needs" of European civilization on the one hand, and the natives' need for "racial progress" on the other. After speaking of the benefits of the arrangement to the colonized, he then calculated the benefits to the colonizer:

> Even when the economic pressure caused by the rapidly increasing population of Europe began to exert inevitable influence, in driving men to seek for new markets and fresh supplies of food

and raw material, the discovery of America, and the new fields
for commerce in India [and Africa], more than met the demand
for several centuries.

Specifically, "one of the immediate causes [for] opening up" Africa was, in
Lugard's account, an entirely European affair, the Franco-Prussian War of
1870.

> Crippled by her defeat France proclaimed by the mouth of her
> principal statesmen and writers . . . that it was to the Greater
> France beyond the seas, and especially in West and North-West
> Africa, that she must look for rehabilitation. At that time, more-
> over, colonization in tropical Africa was believed to be both pos-
> sible and desirable. Germany, on the other hand, found herself
> with a great and increasing industrial population in urgent need
> of raw materials and additional food supplies. Not content with
> the wholly unrestricted market offered by British colonies, where
> Germans were welcomed and exercised every privilege equally
> with their British rivals, she not unnaturally desired to have
> colonies of her own.[90]

These political and economic motives for "the scramble for Africa" should
be familiar to philosophers from Hegel's *Philosophy of History* and *Philosophy
of Right*, Eric Hobsbawn's multivolume *The Age of Revolution*, and Hannah
Arendt's *Origins of Totalitarianism*, or the works of African political scientists and political economists such as Ali Mazrui and Samir Amin. Lugard,
a more practical-minded theorist as well as a consummate administrator,
supplies the data, accumulated from the everyday, which portrays the
balance sheet from what he called "competitive trade" with the dark race of
Africa.

He explains, "The conquest of the ocean . . . directly led to the
expansion of the peoples of Europe, and relieved them from the age-long
pressures of Asia on their frontier." Calculating the increased opportunities
available to Europeans to make a living and support families, beginning
from after 1492 (when Columbus had reached America) and 1494 (when
Vasco da Gama had rounded the African Cape), Lugard stated:

At that time the population of Europe was about 70 millions. At the end of the next three centuries it is said to have been 150 millions, and additional 10 millions having migrated overseas. But [at] the close of the succeeding century—which witnessed the industrial revolution, and the advent of steam navigation—it is estimated at nearly 450 millions, with 100 millions additional emigrants. Thus, while the population of Europe only doubled itself in the three centuries prior to 1800, it more than trebled itself in the following century. The figures for the Great Britain [England only] are: population in 1600, 4,800,000; in 1800 about 16,000,000; and in 1900 about 42,000,000.[91]

These, then, are the benefits of imperial conquest and colonization created by the nascent capitalism for the industrial class and the once "penurious rabbles" (in Hegel's phrase).[92] It is a success story made possible by what Arendt called an "alliance between mob and capital."[93] It is also instructive to compare the number of immigrants from Europe to the colonies to the number of ex-colonized who are currently denied a chance to make a living in Europe.

The calculations reflected the "reward" reaped by the white, civilized, and colonizing nation-states from their "paying" dark, barbaric, and colonized natives. "The demand for increased supplies of food and raw materials at the close of the nineteenth century," Lugard concluded, was to be explained by the expanding population as well as "the immensely improved standard of living" in Europe, a Europe he always thought of as white. To this effect, he corroborates most of his figures with statistics from a contemporary publication entitled *The Rising Tide of Colour*.[94]

Philosophy and Racial Colonialism

Ernest Gellner recently wrote, "The industrial age is based on economic growth. This in turn hinges on cognitive growth, which was ratified and perhaps even significantly aided by Cartesian and empiricist philosophies."[95] I propose that modern philosophy "ratified" and "aided" not only industrial and economic growth; it also cognitively formed—through concepts such as "reason," "man," "culture," and "civilization"—the modern idea of race.

In its effort to posit the path to a true nature of "man"—the transformations that an individual must undertake to achieve humanity—modern philosophy has conceptually fashioned something *against* which man must become. When modern philosophy speaks of reason, for example, it refers not simply to "science," "knowledge," "method," or "critique"; it is, more fundamentally, the meaning of humanity, the anthropos, that is at stake. Sartre understood this quite well when he elegantly described his *Critique of Dialectical Reason* as "a prolegomena to any future *anthropology*." For Sartre, in fact, "La Raison est un certain rapport de la connaissance et de l'être." He continued:

> We assert simultaneously that the process of knowledge is dialectical, that the movement of the object (whatever it may be) is *itself* dialectical, and that these two dialectics are one and the same. Taken together, these propositions have *material content*; they themselves are a form of organized knowledge, or, to put it differently, they define a rationality of the world.[96]

Questions about reason and human identity, including racial identity, have always clung together in modern thought, so that the dialectical movements of thought which organize the world, including our racial consciousness, present race to us as itself a domain of the rational.

Léopold Sédar Senghor's theoretical work shows how race plays itself out in the modern dialectical constitution of the ideas of reason and "man." The former president of Senegal and the only African ever to sit on the Académie Française, Senghor may have been disingenuous but not at all innocent of modern racial battles over the meaning of reason and humanity when he notoriously defended a thesis that, *on the surface*, is unsurpassably droll: "Emotion is Negro, and reason Greek." This statement recapitulates a strain of irrationality in modern African thought, an African response to an earlier European rejection of the African as not rational enough to be human enough. It is as if Senghor said, "Well, you keep your Reason; we have our Emotion. Besides, our Emotion is superior to your Reason." The *sous-entendu* in Senghor's statement is more explicit in the thought of his friend and colleague, the Martinician Aimé Césaire, a former teacher of Frantz Fanon and one of the intellectual influences on Fanon's early understanding of racial consciousness. Césaire strongly declared in one of his poems, "*Je suis un homme aussi*" (I am also human).[97] Césaire and Senghor developed Négritude, the Africanist and black movement whose philosophical significance I discuss in detail in chapters 4 and 5. Négritude was a response to the Age of Enlightenment's discourses on man and reason.

The Enlightenment, under the aegis of race knowledge, produced in Africa a realm of darkness where some humans could quite conveniently be philosophically judged as incapable of reason and freedom and unworthy of responsibility. When those who were racially frozen as Other uncritically accepted this identity, it became difficult to find philosophico-theoretical grounds to think of oneself as free and responsible. The false choice was either to succumb to racial degradation or to seek an essence that never existed—now the essence of "emotion," then the essence of "blackness," and then again the essence of "sun people." Thanks to modern racial encounters, unreason, whether in the form of emotion or irresponsibility in European anthropology and philosophy, was no longer thought of as located within Europeans. Unreason remained strange, dreadful, even exotic; but henceforth its representations would be conveniently located in cultures outside of Europe, against whom anthropology and philosophy must now heteronomously manifest a racialized, white, sovereign reason, order, and humanity.

When he writes mockingly about a representative work (Placide Tempels's *Bantu Philosophy*) from this whitened school of anthropology and philosophy, Césaire illuminates the cunning nature of the colonizing Reason: "You are going to the Congo? Respect—I do not say native property, I do not say the freedom of the natives, I do not say the Congolese nation,—I say: You are going to the Congo? Respect the Bantu philosophy!" Furthermore:

> Let them plunder and torture in the Congo, let the Belgian colonizer seize all the natural resources, let him stamp out all freedom, let him crush all pride—let him go in peace, the Reverend Father Tempels consents to all that. But take care! . . . Since

Bantu thought is ontological, the Bantu only ask for satisfaction of an ontological nature. Decent wages! Comfortable housing! Food! These Bantus are pure spirits, I tell you: "What they desire first of all and above all is not the improvement of their economic or material situation, but the white man's recognition of and respect for their culture." In short tip your hat to the Bantu life force, you give a wink to the immortal Bantu soul. . . . You have to admit you're getting off cheap![98]

For many centuries, Europeans produced similar "Bantu philosophies" to justify the colonial subjugation of Africans, slavery and segregation in the United States, and apartheid in South Africa. Instead of educating and empowering the "natives" for economic and political equality, Europeans found it cheaper to confine "black" populations to the plantations, the "other" side of town, or "native" quarters and "homelands"—or in the case of today's United States, jails. Blacks, the argument goes, either are equipped with inherently below-capacity brains and are therefore "naturally" less qualified for culture and humanity, or have a different "soul" than whites, and little else but soul. Should one assume that whites are equipped with brains or minds "naturally" given to delusions of racial superiority?

The question "What is Enlightenment?" that Kant and other philosophers tried to answer could not have been answered for all times and for all peoples. My kind of critique of capitalism-driven modern European encounters with Africa and of the conceptual deficiencies of the Enlightenment projects can, therefore, hardly be seen as "criticism" in the negative, everyday use of the word. What we must investigate is far more technical and scientific. We must examine the philosophical principles that inspired and continue to inspire both the Enlightenment ideas of reason and humanity, and the processes of modernization in order to identify for philosophy the root causes of its principles' historical deficiencies—deficiencies most evident in the histories of tragedies such as racial slavery, racism, and virulent white ethnocentrism. It would seem to me that since the modern idea of humanity is irrevocably linked to a theory of race, in order to more nearly realize modern aspirations to humanity, the present-day attendant concept of race must be reformed or, preferably, jettisoned.

NOTES

1. René Descartes, "Letter of Dedication," *Meditations on First Philosophy* [1641], trans. Lawrence J. Lafleur, New York: Library of Liberal Arts, Macmillan, 1951, pp. 3 and 5; my emphasis.
2. Ibid.
3. Ibid., p. 19; first italics in the original.
4. Blaise Pascal, *Pensées and Other Writings*, trans. Honor Levi, New York: Oxford University Press, 1995, p. 59.
5. Paul Ricoeur, *Freud and Philosophy*, New Haven, CT: Yale University Press, 1970, p. 419.
6. Immanuel Kant, *Logic*, trans. Robert S. Hartman and Wolfgang Schwarz, New York: Library of Liberal Arts, Bobbs-Merrill, 1974; my emphasis.
7. Immanuel Kant, *Anthropology from a Pragmatic Point of View*, trans. Mary J. Gregor, The Hague: Martinus Nijhoff, 1974, p. 3.
8. Ibid.
9. Kant, *Anthropology*, pp. 18–19.
10. Immanuel Kant, *Critique of Pure Reason*, trans. Norman Kemp Smith, New York: St. Martin's Press, 1929, B134 and B135. Kant is, however, more elaborate in B138: "To know anything in space (for instance, a line), I must *draw* it, and thus synthetically bring into being a determinate combination of the given manifold, so that the unity of this act is at the same time the unity of consciousness (as in the concept of a line); and it is through this unity of consciousness that an object (a determinate space) is first known. The synthetic unity of consciousness is, therefore, an objective condition of all knowledge. It is not merely a condition that I myself require in knowing an object, but is a condition under which every intuition must stand in order *to become an object for me.* . . . Although this proposition makes synthetic unity a condition of all thought, it is, as already stated, itself analytic. For it says no more than that all *my* representations in any given intuition must be subject to that condition under which alone I can ascribe them to the identical self as *my* representations, and so can comprehend them as synthetically combined in one apperception through the general expression, '*I think.*'"
11. Kant, *Anthropology*, pp. 18–19.
12. Mary J. Gregor's notes to her translation of the *Anthropology* provide useful clues for anyone who wishes to investigate further such relationships between the *Anthropology* and the *Critiques*. It is difficult to say whether it is the *Anthropology* that influenced the *Critiques* or vice versa; I am however inclined to think that, since the *Anthropology* was already in development as lecture notes before any of the *Critiques* were composed and continued to be re-edited and augmented even after the *Critiques* had been written, it is fair to assume that the *Critiques* constituted specific, detailed studies of an overall Kantian project whose overarching conception and execution could be clearly perceived only from the *Anthropology*.
13. Further, Kant himself explained how his approach relates to Descartes's: Anthropology "can adopt either a physiological or a pragmatic point of view. Physiological knowledge of man investigates what nature makes of him: pragmatic, what man as a free agent makes, or can and should make, of himself. If we ponder natural causes—for example, the possible natural causes behind the power of memory—we can speculate to and fro (as Descartes did) about traces, remaining in the brain, of impressions left by sensations we have experienced. But since we do not know the cerebral nerves and fibers or understand how to use them for our purposes, we still have to admit that we are spectators at this play of our ideas

and let nature have its way. . . . But when we use our observations about what has been found to hinder or stimulate memory in order to increase its scope or efficiency, and need knowledge of man for this purpose, this is part of anthropology for pragmatic purposes; and that is precisely what concerns us here" (*Anthropology*, p. 3).

14. Kant, *Critique of Pure Reason*, p. 472, B574.
15. David Hume, *Treatise of Human Nature* [1739–40], ed. L. A. Selby-Bigge, Oxford: Clarendon Press, 1978, pp. xv, xvi, xviii, 273, 645, et seg.
16. David Hume, *On Human Nature and the Understanding* [1739–40 and 1748], ed. Anthony Flew, New York: Collier Books, 1962, p. 290.
17. Ibid., p. 273.
18. Hume, *Treatise*, p. xv.
19. Ibid., p. 273; my emphasis.
20. Vincent Potter, *Readings in Epistemology: From Aquinas, Bacon, Galileo, Descartes, Locke, Berkeley, Hume, Kant*. New York: Fordham University Press, 1993, p. xii.
21. Ibid.
22. Patrick J. Ryan, "Sailing beyond the Horizon," in *America*, May 23, 1998, pp. 14–24.
23. Determining the beginning and end of the "medieval period" is notoriously unpleasant business; for most people this is the period from the fifth century A.D. to 1350, though others would restrict the properly medieval to 1100 to 1450 or 1500. I have reconciled these diverging systems of dating by speaking of the "early" and "late" medieval period, spanning the fifth century A.D. to the twelfth century. From the end of the twelfth century onward, I would rather speak of the Renaissance, until the early Modern period in the 1500s and the 1600s. For more technical discussions, see the sixth edition of Thomas Greer and Gavin Lewis's *History of the Western World*, New York: Harcourt Brace, 1992, Part Two.
24. John Block Friedman, *The Monstrous Races in Medieval Art and Thought*, Cambridge, MA: Harvard University Press, 1981, p. 1.
25. Ibid., p. 3.
26. Vincent of Neauvais, *Speculum Naturale* (Douai, 1624), 1.31.118, pp. 2387–2388.
27. St. Augustine, *City of God*, trans. Marcus Dods, in *Works of Augustine*, Edinburgh, Scotland: 1934, II, 118–119; Bk. xvi, chap. 9.
28. S. E. Morison, *Journals and Other Documents on the Life and Voyages of Christopher Columbus*, New York: 1963, p. 65.
29. H. F. Augstein, *Race: The Origins of an Idea*, Bristol, U.K.: Thoemmes Press, 1996, p. 7.
30. Marco Polo, *The Travels of Marco Polo*, trans. R. E. Latham, New York: Penguin Classics, 1958, p. vii.
31. Ibid.
32. " 'Savage,' from the late latin *silvaticus* . . . is equivalent to marginality and, from a cultural normative space, designates the uncultivated" (V. Y. Mudimbe, *The Idea of Africa*, Bloomington: Indiana University Press, p. 27).
33. John Burcke, "The Wild Man's Pedigree," in *The Savage Within*, p. 262.
34. Hannah Arendt, *The Human Condition*, Chicago: University of Chicago Press, 1958, p. 277.
35. Ibid.
36. I do not suppose that the account I have provided of the relationship between the Renaissance or the Enlightenment worldview is controversial. Other literature exists on the subject, and I shall give only one, impressive example: Donald F. Lach and Edwin J.

Van Kelly's study of relations between Asia and Europe during the same periods of European expansion, entitled *Asia in the Making of Europe*, published by University of Chicago Press from 1965 to 1993. The first volume, *The Century of Discovery*, in two books of more than fifteen hundred pages, comprises the chapters "Antiquity and the Middle Ages," "The Renaissance Before the Great Discoveries," "The Spice Trade," "The Printed Word," "The Christian Mission," "India," "Southeast Asia," "Japan," "China," and an epilogue, "A Composite Picture." The second volume, *A Century of Wonder* (in three books: *The Visual Arts*, *The Literary Arts*, and *The Scholarly Disciplines*), is more than fourteen hundred pages and consists of sixteen chapters: "Collections of Curiosities"; "The Individual Arts"; "The Iconography of Asian Animals"; "Naturalism, Symbolism, and Ornament"; "Heralds of Empire"; "Books, Libraries, and Readings"; "The Inherited Themes"; "Portuguese Literature"; "Spanish Literature"; "Italian Literature"; "French Literature"; "German Literature"; "Technology and the Natural Sciences"; "Cartography and Geography"; "Language and Linguistics"; and "Epilogue." The third and last volume, *A Century of Advance* (also in three books: *Trade, Missions, Literature*; *South Asia*; and *Southeast Asia*), is more than sixteen hundred pages. Chapters range from "Empire and Trade" through "The Iberian Literature" to "Vietnam." In contrast to Lach and Van Kelly's ambitious Chicago project, my argument shall remain, without doubt, a modest contribution from philosophy to a related area of study where, unfortunately, there are still so many more mysteries than knowledge.

37. Léopold Sédar Senghor, *On African Socialism*, trans. Mercer Cook, New York: Praeger, 1964, p. 81.

38. V. Y. Mudimbe, *The Invention of Africa*, Bloomington: Indiana University Press, pp. 69–70.

39. Emmanuel C. Eze, *Race and the Enlightenment*, Oxford: Blackwell, 1997, p. 4.

40. Orlando Patterson, *Ethnic Chauvinism: The Reactionary Impulse*, New York: Stein and Day, 1977, p. 51.

41. Ibid., p. 71.

42. J. Huizinga, *The Waning of the Middle Ages: A Study of the Forms of Life, Thought and Art in France and the Netherlands in the Dawn of the Renaissance* [1924], New York: Anchor Doubleday, 1949, pp. 5–6.

43. Orlando Patterson, who uses the word ethnic to refer to "racial" identities, argues, "We must agree with Brunt that the Romans were less generous with the grantings of citizenship than some earlier authorities would lead us to believe. Compared to the Greeks, the Romans seem a model of imperial tolerance and generosity, but also most any group of people would appear favorable in comparison with the Greeks in ethnic matters." However, Mudimbe asks, "In the same vein as Snowden's argument, one could emphasize, as did A. Bourgeois, evidences of assimilation and cultural integration. . . . Yet what do these [evidences] demonstrate? Here is just one of numerous counterexamples: during the reign of Hadrianus (A.D. 76–138), the poet Florus from the African province was denied a prize because, according to a witness, 'the emperor . . . did not want to see Jupiter's crown going to Africa'" (*The Invention of Africa*, pp. 69–70). We should point out that Patterson also recognized that "the Romans in the provinces . . . formed a distinct ethnic group, incorporating only a very limited degree cooperating elements of the displaced native elite" (*Ethnic Chauvinism*, p. 60). The matter as it stands is, indeed, "an invitation to further research and not closure" (Mudimbe, *The Invention of Africa*, p. 70).

44. I am using the word anthropology in two senses: (a) the science of "man," physical (as in

physical anthropology) or moral and psychological (as in moral, rational, or philosophical anthropology); and (b) the study of human cultures (cultural anthropology).

45. David Hume, *Essays Moral, Political, and Literary* [1777], ed. Eugene F. Miller, Indianapolis: Liberty Fund, 1987.

46. Kant's "Reviews of Johann Gottfried Herder's *Ideas on the Philosophy of the History of Mankind*" or *Observations on the Feeling of the Beautiful and Sublime* easily belong to this category. For a bibliographic guide on Kant's anthropological writings, see Howard Caygill, *A Kant Dictionary*, Oxford: Blackwell, 1995, pp. 418–427.

47. Kwame Anthony Appiah, "Philosophy and the Study of Africa," *Encyclopedia of Africa South of the Sahara*, Vol. 3, ed. John Middleton, New York: Charles Scribner's Sons, 1997, pp. 399–404.

48. K. (J. E.) Wiredu, "How Not to Compare African Thought with Western Thought," in *African Philosophy: An Introduction* (3rd edition), ed. Richard Wright, New York: University Press of America, 1984, p. 159.

49. Ibid.

50. Kwame Anthony Appiah, "Race, Culture, and Identity: A Misunderstood Connection," in *Color Conscious: The Political Morality of Race*, ed. K. A. Appiah and Amy Guttman, Princeton, NJ: Princeton University Press, 1996, pp. 90–91.

51. Ibid., p. 2.

52. Ibid., p. 1.

53. Regarding Karl Marx's comment: "This combination of Jewry and Germany with a fundamental Negro streak . . . The fellow's self assertiveness is Negro too," Wiredu responded: "It is sometimes understandable for a man to chide his own origins, but to condemn a down trodden people like this is more serious. Would that black men everywhere had more of the self assertiveness which Marx here deprecates" (Wiredu, "How Not to Compare," p. 159).

54. David Hume, *The Philosophical Works*, ed. T. H. Green and T. H. Grose, London: 1882, III, p. 253.

55. Kant, "Innate Characteristics of Human Beings," in *Race and the Enlightenment: A Reader*, ed. E. C. Eze, Oxford: Blackwell, 1997, pp. 62–64.

56. Hegel, "Geographical Basis of World History," in *Race and the Enlightenment: A Reader*, ed. E. C. Eze, Oxford: Blackwell, 1997, pp. 110–149.

57. Hannah Arendt, *Kant's Political Philosophy*, ed. Ronald Beiner, Chicago: University of Chicago Press, 1982, p. 7.

58. Augstein, *Race*, p. ix. Anthropological and sociological works that accept this point of view include George Stocking, *Victorian Anthropology* (New York: Free Press, 1987); Michael Banton, *Racial Theories* (Cambridge: Cambridge University Press, 1987); and Nancy Stepan, *The Idea of Race in Science: Great Britain 1800–1960* (London: Macmillan, 1982).

59. Banton, *Racial Theories*, pp. ix–x.

60. Thomas Jefferson, *Notes on the State of Virginia*, ed. William Peden, New York: Norton, 1972, p. 143.

61. Ibid., pp. 138 and 142.

62. Quoted in Banton, *Racial Theories*, p. 1

63. See Robert Knox, *The Races of Men: A Fragment*, 2nd ed., London: Renshaw, 1850.

64. J. C. Nott and G. R. Giddon, *Types of Mankind; or, Ethnological Researches*, Philadelphia: Lippincott, 1854; and J. C. Nott and G. R. Giddon, *Indigenous Races, or New Chapters of Ethnological Enquiry*, Philadelphia: Lippincott, 1857.

65. Comte de Gorbineau, *Essai sur l'inégalité des Races humaines*, Paris: [Firmin-Didot, 1853–1855] Belfond, 1967.

66. All references to *Systemae naturae* in this section are from the English translation of the same in Eze, *Race and the Enlightenment* (Oxford: Blackwell, 1997).

67. Robert J. C. Young, *Colonial Desire: Hybridity in Theory, Culture and Race*, New York: Routledge, 1995.

68. Friedman, *The Monstrous Races*, p. 203.

69. Race thinking in the eighteenth and nineteenth centuries, from Georges Louis Leclerc Buffon and Lord Henry Home Kames through Kant to Cuvier, though varied one from the other, are indebted to Linnaeus's original outlines. While disagreeing with Buffon on the issue of whether there is one origin or many origins of mankind (the famous mono-genesis versus polygenesis argument), Kames, like Buffon, produced a system of classifi-cation whose general order mirrors Linnaeus's definition of *kinds*. There is also a continuity between Linnaeus's system and Knox's "transcendental anatomy," a program Knox designed "to explain in a connected chain the phenomena of the living material world," and to show that "all animals are formed upon one plan." In Linnaeus as in his suc-cessors, the idea of "variety" among human species was quickly reduced to "monstrosity" and "deformity"—a deviance.

70. Elazer Barkan, *The Retreat of Scientific Racism: Changing Concepts of Race in Britain and the United States between the World Wars* (Cambridge: Cambridge University Press, 1992), p. 42.

71. See, for example, Robert E. Park and E. W. Burgess, eds., *Introduction to the Science of Sociology* [1921], Chicago: University of Chicago Press, 1969; or Park, "The Nature of Race Relations," in *Race Relations and the Race Problem: A Definition and an Analysis* [1939], ed. Edgar T. Thompson, New York: Greenwood Press, 1968. pp. 3–45. Park's work should alert us to another way of talking about "race" after the science of genetics: a *recon-struction* of what race could mean, such as Lucius Outlaw's *On Race and Philosophy*, New York, Routledge, 1996.

72. Park, "The Nature of Race Relations," pp. 3–45.

73. Ibid., p. 5.

74. Lewis Copeland, "The Negro as a Contrast Conception," in *Race Relations and the Race Problem*, ed. Edgar T. Thompson, 1968, pp. 152–179.

75. Ibid., p. 152.

76. Ibid., p. 152–153.

77. Maurice Evans, *Black and White in South East Africa*, London: Longman, Green & Co., 1911, pp. 15–13.

78. Tzvetan Todorov, *On Human Diversity: Nationalism, Racism, and Exoticism in French Thought*, Cambridge, MA: Harvard University Press, 1993; Jacques Barzun, *The French Race: Theories of Its Origin and Their Social and Political Implications, Prior to the Revolution*. New York: Columbia University Press, 1932; and Léon Poliakov, *The Aryan Myth: A History of Racist and Nationalist Ideas in Europe*, London: Chatto, Heinemann, 1974.

79. H. D. Perraton, "British Attitudes towards East and West Africa, 1880–1914," *Race* 8: 223–246.

80. Quoted in Banton, *The Idea of Race*, Boulder, CO: Westview Press, pp. 60–61.

81. Augstein, *Race*, p. xi. See also G. S. Rousseau and Roy Porter, *The Ferment of Knowledge: Studies in the Historiography of Eighteenth-Century Science* (Cambridge: Cambridge University Press, 1980); Londa Schiebinger, *Nature's Body: Gender in the Making of Modern Science* (Boston: Beacon Press, 1993); and Christopher Fox, Roy Porter, Robert Wokler,

eds., *Inventing Human Science: Eighteenth-Century Domains* (Berkeley: University of California Press, 1995).

82. Michael Banton, professor of sociology at the University of Bristol, director of England's Social Science Research Council Unit on Ethnic Relations, and a member of the United Nations Committee for the Elimination of Racial Discrimination, contends that it is quixotic to try to produce a particular date as *the* day when modern "racial consciousness" developed. See Banton, *The Idea of Race*, pp. 13–26.

83. Patterson, *Ethnic Chauvinism*, p. 43.

84. Mircea Eliade, *The Sacred and the Profane*, New York: Harvest Books, 1959, pp. 29–31.

85. Margery Perham, in introduction to Lord Lugard, *The Dual Mandate in British Tropical Africa*, 5th ed., London: Archon Books, 1965 [1922].

86. Lugard, *The Dual Mandate*, p. 617.

87. Ibid.

88. Ibid., p. 618.

89. Ibid.

90. Ibid., p. 3.

91. Ibid., p. 3, n1.

92. Hegel, *Elements of Philosophy of Right*, ed. Allen W. Wood, trans. H. B. Nisbet, Cambridge: Cambridge University Press, 1991.

93. Hannah Arendt, *The Origins of Totalitarianism*, New York: Harcourt Brace Jovanovich, 1973, p. 147; see also the section of the same chapter entitled "Expansion and the Nation-State."

94. Lugard, *The Dual Mandate*, p. 3, n1.

95. E. Gellner, *Nations and Nationalism*, Ithaca: Cornell University Press, 1983, pp. 77–78.

96. Jean-Paul Sartre, *Critique de la Raison Dialectique*, Paris: Gallimard, 1960, p. 10. For the English translation by Alan Sheridan-Smith (*Critique of Dialectical Reason*, Atlantic Highlands, NJ: Humanities Press, 1976), see Part 1 ("Theory of Practical Ensembles"). In the preface to the French edition, Sartre was yet more eloquent: "si quelque chose comme une Vérité doit pouvoir exister dans l'anthropologie, elle doit être *devenue*, elle doit se faire *totalisation*. Il va sans dire que cette double exigence définit ce mouvement de l'être et de la connaissance (ou de la compréhension) qu'on nomme depuis Hegel "dialectique" . . . Y a-t-il une Vérité de l'homme?" (p. 10).

97. Aimé Césaire, *The Collected Poetry*, trans. Clayton Eshleman and Annete Smith; Berkeley: University of California Press, 1983.

98. Césaire, *Discourse on Colonialism*, New York: Monthly Review Press, 1973; pp. 37–38, 39.

CHAPTER 2

HUME, RACE, AND REASON

INTRODUCTION

In "The Racial Contract Hypothesis," an otherwise useful analysis of Charles Mills's *The Racial Contract*, J. L. A. Garcia claims that Mills "echoes uncritically Emmanuel Eze's complaints about the (all too real) racism of Enlightenment *philosophers*, but provides no serious inquiry into the crucial question of what it would mean for . . . *philosophies* to be racist."[1] But several years earlier, John Immerwahr had suggested, if only cryptically, "While Hume is generally known as an enemy of prejudice and intolerance, he is also infamous as a proponent of *philosophical* racism."[2] I wonder, then, how many brands of racism exist? What does "philosophical" racism mean? If philosophical racism is something about which one wishes to care, what part of Hume's philosophy sustains this racism?

Hume wrote little that directly addresses race, although his footnote to the essay "Of National Character" is notorious. Ironically, the footnote was not part of the original essay; it was added between 1753 and 1754 to a revised version. The original was written in 1748. A final, third version was edited by Hume shortly before he died in 1777, and formed part of the collection published as *Essays: Moral, Literary, and Political*.[3] This background is important because it is relevant to the question of whether Hume's interests in racial issues were merely passing, or persistent.

The footnote is not, as some would like to think, philosophically insignificant. Its addition to the original essay and maintenance throughout subsequent revisions indicate that the ideas expressed were important to the author, and that he believed them to be equally important to his audience. By 1770, the essay was so popular that University of Aberdeen professor James Beattie, in *An Essay on the Nature and Immutability of Truth, in Opposition to Sophistry and Skepticism*, devoted several pages to refuting the views expressed by Hume in the footnote. Hume responded to Beattie's criticisms, though dismissively. In a letter to William Straham, later published in the *London Chronicle* of June 12–14, 1777, Hume reacted by calling Beattie "a bigoted silly fellow."[4] This exchange shows that Hume was not unaware of the controversial nature of his racial views, or why some of his contemporaries might have considered them troubling. Since he continued to defend these views, they must have represented his considered judgment.

Race and Empiricism

Some critics think that Hume's racist views were merely his, but others believe that the racism Hume expresses is rooted in the epistemology of empiricism, a philosophical movement that Hume vigorously promoted. The arguments are usually stated in two forms: first, some historians of philosophy think that Hume was merely repeating prejudices that were common among intellectuals of his time. In "Hume's Racism,"[5] for example, Richard Popkin traces the sources, contexts, and consequences of Hume's race-related ideas—an approach not unlike Cornel West's in "The Genealogy of Modern Racism."[6] In fact, Popkin's questions are typical of the genealogical perspective: Who influenced Hume? Who was influenced by Hume? What are the continuities in this development of racialist and racist ideas? The underlying question is how to establish that Hume's racism might have been a textual repetition of what most intellectuals of the time thought, but perhaps did not voice (or at least did not write down) as Hume did. Popkin explained, for example, that Hume "held to the prejudices of the time; he had a view that fitted with them. He stated more forcefully than any of his contemporaries what they believed, and because his views fitted too well with racist ideology he became the spokesman."[7] If this interpretation is accurate, the lesson to be drawn seems clear-cut: philosophers,

Popkin cautioned, "should be more careful about throwing prejudicial beliefs into even the footnotes of [their] writings." Popkin in fact believed that Hume's footnote was simply a "casual addition" which, accidentally, became "the rallying point of the polygenetic racists."[8]

The second form of historical interpretation seems more appealing, because it appears to overcome the obvious difficulties in Popkin's perspective. In what ways, for example, could the footnote be said to have been "casual"—after all, it was deliberately added to an already self-standing essay; it was revised but maintained in numerous subsequent editions; and it was on numerous occasions publicly defended by Hume against criticisms. Do not these facts suggest that the footnote was not casual, but premeditated, and fastly held unto? I shall have explored several reasons—both philosophical and historical—why this must have been the case, by the end of this chapter. The footnote, I shall argue, is rooted both in Hume's epistemology and in his political thought.

For those who believe that Hume's views were rooted in empiricism, the key question is to establish that empiricism, as a philosophical method and a body of doctrines, is historically linked to racism (and forms of exploitation based on sex, religion, class, and ethnicity). Harry Bracken and Noam Chomsky are outspoken proponents of this position. Bracken argues: "Racism is easily and readily stateable if one thinks of the person in accordance with empiricist teaching because the essence of the person may be deemed to be his colour, language, religion, etc." To empiricism Bracken opposed Cartesianism: "the Cartesian dualist model provided what I called a modest conceptual brake to the articulation of racial degradation and slavery." This argument is therefore based on the claim that empiricism's account of concept acquisition and learning and its distinctions between fact/value provide "ideological bulwark behind which racially biased pseudo-science continues to flourish."[9] By contrast, it is presumed that one would not find in Cartesianism (its universalist doctrine of a human essence, in particular) a basis for philosophically justifying racialism and therefore racism. "Historically," writes Bracken, "the most significant feature of the shifts in ideas between the sixteenth and nineteenth centuries is that racism not only runs counter to the three major religious traditions which have dominated the west, it runs counter to the doctrines of man still being articulated within the seventeenth century."[10] Cartesianism was one such older doctrine that was supplanted, in England at least, by empiricism. Bracken claims that "if one is a Cartesian, a defender of mind/body dualism . . . it becomes impossible to state a racist position" because "man's essential properties reside finally in his spirit. His colour, his language, his biology, even his sex are in the strictest sense *accidental*."[11]

To better appreciate Bracken's argument, recall that Descartes had argued: "Reason is found whole and entire" in every human.[12] For the ardent Cartesian, therefore, human differences of skin color or sex are merely accidents, inessential, and are illegitimate criteria for determining the essential and true worth of the person. Bracken claims to have found an intriguing historical correlation between the rejection of Cartesianism in England and the simultaneous growth in that country of empiricism, colonialism, and racism.

Hume, unlike Descartes, denied the existence of a metaphysical essence of human nature, and this shows, according to Bracken, that empiricism could provide no conceptual tools to a universal defense of some basic rights to all humans. For example, if the Locke-Hume empiricist "doctrine of substance and the consequent denial of thinking substance" leads to an amoral philosophical conception of human nature, where subjection and manipulation of human beings by experts are easily philosophically justified, then could not one assert a clear philosophical relationship between the rise of empiricism and the "techniques of manipulation," on the one hand, and the shrinking of rationalism and freedom on the other? Of course Bracken cautioned: "I am not claiming that empiricism is responsible for slavery; or that a return to the rationalism would herald a new age of human freedom," and "The connection between empiricism and the rise of manipulative models of man may be considered historical, not logical." But there is no doubt that *some* logical argument is proposed here: it is assumed, in principle, that when a philosopher rejects Cartesianism in favor of empiricism, he or she is left with a philosophical doctrine that, *a priori*, is said to be compatible with techniques of manipulation. Bracken also seems to have no doubt that it is empiricism, not rationalism, that ushered in "methods of control . . . whereby people have been [on the basis of race] merchandised."[13]

In 1784 James Ramsay wrote that there were relationships between arguments produced in favor of African slavery and the arguments of British empiricism.[14] Ramsay was aware of the public stands of key philosophers on the question of slavery, and the public debates about "the Negro mind" as they related to the issue of whether the Negro was a legitimate "article of trade." In a less than subtle reference to Hume, Ramsay had written: "It is ludicrous to equate or correlate capacity for arts and the sciences with skin colour." Like Bracken after him, Ramsay exhibited a preference and passion for Cartesianism, and justified his antislavery arguments on grounds that "the soul is a simple substance, not to be distinguished by squat or tall, black, brown, or fair." He even asked how it would look if one argued, at Hume's expense, that only nonfat people are capable of "metaphysical subtlety."[15]

Unlike Bracken, Chomsky joined the debate about the relationship between empiricism and slavery and racism from an indirect route. In *Reflections on Language* he provides arguments that reinforce Bracken's intuitions about empiricism—but on the bases of the well-known universalist claims of his linguistic theory. Paul Rabinow eloquently captures Chomsky's position on this issue in his summary of the famous debate between Chomsky and Michel Foucault (a debate that was conducted on a Dutch television program):

> For Noam Chomsky, there is a human nature . . . unless there is some form of relatively fixed human nature, true scientific understanding is impossible. Starting from his own research, Chomsky asked: How is it that on the basis of a partial and fragmentary set of experiences, individuals in every culture are able not only to learn their own language, but to use it in a creative way? For Chomsky, there was only one possible answer: there must be a bio-physical structure underlying the mind which enables us, both as individuals and as species, to deduce from the multiplicity of individual experiences a unified language. There must be, Chomsky insists, a "mass of schematisms, innate governing principles, which guide our social and intellectual and individual behavior . . . there is something biologically given, unchangeable, a foundation for whatever it is that we do with our mental capacities." Chomsky's scientific

career has been devoted to uncovering these structures. His aim: a
testable mathematical theory of mind. His lineage: Cartesian
rationality.[16]

Chomsky saw in Bracken's work an opportunity to reject linguistic theories
that compete with his own—those based on empiricist postulates. For
Bracken as for Chomsky, if it is assumed that there is no innate human
nature, then there is no conceptual support to one culture's or even one person's protests against treating others or oneself as racial, sexual, class, or ethnic objects, to be manipulated or "cleansed" according to the whims of those
who have the power to attempt such manipulation and cleansing. "The concept of the 'empty organism,' plastic and unstructured," Chomsky claims,
"apart from being false, also serves naturally as the support for the reactionary social doctrines. If people are, in fact, malleable and plastic beings
with no essential psychological nature, then why should they not be controlled and coerced by those who claim authority, special knowledge, and a
unique insight into what is best for those less enlightened?"[17]

A CONVERSATION BETWEEN THE DEAF AND THE BLIND?

It is difficult not to feel that Bracken's and Chomsky's case against empiricism—Hume, in any case—is too diffuse and weak. But even those who
have remarked on this fact appear to be too much on the defensive to be able
to provide a more coherent account of the historical relationships between
modern philosophy and racism, or a clearer picture of empiricism and the
individual empiricist's position in the modern English arguments in favor of
racism and slavery. John Searle, for example, offers an "argument" that runs
like this: between empiricism and rationalism, the latter was historically
more likely to promote racism. Why? Because if one assumes, as Descartes
did, that there exists a substance of human nature, it is only a short step from
this to conclude that there are as many kinds of these substances as there are
races, and that some of the racialized substances are intellectually, morally,
and aesthetically superior to others. This, Searle concludes, means that
Cartesianism might have been prone to a harsher form of racialism and
racism. In his own words:

> I have now read over these passages alleging a connection between racism and empiricism on the one hand and Cartesianism and freedom on the other. . . . I would very much like to think I am misunderstanding what Chomsky is saying. Otherwise, it is hard to interpret them in ways that do not render them quite unacceptable. . . . If anything, it is a shorter step from the Cartesian theory of the mind to the theory of racial inferiority than from the Humean, because once you believe that there are innate human mental structures it is only a short step to argue that the innate mental structures differ from one race to another.[18]

Searle in fact claims that Bracken and Chomsky merely wanted "to smear the great empiricists with . . . veiled accusations of racism."[19]

Searle's argument is strained because he doesn't really deny that the empiricists, some of whom he acknowledged were in their "*professional* lives" involved "in the creation of the colonial system," were racists, promoted slavery, and fashioned epistemologies and metaphysics that suited these professional activities. In fact, it is easy to see that Searle *expanded* the field of possible applications of Bracken's and Chomsky's argument: Cartesianism, *too*, could have been equally suitable for arguing in favor of racist, proslavery, or sexist positions. Bracken did not fail to pick up this opportunity in a rejoinder:

> Those of us who have tried to discover whether racism has any roots in the philosophical traditions have not been in the "smear" business. We probably share a belief that racism is an evil—but the "ultimate" question has to do with the ways in which racism has, in the course of our history, become so comfortably institutionalized within Anglo-American liberal culture.[20]

Even when Bracken's focus became more pointed: "The conceptual building blocks which were initially used in the construction of racism within this culture were initially provided, I have contended, not only by empiricists but by *racist* empiricists," those who came to Searle's defense fared no better. Bernard Williams, the ethicist, is one. In a review of Chomsky's *Reflections*, he noted, with appropriate echo of the notorious historical debate about "the Negro mind": "It seems odd that anyone should need reminding at the moment that it is the environmentalists' [i.e., empiricists'] view of matters of 'intelligence' which has been identified as the liberal one."[21] The problem, however, is that it is just this "liberal" view that Bracken has explicitly characterized as racist. Bracken responded: "Williams is correct . . . the environmentalist view has been so identified. However, I have been concerned that several ingredients in empiricism, including the environmentalism of the blank-tablet thesis, have in fact facilitated the articulation of racism even while being identified as 'liberal.'"[22]

To make our way out of these claims and counterclaims, consider the presumption that only a religious, metaphysical, or biophysical conception of "essence" of the human nature can deliver philosophy from racism, sexism, classicism, and so on. Critics charge that "empiricist doctrine can easily be molded into an ideology for the vanguard party that claims authority to lead the masses to a society that will be governed by the 'red bureaucracy' . . . just as easily for the liberal technocrats or corporate managers who monopolize 'vital decision-making' in the institutions of the state capitalist democracy."[23] But this way of raising the issue obscures another, more subtle one: Does empiricism offer another kind of nonessential conception that could equally promote social equality and universal defense of human rights? Instead of dogmatically pitting empiricism and rationalism against each other, should we not also inquire if *any* philosophical doctrine can cure humans of cruelty—such as those evident in racism, sexism, and slavery, of both ancient and modern kinds?

The fear of every kind of "manipulation" could also be exaggerated: individuals dialectically shape one another (the whole meaning of society), just as groups shape one another (in intertribal as in international relations), and these "shapings" are sometimes benevolent, sometimes malevolent, but most likely they are more often indifferent. If philosophy cannot cure humans of malevolence and indifference, is it justified to attribute to it as much historical power over national and international social problems—especially the problems of racial exploitation and inequality? Without a corresponding study of actual histories of racism, colonialism, or the elitism implied in the class structures of a society—structures which, it is claimed, either empiricism or rationalism initiates or promotes—it would be impossible to evaluate which of the claims is true.

Of course, in principle, nonessentialist metaphysics or theory of mind may promote social equality. When Richard Rorty gave up foundationalist epistemology and essentialist metaphysics in favor of a pragmatic conception of truth and rights, when he gave up thinking of principles of social movements promoted in the name of God or the Universal, he continued to argue for campaigns for social justice—"campaign" understood as small, tactical mobilizations around issues that are socially progressive. The metaphysical question of "essence-accident," or "fact-value," appears remote from Rorty's point of view: either has been replaced by the pragmatic concepts of "useful-useless." For Rorty, philosophy will get along better without theories of the intrinsic nature of reality—including human reality. And "once one gives up the appearance-reality distinction, and the attempt to relate such things as predictive success and diminished cruelty to the intrinsic nature of reality, one has to give separate accounts of progress in science and morals."[24] It is the question of alternative accounts of human nature and morals, outside of the traditional parameters set by French rationalism and British empiricism, that neither Bracken nor his critics considered.

But to believe, as I do, that empiricist positions on the nature of "mind" do not automatically entail racism is not to absolve specific empiricist doctrines, in their political and historical commitments, from being complicit with cultural and intellectual infrastructures that sought to normalize racialism and racism. Such an absolution whether pleaded for empiricism or for any other strand of modern philosophy could hardly be justified without careful attention to the particular philosophical methods or doctrines and their peculiar histories.

HUME AND HUMAN NATURE

Was Hume's theory of human nature racist? Yes. But some who ostensibly seek to protect Hume's thought from "smear" have gone as far as to argue that Hume had no positive theory of human nature, and that he was merely a skeptic, a "negative" thinker. This is, however, a point of view that does not square even with establishment scholarship on Hume. Barry Stroud, for example, rejects as a caricature the image of Hume as "the arch sceptic whose primary aim and achievement was to reduce the theories of his empiricist predecessors to the absurdity that was implicitly contained in them all along." Hume, Stroud argues, was "a philosopher of human nature [who] puts forth a new theory or vision of man."[25] Hume's vision of "man" is new because it was different from those of his predecessors, especially Descartes.

In a study entitled *Descartes and Hume*, Ezra Talmor showed that the young Hume's sojourn in France—at the Jesuit College at la Flèche, to be precise—were more than pilgrimages to the heartland of Cartesianism solely to "attack" it. La Flèche was the heartland of Cartesianism, and it is true that Hume developed an enthusiasm for Descartes's ideas, and often referred to them as "the most profound philosophy" of the time. Hume wanted to avail himself of the new ideas in view of undertaking a general scientific study of man—which he called "anatomical philosophy." Anatomical philosophy would combine Cartesianism and Newtonian theories, a synthesis Hume hoped would yield "a completely general theory of human nature to explain why human beings act, think, perceive and feel in all the ways they do."[26]

From the point of view of this project, the skepticism in Hume's study of human nature can only be considered methodological and academic. Hume admitted that "total" skepticism regarding the existence of human nature, and human knowledge, is impossible—on natural grounds. In Part IV of Book I of the *Treatise*, in the section "Of the Sceptical and other Systems of Philosophy," he stated: "Shou'd it be ask'd of me, whether I sincerely assent to this argument, which I seem to take such pains to inculcate, and whether I be really one of those skeptics, who hold that all is uncertain, and that our Judgment is not in *any* thing possest of *any* measures of truth and falsehood; I shou'd reply, that this question is entirely superfluous, and that neither I, nor any other person was ever sincerely and constantly of that opinion." Total skepticism is superfluous because nature could not permit it:

> Nature, by an absolute and uncontroulable necessity has determin'd us to judge as well as to breathe and feel; nor can we any

more forebear viewing certain objects in a stronger and fuller light, upon account of their customary connexion with a present impression, than we can hinder ourselves from thinking as long as we are awake, or seeing the surrounding bodies, when we turn our eyes toward them in broad sunshine.[27]

The "proof" offered here against skepticism on natural grounds is similar to Descartes's conclusion, on logical grounds, in "I think, therefore I am"; as by the very act of doubting one proves that one exists, one could not, according to Hume, have a mind and body structured by nature in certain ways and deny that this structure of this mind and this body inescapably leads one to think, judge, breathe, feel, and so on, in specific ways. A philosopher must recognize and, according to Hume, "anatomically" describe these natural processes and the structures of their organization.

This was why the task of moral philosophy, as Hume understood it, was complementary to natural philosophy. Whereas natural philosophy encompasses the domains we would assign to physics, chemistry, and biology, moral philosophy studies human thoughts, actions, and feelings, and conventions, customs, and traditions. The belief that the objects of both natural and moral sciences are subject to scientifically describable general laws of nature is a consistent theme in Hume's work. Why then did he "take such pains," in his own words, to cultivate arguments that were "skeptic[al] with regard to reason . . . the senses . . . [and] personal identity"?[28] Hume himself provided the answer: "My intention in displaying so carefully the arguments . . . is only to make the reader sensible of the truth of my hypothesis, that all our reasoning concerning causes and effects are deriv'd from nothing but custom; and that belief is more properly an act of the sensitive, than of the cognitive part of our natures."[29] The strategic intent of this skepticism couldn't be more clearly stated.

In fact, David Norton believes that "Hume . . . may be best understood as the first *post*-sceptical philosopher of the early modern period." Arguing that Hume's thought is both "fundamentally sceptical *and* fundamentally constructive," Norton asserts that Hume's position "is sceptical in so far as he shows that knowledge has nothing like the firm, reliable foundation the Cartesians or other rationalists had claimed to give it"; but the position is also "constructive in so far as he undertook to articulate *a new science of human nature* that would provide for all sciences, including morals and politics, a unique and defensible foundation."[30] To answer the question, "Is there a philosophical racism in Hume?" we must examine his "science of human nature."

Hume's theory of the mind is at the heart of his analysis of human nature, for the mind constitutes what he calls the "self." Yet scholars are not agreed as to what, exactly, Hume says the mind is.

> To some it is plain that Hume reduces matter to mind, that he adopts a radical subjective idealism without benefit of Berkeley's God or Berkeleyan minds. In the view of others he reduces both minds and bodies to some natural stuff, anticipating the neutral monism of James and Russell. Some recent writers see Hume as flirting with a reduction of mind to matter in the manner of behaviorism or, more plausibly, so-called identity theories. Some think that as a consistent sceptic, he has no constructive view about the matter of mind.[31]

The last suggestion stems from the view of Hume as a total skeptic, a view we already rejected because it neglects the constructive orientation in his view of human nature. The first option—Hume the radical subjective idealist—is far from convincing: the idea of God or its conceptual likeness plays no part in Hume's theory of mind; and the second option, Hume-the-monist, fares no better than the first, for Hume's idea of mind does not depend on the existence of a "stuff," "the one," or anything resembling Berkeley's notion of "Spirit." Finally, the naturalistic aspects of Hume's theory of mind do not qualify it as positivism or "behaviorism" in the ways we understand the terms today, for Hume's idea of "science," for example, remained—unlike what we think of as science nowadays—highly reflective and philosophical. In fact, Hume's science sought to build a bridge between Descartes and Newton, hence the subtitle of the *Treatise*, "Being an attempt to introduce the experimental method of reasoning into moral subjects."

For Hume the mind is not a "thing"; in fact, he denies the very idea that there exist "substances," material or immaterial, as previously advocated by Locke and Malebranche. Against these predecessors, Hume argues: "These philosophers are the curious reasoners concerning the material or immaterial substances. . . . In order to put a stop to these endless cavils on both sides [the objectivist Locke and the spiritualist Malebranche], I know no better method than to ask these philosophers in a few words, *What they mean by substance. . . .* This question we have found impossible to be answered."[32] Hume also explicitly rejected Descartes's definitions: "Descartes maintained that thought was the essence of the mind—not this thought or that thought, but thought in general. This seems to be absolutely unintelligible, since everything that exists is particular; and therefore it must be our several particular perceptions that compose the mind. I say *compose* the mind, not *belong* to it. The mind is not a substance in which the perceptions inhere."[33]

If the mind is not a thing existing as identical to itself (it is a series of perceptual activities), so is the self. Hume rejects the position that "we are every moment immediately conscious of what we call SELF; that we feel its existence and its continuance in existence and are certain, beyond the evidence of a demonstration, both of its perfect identity and simplicity."[34] These assertions, Hume continues, "are contrary to that very experience which is pleaded for them, nor have we any idea of *self*, after the manner it is here explain'd"; he queries: "From what impression cou'd this idea [of the self] be deriv'd? This question 'tis impossible to answer without a manifest contradiction and absurdity."[35] In place of the traditional conceptions of mind, soul, or self, Hume therefore proposes, "What we call a *mind* is nothing but a heap or collection of different perceptions, united together by certain relations."[36]

What are these relations? The idea that there are relations that unite otherwise disparate sensual impressions or ideas is an important one. Sometimes Hume compared the mind to a theater, "where several perceptions successively make their appearance; pass, re-pass, glide away, and mingle in an infinite variety of postures and situations."[37] But the image of space evoked in the metaphor of theater could be misleading. Is the mind an empty space where impressions and ideas, as characters, relate to one another? Hume warned against this interpretation. "The comparison to theatre must not mislead us," he said. "They are the successive perceptions only that constitute the mind."[38] We must rely therefore simply on the idea of "relations" to account for the relative unity enjoyed by the mind or self. "The true idea of the human mind," Hume insisted, "is to consider it a system of different perceptions or different existences, which are link'd together by the relation of cause and effect, and mutually produce, destroy, influence, and modify each other." More poetically, Hume admits that he "cannot compare the soul to anything than to a republic or commonwealth, in which the several members are united by the reciprocal ties of government and subordination, and give rise to other persons, who propagate the same republic in the incessant changes in parts."[39] Reciprocal ties, the idea of relations, is therefore the single most important ingredient of the human mind.

But what, precisely, are those "ties" that bind "perceptions which succeed one another with an inconceivable rapidity and in a perpetual flux and movement"?[40] In other words, how does the mind "compose" itself? How does the individual achieve and maintain a fairly stable *sense* of identity, of being the same person over time? Hume said that this process of self-composition occurs at two levels: first, at a level of "common relations," attributed to processes of unreflective nature; and second, at a level of "union of ideas," where the mind actively generates (self)reflection in the form of combination or comparison—in fact, by self-doubling, as of a wall of mirrors—of ideas. Hume explained:

> The word relation is commonly used in two senses considerably different from each other. Either for that quality, by which two ideas are connected together in the imagination, and the one naturally introduces the other . . . or for that particular circumstances, in which, even upon the arbitrary union of two ideas in the fancy, we may think proper to compare. In common language the former is always the sense in which we used the word, relation; and 'tis only in philosophy, that we extend it to mean any particular subject of comparison.[41]

Let us set aside, for the moment, the common relation which occurs naturally, and focus instead on the "philosophical" relation—the one that makes possible active combination and comparison of ideas. According to Hume there are many kinds of philosophical relation—about seven of them. He believed that "it may be esteemed . . . an endless task to enumerate all those qualities which make objects admit of comparison, and by which the ideas of philosophical relations are produced. But if we diligently consider them we shall find that without difficulty they may be compriz'd under seven general heads, which may be considered the source of all philosophical relation." Hume enumerates these as follows: resemblance, identity, space and time (distant, contiguous, above, below, etc.), quantity, quality, contrariety, and cause and effect. These are the relations that lend themselves to "the determination of the mind."[42] As the highest recesses of the mind, these relations account not only for the *relative* unity of the mind or sense of selfhood, but also form the foundations of knowledge, science, and the arts.

Existentially, the mind organizes itself as uniquely human at the moment when, transcending the "common" relations, it emerges as self-reflective: a self-mirroring bundling of perceptions. Knowledge derives its formal validity from these processes of development and growth in psychological awareness. In fact, just as the possibility of a sense of self depends upon capacity for knowledge, so are the conditions of knowledge and science nonexistent without the self-constituting activities of the mind. Knowledge, understood in this way, is indirectly what Hume regarded as the "key feature of human nature"—because knowledge is coeval with, and represents, the unique aspects of the human subjectivity.

Epistemologically, then, Hume achieved an objective he had announced when he said, "There is no question of importance, whose decision is not compriz'd in the science of man; and there is none, which can be decided with any certainty, before we become acquainted with that science." He added, "In pretending . . . to explain the principles of human nature, we in effect propose a compleat system of the sciences." For the "science of man," Hume says, is "a foundation almost entirely new, and the only one upon which they [the sciences] can stand with any security."[43]

This is not the place to delve into the problems created by Hume's epistemology for classical theories of knowledge (cause and effect, for example, are said by him to derive their connection from the "understanding" rather than from "nature");[44] but we must observe, for reasons that will become obvious shortly, that the first three of the seven types of philosophical determination of the mind (resemblance, identity, and space and time) are characterized by Hume as marginal—"antecedent"—to the activities of understanding. We are then left with only four relations (quantity, quality, contrariety, and cause and effect) that are essentially philosophical and that provide the best foundations for self- and knowledge-constitution.[45] These higher levels of the processes of association or combination of ideas are the ones that make possible certainty and objectivity of knowledge and, therefore, the possibility of the sciences and the arts.[46] We should keep in mind, therefore, that when Hume says that some races are inferior to others, and the evidence for this is that the inferior ones lack the science and the arts, he is saying, in effect, that members of the inferior races are ontologically (psychologically) and functionally (cognitively) deficient. The Negro, for Hume, is the paradigm of this racial inferiority.

HUME'S NEGRO'S MIND

The double uses, psychological and epistemological, that Hume makes of his theory of mind underlie his remarks about the "nature" of the races. He believed that the races—of which he said there are about four or five— are endowed naturally with different *kinds* of psychological and cognitive constitutions. The differences in kind essentially yield different kinds of human beings—the "varieties of men."

Since nature produced not only differences among humans by race but also unevenly endowed the races with the resources required for mental development and cultural progress, Hume thought that some races have high levels of mental capacities and that others do not. Although he believed that mind or the self is not a fixed substance, Hume nevertheless thought that nature itself did not establish in some humans, as it did not in nonhuman animals, the capacity to develop or use levels of intelligence available in the higher philosophical determinations of the mind—the spheres of perception responsible for production of the sciences, the arts, and "eminent" (i.e., moral) action.

When Hume asserts, in the first version of the renowned footnote, "I am apt to suspect the Negroes and in general all other species of men . . . to be naturally inferior to the white," he was claiming *by race* superior status for whites and inferior status for nonwhites. He also wrote: "There never was a civilized nation of any other complexion other than white."[47] But in the second version, modified to exclude the Mexicans from the category they had shared with the Negroes in the original, Hume still maintained: "There are NEGRO slaves dispersed all over EUROPE, of which none ever discovered any symptoms of ingenuity; tho' low [white] people, without education, will start up amongst us, and distinguish themselves in every profession." He draws then the following conclusion: "the uniform and constant difference could not happen, in so many countries and ages, if nature had not made an original distinction betwixt these breeds of men."[48]

The implications of the above, philosophically, are as follows. Whites are capable of active uses of reason, but blacks are incapable of these; blacks are susceptible to only the passive processes of the mind. Hume explains:

> All kinds of reasoning consist in nothing but *comparison*, and a discovery of those relations, either constant or inconstant, which two or more objects bear to each other. This comparison we may make, wither when both objects are present to the senses, or when neither of them is present, or when only one. When both the objects are present to the senses along with the relation, we call this perception rather than reasoning; nor is there in this case any exercise of the thought, or any action, properly speaking, but mere passive admission of the impressions thro' the organs of the sensation.[49]

The first type of mental activity occurs when objects compared are physically present together, so that the mind merely registers them as together; the second occurs when only one of the objects of comparison is physically present; and the third when no object of the comparison is physically present, so that the association is purely abstract mental representations. Hume calls the first "perception" rather than reasoning, because there is, properly speaking, no thought.

Now if Negroes as a race lack "eminence" in thought, it means that each Negro can experience "mere passive admission of impression" through the senses, but none can undertake the third type of mental function. As to the second type, one could guess what the Negro might do: sensually ravish the object physically present, unaware that it has or could have any formal relation to an abstract representation? Thus, without denying all mental functions to the Negro, Hume nevertheless theorizes that the race is endowed by nature with only a passive sort of mind.

When he wrote about nonhuman animals, Hume argued that they are certainly capable of enjoying the lower levels of relations of ideas which, without doubt, he thought the Negro could experience. Hume explained:

> There is evidently the same relation of ideas, and derived from the same causes, in the minds of animals as in those of men. A dog that has hid a bone often forgets the place; but when brought to it, his thought passes easily to what he formerly conceal'd, by means of the contiguity, which produces a relation among his ideas. In like manner, when he has been heartily beat in any place, he will tremble on his approach to it even tho' he discover no signs of any present danger. The effects of resemblance are not so remarkable, but as that relation makes a considerable ingredient in causation, of which all animals shew so evident a judgment, we may conclude that the three relations of resemblance, and continuity and causation operate in the same manner upon beasts as upon human creatures.[50]

But Hume cautioned, "We ought not to receive as reasoning any of the[se] observations . . . since in none of them the mind can go beyond what is immediately present to the senses, either to discover the real existence or the relations of objects."[51]

In the *Treatise*, in the section "Of the Reason of Animals," Hume further noted that "experimental reasoning which we possess in common with beasts, and on which the whole conduct of life depends, is nothing but a species of instinct or mechanical power that acts in us unknown to ourselves, and in its chief operations is not directed by any such relations or comparison of ideas as are the proper objects of our intellectual faculties."[52] But it is precisely this "species of instinct or mechanical power" that make up about all that Hume thought individuals who belong to "inferior" races could have in common with humans of "superior" races. If, then, for Hume the mental capacity of Negroes as a race—which is to say, the level of their humanity—is more nearly animal than white, is there any reason why the Negro could not be sold by the white like a horse or, to use Hume's example, a dog? For Hume the Negro was, in the language common at the time, a legitimate "article of trade."

In October of 1769, Charles Stewart brought his slave James Sommerset from Virginia to England, and, after two years of service to the master in country, Sommerset absconded. Notices were put out for his capture. When Stewart was once again in possession of the disobedient slave, he decided that the best course of action was to sell him to a planter in Jamaica. Sommerset had, however, consulted antislavery activist Granville Sharp, so that by November 28, 1771, a suit had been filed at the Court of King's Bench in Westminster Hall, challenging the legality of Stewart's planned sale of Sommerset. The lawyers for the plaintiff argued that such a sale constituted a deportation and was therefore against habeas corpus, a law enacted a hundred years earlier "for the better securing of the Liberty of the subject, and for Prevention of Imprisonment beyond the Sea." When the case was argued on February 7, 1772, the defendant's lawyers claimed that habeas corpus did not apply to Sommerset because in Britain the Negro was not a "subject" but only a commercial property, a "legal Property, vested in the planter-owner by the law of Great Britain."[53] They also argued, forcefully, that the Negro could not be considered sufficiently human. "Perceiving the corporeal as well as the intellectual differences of Negroes from other people, knowing the irreclaimable savageness of their manners, and of course supposing that they are an inferior race of people," the defendants pleaded, "the conclusion was, to follow the commercial genius of this country, in enacting that they should be considered and distinguished (as they are) as articles of its trade and commerce only."[54]

Sharp's account of the proceedings suggests that he challenged both arguments of the defense. Addressing the idea that a Negro is not a citizen, he asked, "Would it not be esteemed a great injustice, if any one was to allege, that a Hungarian, Pole, Muscovite, or alie of any other European nation, is not protected by our laws when in England, because there is a possibility of supposing, that his countrymen might not have been 'had in consideration or contemplation at the time of making these laws'?" Given the fact that any white foreigner in England would be protected by habeas corpus, Sharp suggested that it was only racial discrimination that would lead the defendant's counsel to argue that the Negro could not be granted such protection. For Sharp, only casuistry would allow one to claim "that the most invaluable blessing which humanity lays claim to should be confined to any particular country, or that MEN are excluded from it, whose crime is to have been born with darker skin."[55] In response to the argument that the court was being asked to protect a "commercial property," Sharp countered that it made no difference whether the words "slavery" or "commercial property" were employed, for "What signifies the name since the thing is the same?" For Sharp, "The laws of England will impartially judge between Master and Slave as between *Man and Man*, and will prefer the superior (because natural) Claim of property in his own person, to the mere pecuniary Claim of the Slaveholder."

To the argument that Sommerset lacked sufficient human attributes to claim equality to whites under law, Sharp explained that the claim was not unconnected to an earlier one, which wished to regard the Negro solely as property. The opposing counsel, Sharp suggested, "seems sensible of this himself, that the Negro cannot be property, and has endeavored to rob the Negroes of their just claim to humanity by insinuating that they are a different and inferior species of Men from the Whites and that 'the Negro Man' is incapable of moral sensations, or perceives them only as Beasts do simple ideas, without the power of combination."[56]

The language of these claims and counterclaims are, of course, of interest. In the *History of Jamaica*, Edward Long, a proponent of the view that the Negro was merchandise and that the rights of the owner were "just, legal, and indefeasible, and compleat, as that of any other British merchant over goods in his warehouse," made the continuities between the arguments of philosophers and proslavery positions more explicit. "Mr. Hume," wrote

Long, "presumes, from his observations of the native Africans, to conclude, that these are inferior to the rest of the species, and utterly incapable of all the higher attainments of the human mind."[57]

Some may argue that even if Hume wrote that blacks were inferior to whites, it does not mean that he stated that blacks had no rights and, therefore, should be legitimate targets of the peculiar system of racial slavery. They might even say that Hume suggested only that human and nonhuman animals share "brotherly" or "sisterly" bonds since nature treats both alike in their sensitive bodiedness. In fact Hume had argued that "there are instances of the relation of impressions, sufficient to convince us, that there is a union of certain affections with each other in the inferior species of creatures as well as in the superior."[58] Thus, if both the "superior" and the "inferior," human and nonhuman animals share similar emotional and "mental" lives, why should one be concerned that Hume happened to classify the Negro among inferior rather than superior human animals? Couldn't emotions and affections, such as pleasure, pain, joy, and fear which Hume stated belong to both beasts and humans be regarded as a common basis for affirming a common "humanity"—a humanity of both whites and blacks? What then does it matter if Hume just happened to believe that blacks were the missing link between bestial inhumanity and white humanity? What philosophical difference does such a system of classification make since, in any case, as if by a compromise with the inferior races, Hume argued that it is not reason but passion that determines social solidarity? In fact in his writings on *sympathy*, Hume strongly argued that the foundation of sympathy is the relation, at affective levels of perception, between ourselves and others.[59] That is why he said that passion and custom, rather than reason, are the durable bases of social cohesion.

So let us assume, for the argument, that all the above are Hume's views. But we would still be in difficulty to determine a common "humanity" between, to stay with the examples, humans and dogs or, as Hume's explicit theory frames them, whites and blacks. Though he recognized the value of passion and habit, Hume also stressed the role of reason as a uniquely human capacity. *If* whites and blacks, like humans and dogs, are separated by some "original distinction" which "nature had . . . made," then, would there not be little or no "rational" basis for a shared life across the kinds?

To argue that in Hume's thought the Negro and the white races share a common humanity on the basis of "sympathy" rather than "reason" is trivial. It requires abandoning the status of reason, even as described by Hume, as a possible basis for affirming—or achieving—a universal humanity. Though Hume wrote, "'Tis not, therefore, reason, which is the guide of life, but custom," he also wished that philosophy would enable humans to "shake off the yoke of authority, and accustom them to think for themselves."[60] He insisted that one must "assent to our faculties, and employ our reason only because we [as humans] cannot help it."[61] Could Hume have meant only a white "we"?

CONCLUSION

Instead of asking whether or not racism has any roots in philosophical traditions, it might be more worthwhile to ask: Could philosophical thought have roots in racism? Instead of *ad hominem* arguments about "racist empiricists," philosophical knowledge could more easily be related to their conditions of origin, in view of determining the roots of the content. The paradigmatic image of a "universal" modern philosophical reason has always been connected to particular cultures, societies, and economic conditions out of which philosophy attempts to carve for itself a space—a critical space, but nonetheless one that is always part of its world. What we learn from this reading of Hume on the subject of race, I think, is better considered in the context of other works that aim to show that philosophy's hankering after ahistorical reason is itself a *historical* longing. To formulate well a question about race, or about what the eighteenth- and nineteenth-century philosophers sometimes called "nation," and to formulate these racial or national questions within the very resources of modern philosophy, is nothing but an extension—we shall call mine an Africanist extension—of a "historical turn" in philosophy that was most evident in Hegel in the West or in the Igbo concept of *Agwu* as developed by Achebe or the Yoruba *Esu-Elegba* as developed by Soyinka in the African systems of thought. Philosophy, I am convinced, is the most fruitful when it dialectically faces its own demons, and most enlightened when it understands the Others it produces by its own inevitable shadows.

NOTES

1. See J. L. A. Garcia, "The Racial Contract Hypothesis," *Philosophia Africana*, vol. 4, no. 1 (March 2001).
2. John Immerwahr, "Hume's Revised Racism," *Journal of the History of Ideas* (1992): 1–23, 481.
3. In the alterations, Hume did not abandon the idea that some *races* are by nature incapable of reflective reason and moral action; he simply restricted the number of races included in this category. Since my interests concern Hume's arguments about racial categories in general, rather than who belongs to the superior or inferior groups, my references are to the original as well as the revised versions. I shall, with each reference, indicate which version am referring to. While Hume referred to the African only as "the Negro" and the "Negro race," I use the term "black" in addition to "African" in my commentaries.
4. See *Letters of David Hume*, Vol. II, 1766–76, ed. J. Y. T. Greig, Oxford: Clarendon Press, 1932, pp. 299–302.
5. Richard Popkin, "Hume's Racism," in *Philosophical Forum* 9, 2–3 (1977/78): 211–226; and Harry M. Bracken, "Minds and Learning: The Chomskyan Revolution," in *Metaphilosophy* 4 (July 1973). Bracken, Popkin, and David Fate Norton started the discussions leading to these articles in 1970, particularly at that year's meeting of the American Society for Eighteenth-Century Studies.
6. Cornel West, *Prophesy Deliverance!*, Philadelphia: Westminster Press, 1982, chapter 2.
7. Popkin, "Hume's Racism," p. 224.
8. Ibid.
9. Harry M. Bracken, "Essence, Accident and Race," in *Hermethena* (Dublin) (1973): 81–96; 93. "Value-free descriptions of certain peoples as essentially inferior, grounded in some 'science,'" Bracken explains, "facilitate treating them as inferior" (ibid.).
10. Ibid.
11. Ibid., pp. 83–84; emphasis in original.
12. Descartes, *The Meditations*, "Introduction."
13. Ibid., passim.
14. James Ramsay, *An Essay on the treatment and conversion of African slaves*, Dublin, 1784, chapter 5, passim.
15. Ibid., p. 182.
16. Paul Rabinow, introduction to *The Foucault Reader*, ed. Rabinow, New York: Pantheon, 1984.
17. Noam Chomsky, *Reflections on Language*, New York: Pantheon, 1975, p. 126.
18. Searle's conclusion: "It would not be proper to conclude from this that Descartes and his followers 'facilitated the expression of the racist ideology,' and I am unable to see that it is any more acceptable to smear the great empiricists with these veiled accusations of racism" (Searle, quoted in Bracken, "Philosophy and Racism," p. 254).
19. Ibid.

20. Bracken, "Philosophy and Racism," p. 251.
21. Bernard Williams, "Where Chomsky Stands," *New York Review of Books*, Nov. 11, 1976, pp. 43–45.
22. Bracken, "Philosophy and Racism," p. 260.
23. Chomsky, *Reflections on Language*, pp. 126–134.
24. Richard Rorty, *Truth and Progress*, New York: Cambridge University Press, 1998, p. 2. Rorty's preferred alternative account of human nature is, of course, very Freudian: it consists "in an ability to seek out new redescriptions of one's own past—an ability to take a nominalistic, ironic view of oneself." As he argued this point in an earlier work: "Freud did for the variety of interpretations of each person's past what the Baconian approach to science and philosophy did for the variety of descriptions of the universe as a whole. He let us see alternative narratives and alternative vocabularies as instruments for change, rather than as candidates for a correct depiction of how things are in themselves" (Rorty, *Essays on Heidegger and Others: Philosophical Papers Vol. 2*, New York: Cambridge University Press, 1991, p. 152).
25. Barry Stroud, *Hume*, London: Routledge and Kegan Paul, 1977, p. 1.
26. Stroud, *Hume*, p. 4.
27. David Hume, *Treatise on Human Nature*, p. 183.
28. On reason, see Hume, *Treatise*, part 4, pp. 180–263; on the senses, see pp. 188, 189 (for example, "To begin with the SENSES, 'tis evident these faculties are incapable of giving rise to the notion of the *continu'd* [i.e., enduring] existence of their objects. . . . That our senses offer not their impressions as the images of something *distinct*, or *independent*, and *external*, is evident. . . . If our senses, therefore, suggest any idea of distinct existences, they must convey the impressions as those very existences, by a kind of fallacy or illusion"); and on the self, pp. 251–262.
29. Ibid., p. 183.
30. David Fate Norton, "An Introduction to Hume's Thought," in *Cambridge Companion to Hume*, ed. D. F. Norton, Cambridge: Cambridge University Press, 1993, p. 1. Norton laments, "For nearly two centuries the positive side of Hume's thought was routinely overlooked—in part as a reaction to his thoroughgoing religious skepticism—but in recent decades commentators, even those who emphasize the sceptical aspects of his thought, have recognized and begun to reconstruct Hume's positive philosophical positions."
31. John Bricke, *Hume's Theory of Mind*, Edinburgh: Edinburgh University Press, 1980, p. 1.
32. Ibid., p. 232, italics in original; see also the section "Of immateriality of the Soul."
33. David Hume, *On Human Nature and the Understanding*, ed. Anthony Flew, New York: Collier Books, 1962, pp. 298–299.
34. Ibid.
35. Hume, *Treatise*, p. 251.
36. Ibid., p. 207.
37. Ibid., p. 253.
38. Ibid.
39. Ibid., pp. 252, 259, 261.
40. Ibid., p. 261.
41. Ibid., p. 14.
42. Ibid.
43. Ibid., *Treatise*, introduction.

44. Anticipating objections to his inclusion of cause and effect under "philosophical" relations, Hume represented the views of a hypothetical opponent: "What! the efficacy of cause lie in the determination of the mind! As if causes did not operate entirely independent of the mind, and wou'd not continue their operation, even tho' there was no mind existent to contemplate them, or reason concerning them. Thought may well depend on causes for its operation, but not causes on thought. This is to reverse the order of nature, and make that secondary, which is really primary." To this he responded: "As to what may be said, that the operations of nature are independent of our thought and reasoning, I allow it; . . . that like objects may be observ'd in several instances to have like relations; and that all this is independent of, and antecedent to the operations of the understanding. But if we go farther, and ascribe a power of necessary connexion to these objects; this is what we can never observe in them, but must draw the idea of it from what we feel internally in contemplating them" (Hume, *Treatise*, p. 169). In a later passage, he wrote: "My hypothesis [is] that all our reasoning concerning causes and effects are deriv'd from nothing but custom" (Hume, *Treatise*, p. 183). This was a problem that Kant tried to resolve in the *Critique of Pure Reason*.
45. He succinctly stated, science "[must] confine [itself] to these four relations, which alone admit of that degree of evidence" (Ibid., p. 463).
46. Hume said, "Of these seven philosophical relations, there remain only four which, depending solely upon ideas, can be objects of knowledge and certainty" (Ibid., 69–70.)
47. Hume, "Of National Character," in *Race and the Enlightenment*, ed. Emmanuel Eze, Oxford: Blackwell, 1997, chapter 3, pp. 30–33.
48. Ibid.
49. Ibid.
50. Hume, *Treatise*, p. 327.
51. Ibid.
52. Ibid.
53. Samuel Estwick, *Considerations of the Negro Cause, commonly so called, addressed to the Right Honourable Lord Mansfield, Lord Chief Justice of King's Bench, & C.*, London: J. Dodsley, 1772, pp. 32–33.
54. Ibid., p. 82.
55. Granville Sharp, *A Representation of the Injustice and the Dangerous Tendency of Tolerating Slavery; or of Admitting the Least Claim of Private Property in the Persons of Men, in England*, London: Benjamin White, 1769, p. 38.
56. Ibid.
57. Edward Long, *History of Jamaica*, London, n.d., Book III, chap. 1, p. 376. Interestingly, Long explains the motives of the proslavery arguments (after explicitly acknowledging that he was "a Planter") in the warning that "the advantages derived to this kingdom from her plantations, and principally by means of Negro labour, are so well known and understood, that it is superfluous for me to expatiate upon them; . . . The failure of our West Indian trade would of course be followed by a great diminution in . . . the duties and customs upon which no mean figure in the revenue account; . . . These are considerations which seem to merit the notice of all the pretended reformers of the age; who under the cloak of furious zeal in the cause of religion and liberty, do all they can to throw down those essential pillars, commerce, trade, and navigation, upon which alone must depend their own enjoyment of any freedom, civil or religious" (Ibid.). See also the diatribe from the same author upon the court's ruling in favor of plaintiff: Edward Long, *Candid*

Reflections upon the Judgment Lately Awarded by the Court of King's Bench in the Westminster Hall on What Is Commonly Called the Negroe Cause, London, 1772.

58. Hume, *Treatise*, p. 327.
59. Ibid., Book II, "Of the Passions," especially section 9, pp. 316–318, and all of section 12.
60. Ibid., p. 644.
61. Ibid., p. 657.

CHAPTER 3

RACE: A TRANSCENDENTAL?

If there is any science man really needs, it is the one I
teach, of how to fulfill properly that position in creation
which is assigned to man, and from which he is able to
learn *what one must be in order to be a man.*
— Kant, *Gesammelte Schriften* (author's translation)

INTRODUCTION

While Hume compared the Negro poet Francis Williams to a "parrot
who speaks a few words plainly," Kant, despite stated surprise at the
high level of destruction visited by civilized Europeans on colonized non-
Europeans, could not theoretically grant—even as a formality—equality of
humanity to both Europeans and so-called savages. According to Kant, the
existence of the natives had no value beyond that of sheep, so that about the
blacks in Tahiti, for example, he explained that only contact with white
Europeans could elevate them to the human level.[1] While condemning the
avarice of the colonizing merchants and states, and deploring what he called
"the inhospitable actions of the civilized," Kant could blame his fellow
whites for the injustice suffered by others, the victims, but seemed more
pained by the degrading of "mankind"—the white mankind—revealed in a
level of racial cruelty that Kant considered unusual.

> The injustice which they show to lands and peoples they visit
> (which is equivalent to conquering them) is carried by them to

terrifying lengths. America, the lands inhabited by the Negro, the Spice Islands, the Cape, etc., were at the time of their discovery considered by these civilized intruders as lands without owners, for they counted the inhabitants as nothing. In East India (Hindustan), under the pretense of establishing economic undertakings, they brought in foreign soldiers and used them to oppress the natives, excited widespread wars among the various states, spread famine, rebellion, perfidy, and the whole litany of evils which afflict mankind.[2]

But a close examination of Kant's philosophical theories about the varieties of human nature, in particular his theories of international relations and the history and character of the races, show that there is little or nothing in the theories regarding the practices of the civilized that one could condemn as out of order. In the same essay in which he condemned the treatment of non-European populations, Kant described the type of relationship he thought should govern the encounter of the civilized and the uncivilized. Normally, Kant thinks, acts of aggression by one person or nation upon another should be condemned as unlawful; he also sensibly insisted that such normal rules apply only where there is a reciprocal recognition that all parties in the encounter are governed by law. But in the case of those whose existence he called savage, Kant thought that no law existed in their societies, either within their countries or in their relationship to the European intruders. This presumption that the lives of the so-called savages were governed by caprice, instinct, and violence rather than law left no room for Kant to imagine between the Europeans and the natives a system of international relations, established on the basis of equality and respect, and governed by non-unilaterally imposed systems of law. Because Kant presumed the civilized European to be governed by law, as he presumed the non-European to exist in "the state of nature" and lawlessness, it was obvious that the prerequisite for any civil encounter between those he rightly called the intruders and the natives intruded upon must be an initial conquest of the latter by the former, a conquest through which, it is presumed, the native would be subjected by force to law—European kinds of law. Kant explained:

We ordinarily assume that no one may act inimically toward another except when he has been actively injured by the other. This is quite correct if both are under civil law, for, by entering into such a state, they afford each other the requisite security through the sovereign which has power over both. Man (or the people) in the state of nature deprives me of this security and injures me, if he is near me, by this mere status of his, even though he does not injure me actively; he does so by the lawlessness of his condition which constantly threatens me. Therefore, I can compel him either to enter with me into a state of civil law or to remove himself from my neighborhood.[3]

Unexamined is the assumption that the "native" actually lives in a "state of nature" rather than that Kant and some few Europeans thought so. Though the European is acknowledged as the intruder, it is the native whom Kant called the aggressor—the European is the victim; and Kant's "my neighborhood," from which the proud "savage" would be forced to remove himself or be removed could not have been Berlin or London or Paris but Delhi, Guyana, or Onitsha. The native, "by this mere status of his," or in other words, by the mere fact of existing, but now under the label "lawlessness"—a label designed by the European intruder—is now a threat who could either be exterminated or forced into confinement in arid reservations and Bantuslands. The freedom of the native either as individual or as nation was not considered by Kant as worthy of respect by Europeans.

Because of its racial bias, Kant's writing was not able to universally advocate its well-known categorical rules of conduct. In "Kant as an Unfamiliar Source of Nationalism," Isaiah Berlin traced the intellectual origins of European nationalism, including its racism and ethnocentrism. While noting as curious that little or no attention has been accorded to this issue—though admitting that "at first sight nothing would seem more disparate than the idea of nationality and the sane, rational, liberal internationalism of the great Königsberg philosopher"—Berlin argues that Kant was the "father of modern nationalism."[4] In Berlin's estimation the connection between Kant's nationalism and racism is explicit, for Berlin defined nationalism as "the consciousness of national unity . . . rooted in a sharp sense of the differences between one human society and another. . . . In its pathological forms, it proclaims the supreme value of the nation's own culture, history, race, spirit, institutions, even of its physical attributes, and their superiority to those of others."[5]

Of course Berlin had no doubts that Kant was a man of the Enlightenment or that he subscribed to Enlightenment ideals. Berlin admits, too, that Kant politically "hated inequality, he hated hierarchies, oligarchies, paternalism, no matter how benevolent."[6] Kant, for example, praised the French Revolution and its proclamation of universal rights, even as he condemned its descent into terrorism and bloodshed. But in the essay "On the Different Races of Man," Kant argued that there are four races, each with a specific "natural disposition"; but all the races, he claimed, derive from an ideal "stem genus"—a *white* stem existing "between the 31st and 52nd parallels in the Old World," and best approximated by the "very blond, soft white-skinned, red haired, pale blue eyes [of] the northern regions of Germany."[7] Because the genus is model and norm, the humanity of those whose profiles match the geographical, racial, and national specifications given by Kant are, this argument goes, "higher" than the humanity of the rest in beauty and intelligence. How does one reconcile this racial, national, and geographical determinism with Kant's proclaimed "universal" ideas about "unchanging rights of the individual, whoever he may be, whatever his time, whatever his place, his society, his personal attributes"?[8]

It appears that Kant heartily condemned ethnocentrism when he complained as follows about the English: "the Englishman establishes great benevolent institutions, unheard of among other peoples. But if a foreigner whom fate has driven ashore on his soil falls into dire need, he can die on a dung hill because he is not an Englishman—that is, not a man." What he accused the English of doing to others *in practice*, Kant inflicts upon nonwhite peoples *in theory*. For example, why shouldn't the English treat those they consider racial foreigners unequally if, as Kant observed, "The inhabitant of the temperate parts of the world . . . has a more beautiful body, works harder, is more jocular, more controlled in his passions, more intelligent than any other *race* of people in the world"?[9] It is this racial superiority that is assumed when Kant notes that some races, as if by right, "have educated the others and controlled them with weapons." In fact, some of Kant's works simply argue that certain races, by nature, shall forever remain immature and therefore perpetually subordinate. He does not raise the question of whether it is the "education" and superior weapons of the conquering tribe that produce the "immaturity" of the conquered.

Sander Gilman, writing about Kant's racial views, argued that "for the precritical Kant blackness is a state which negatively predetermines the aesthetic sensibility and proclivity of the observer."[10] By my own readings, however, Kant's antiblack prejudice is not limited to the precritical works; nor is it limited to the *Critique of Judgment* (the relevant chapter in Gilman's book was entitled "Towards a Critique of Judgement"). Evidence from *Critique of Practical Reason* and *Critique of Pure Reason*, coupled with passages in *Anthropology from a Pragmatic Point of View*, suggest that it is more accurate to state, simply, that for Kant "the ideal of normative beauty [and intelligence] is racially determined." With a consistency that we see in the *Critique of Judgment*, *Observations on the Feeling of the Beautiful and the Sublime*, and *Anthropology*, Kant claimed that "each race produces an archetype of beauty which constitutes the form of the concept of beauty,"[11] and the universal experience he claimed we have of the law and the divine is equally profoundly race-inflected. In both the precritical and critical works, blacks are never thought of as capable of moral, intellectual, or aesthetic experience "beyond the trifling."[12]

I am often asked, Why "expose" Kant? Or: Why read him "destructively"? But this is neither an exposé nor a destruction. For some of us, old-fashioned you might say, who do not wish to continue to see the word "universalism" regarded as a curse word (to damn nonwhite cultures or as an expletive against white cultures), are interested in separating true from false universalism. In his aesthetics Kant makes an important distinction between *ideal* and *norm*, and between *perception* and *judgment*. But in these distinctions is a gap which allowed him to argue that certain races are incapable of making judgments with regard to the ideal of beauty, even though they have, within their cultures, norms of beauty. In parallel, aesthetic *perception*, a question of taste, is "culturally determined"; but aesthetic *judgment*, a matter of what is universally right or wrong, is philosophically determined. "The correctness of such an ideal of beauty," Kant wrote, "is indicated in that it is not possible to mix sensual charm with satisfaction in the object, and yet allows great interest to be taken. This indicates that such a judgment, in accordance with an ideal of beauty, is not merely a judgment of taste."[13] It is the capacity for judgment that Kant believed is racially lacking among nonwhite groups, just as the corresponding ideal of beauty is supposed to be absent among them.

Members of the "savage" races, because they supposedly live in a state of nature and their existence is accordingly believed to be totally bound up with the sensual, are seen by Kant as incapable of experiencing intellectual appreciation of objects beyond "sensual charm." This is no different from Hume's claim that members of the Negro or Mexican races are incapable of abstract thought or the use of proper reason. For Hume as for Kant, Negroes and Mexicans, because of their racial status, acquire and express only sensual "knowledge" deriving from passion.

Kant's theory of human nature is different, however, from Hume's in one important particular: it transcendentally grounds racialism. Earl W. Count remarked that scholars often forget "that Immanuel Kant produced the most profound raciological thought of the eighteenth century."[14] This scholarly forgetfulness of Kant's raciology might stem from the desire to see Kant only as a pure philosopher, preoccupied only with pure culture- and color-blind themes in the *sanctum sanctorum* of the tradition. It is thereby forgotten that the philosopher developed courses in what he called "Physical Geography," a field with a strong philosophical as well as anthropological component, and taught them regularly for forty years, from 1756 until the year before his retirement in 1797.[15] When Kant spoke about his courses in this area, he explained:

> In my occupation with pure philosophy, which was originally undertaken of my own accord, but which later belonged to my teaching duties, I have for some thirty years delivered lectures twice a year on "knowledge of the world," namely on Anthropology and Physical Geography. They were popular lectures attended by people from the general public. The present

manual contains my lectures on anthropology. As to Physical Geography, however, it will not be possible, considering my age, to produce a manual from my manuscript.[16]

Kant saw his primary duty as teaching about cultures and the peoples of the world, rather than the private "pure" philosophy for which he would become—in our time at least—more widely associated. Yet the critical works, clearly, developed only gradually as various pieces of a construction designed to explain "man" in its cognitive, moral, and aesthetic dimensions.[17] In the course of criticizing his contemporaries who claimed to understand human nature without taking seriously the study of philosophical anthropology, Kant wrote, "They make a great show of understanding *men* . . . without understanding *man* and what can be made of him, for they lack the higher point of view of anthropological observation which is needed for this."[18] Kant strove to provide this universal anthropological point of view, executing the various aspects of this main project from diverse critical angles (the *Critique of Pure Reason, Critique of Practical Reason, Critique of Judgment*). The analytical reception of Kant in our time has, however, tended to ignore the deeper anthropological interests of the critiques.

In fact, it was Kant who introduced anthropology as a self-standing branch of study in German universities. By the winter semester of 1772–1773, he had started teaching anthropology as distinct from physical geography,[19] although he continued to regard both as "twin" sciences. Evidence of his extensive interests in these courses must include the fact that in his long career at Königsberg, he offered seventy-two courses in anthropology and physical geography, fifty-four in logic, forty-nine in metaphysics, twenty-eight in moral philosophy, and twenty in theoretical physics.[20] A second edition of *Anthropology* was the last work he completed before he died; although far less systematic than the "critical" works, *Anthropology*'s content encompasses issues that range from the precritical to critical periods.

What was Kant's fascination with anthropology? What did he mean by the term? How is the discipline related to physical geography, and why did he think that anthropology and physical geography are twins? Moreover, what are the substantive anthropological theories on race espoused by Kant? For answers, we must rely on both the "critical" and "historical" writings (*Anthropology, Physische Geographie*,[21] *Observations on the Feeling of the Beautiful and the Sublime* [1764], the collection of essays *Kant on History*, as well as "Bestimmung des Begriffs einer Menschenrasse" [1785][22] and "On the Different Races of Man" [1775]).[23]

There are recent interests in these aspects of Kant's work, but not on the racial issues. A representative example is Michel Foucault's postdoctoral dissertation.[24] Because the French universities require two theses for a doctoral degree, a main thesis and a *thèse complimentaire*, Foucault submitted what became *Madness and Civilization* as his main thesis, at the Sorbonne, and for the second *thèse*, offered a partial but the first French translation of Kant's *Anthropology*, accompanied by some 120 typed pages of an introductory essay. Foucault experts believe that the origins of *The Order of Things* are to be found in this encounter with Kant's anthropological work.[25] The affinity between Kant's anthropology and major themes in *The Order of Things* is evident in a curious account Foucault gave of philosophical activities in France in the 1930s and 1940s: he distinguished between two orientations, "philosophy of experience" and "philosophy of knowledge"—and then attributed the origins of both to Kant. Whereas the first orientation belonged to Kant's critical work, the second belonged to the anthropological. Thus, French philosophy of the 1930s and 1940s, Foucault claimed, should be divided into "a philosophy of experience, of sense and subject," and "a philosophy of knowledge, of rationality and of concept"; while the "one network is that of Sartre and Merleau-Ponty," the other "is that of Cavailles, Bachelard, and Canguilhem." *The Order of Things*, as Foucault understood it, was situated within the latter camp: "For the first time . . . rational thought was put in question not only as to its nature, its foundation, its powers and its rights, but also as to its history and its geography."[26]

Heidegger, for another example, considered Kant's anthropological studies as key to understanding all the *Critiques*. He debated this position with Ernst Cassirer at Davos in 1929, a debate structured around the question, "What is the significance of Kant's 'philosophical anthropology.'"[27] Cassirer was quite dismissive. He said: "The *Anthropology* of 1798 cannot in any sense take place beside the essential main systematic works by virtue of its content and structure." Cassirer took this position because, according to him, the book "compiles merely 'in pragmatic respect' the rich material on human history and anthropology that Kant had assembled over a lifetime from his own observations and from odd sources, and had enriched over and over by notes and studies for his lectures."[28] But Cassirer's very description of the book and its clear importance to Kant raises questions about the wisdom of dismissing the book as inessential vis-à-vis the projects of the *Critiques*. If the book was philosophically worthless, why did Kant assemble it "over a lifetime"? If the "material on human history and anthropology" is "rich," and if it was indeed used as a "compendium" for lectures on ethics and metaphysics, as Kant intended, why then could not the book "take place" beside the others that, in Kant's words, were intended to teach "what one must be in order to be a man"?

Heidegger provided better insights into the philosophical significance of Kant's anthropology. Against Cassirer's dismissal he protested, in characteristic force of language and self-amazement, "Readers have taken constant offense at the violence of my interpretations. Their allegation of violence can indeed be supported. . . . Philosophicohistorical research is always correctly subject to this charge whenever it is directed against attempts to set in motion a thoughtful dialogue between thinkers."[29] Then he declared his perspective and sought to justify it further: "the following investigation [is] devoted to the task of interpreting Kant's *Critique of Pure Reason* as a laying of the ground for metaphysics and thus a placing of the problem of metaphysics before us as fundamental ontology."[30] But "metaphysics" and "fundamental ontology," for Heidegger, are programs aimed at getting to the problem of "man"—the problem of anthropology. In *Being and Time*, for example, he stated, "Fundamental ontology means that ontological analytic of the finite essence of human beings which is to prepare the foundation for the metaphysics which 'belongs to human nature.'"[31]

In the rest of this chapter I shall try to reopen this Davos debate—but this time with emphasis on the racial structure of Kant's fundamental ontology. In other words, we shall see how race structures in intimate ways that which Kant believed one must be in order to be a "man."

KANT'S UNDERSTANDING OF ANTHROPOLOGY
AND ITS RELATION TO THE *CRITIQUES*

The disciplinary boundaries established by Kant for anthropology are very different from what today we assume to constitute the contours of the discipline.[32] His use of the term, though in German, is close to the Latin *anthropoligica*. This term can be easily traced to the sixteenth century when it meant *doctrina humane naturae*. Although defined by the duality of soul and body, human nature at this time was yet studied as a unified whole.[33] The peculiar character of anthropology, as Kant understood it, is therefore appropriately conjoint with physical geography (and Kant's concept of geography is equally historically distant). For Kant, physical geography is the study of "the natural condition of the earth and what is contained on it: seas, continents, mountains, rivers, the atmosphere, *man*, animals, plants and minerals."[34] Man is included because humans are also natural. Within humans, however, nature manifests itself in two aspects: externally and internally, as body and as soul. Linnaeus had explained the importance of this duality:

> Man, when he enters the world, is naturally led to enquire who he is; whence he comes; whither he is going; for what purpose he is created; and by whose benevolence he is preserved. He finds himself descended from the remotest creation; journeying to a life of perfection and happiness, and led by his endowments to a contemplation of the works of nature. Like other animals who enjoy life, sensation, and perception; seek for food, amusements, and rest, and who prepare habitations convenient for their kind, he is curious and inquisitive: but, above all other animals, he is noble in his nature, in as much as, by the powers of his mind, he is able to reason justly upon whatever discovers itself to his senses; and to look, with reverence and wonder, upon the works of Him who created all things.[35]

It is the capacity to inquire, to reason, and to engage in the work of culture, and thus transcend in some ways mechanically determined aspects of nature, that defines the destiny of the human being. For Linnaeus, the psychological and spiritual aspect of the person is important because "that existence is purely contemptible, which regards only the ratification of infinitive wants, and the preservation of a body made to perish." He believed that "it is the business of a thinking being to look forward to the purposes of all things; and to remember that the end of creation is that God may be glorified in all his works."[36] The study of human nature therefore must take into consideration the dual dimensions.

Kant believed that physical geography and anthropology are, in combination, capable of providing a total knowledge of the human. While physical geography provides knowledge of human bodies and of the customs regulated by causal and customary laws, anthropology provides knowledge of internal psychological structures regulated by moral law. The book *Anthropology*, accordingly, focuses on the analysis of human beings as moral agents. The individual is a moral agent because one is capable of experiencing oneself as a transcendental "I," contemplating nature, and thinking and willing. This capacity for consciousness and agency, much as in Descartes, is what makes possible the unique moral identity of humans and, as Kant states it, elevates humans above mere nature. "The fact that man is aware of an ego-concept," he says, "raises him infinitely above all other creatures living on earth. Because of this, he is a person; and by virtue of this oneness of consciousness, he remains one and the same person despite all the vicissitudes which may befall him. He is a being who, by reason of his preeminence and dignity, is wholly different from *things*."[37] But what is an ego? For Kant, as it was for Descartes, the answer is found in the human capacity to contemplate the world (think) and to will (intend) ends. The ego consists of the beliefs and the desires formed through thinking and intending, both of which endow a life with an individuality and interiority, and a rational character and conscience.

The *Anthropology*, however, also recognized that that which constitutes the person beyond mere things is also part of nature. This is why, for example, geography could also provide moral knowledge of human nature. It also explains Kant's observation, "a systematic doctrine containing our knowledge of man (anthropology) can either be given from a physiological or pragmatic point of view. Physiological knowledge of man aims at the investigation of what Nature makes of man." The distinction between "what Nature makes of man" and "what man makes, can, or should make of himself"[38] (the latter investigated by pragmatic anthropology) is central to understanding the relationship between Kant's anthropology and geography—as well as his theory of the races. Geography, for example, can be either physical or moral. In its physical aspect, it studies physical human attributes (for example, skin color, skull size, facial structure) and in its moral aspects, it studies customs and unreflectively held mores, which Kant also sometimes called "second nature."[39] Anthropology, too, can be either pragmatic or physiological, as it studies humans as moral agents or as part of physical nature.

These conceptual distinctions between and within the twin sciences of geography and anthropology could also be elucidated through a summary of the distinctions between the critical works, even as the critical works themselves are provided with some explanatory backgrounds through the geographical and the anthropological writings. The *Critique of Pure Reason*, for example, is concerned with the structures of reason in its contemplative interactions with physical nature and the causal laws governing them. The *Critique of Practical Reason*, on the other hand, studies the domain of freedom and moral law, as well as the psychological states of the soul and the will concerned with moral conduct. And finally, the *Critique of Judgment* studies the domain of reflective reason as it spans both nature (for example, the bodily senses and the emotions, the feelings of pleasure and displeasure of a living organism in contact with nature of which it is part) and the interior, formal aspects of mind that bring judgment to bear on the natural experience. Aesthetic experience, for Kant, is therefore obtained when one experiences oneself as both "nature and man."

The distinctions between physical and moral geography and physical and pragmatic anthropology, therefore, are reflected in greater detail and precision among the divisions of the *Critique of Pure Reason*, the *Critique of Practical Reason*, and the *Critique of Judgment*. Sprawling and "noncritical" as it may appear, *Anthropology* is in effect an effort to present in a unitary treatment the full range of the human condition, parts of which each of the *Critiques* was intended to address. It is from this unitary perspective that Kant would write, "If there is any science man really needs, it is the one I teach, of how to fulfill properly that position in creation which is assigned to man, and from which he is able to learn what one must be in order to be a man."[40] The *Critiques* are, you might say, subplots in this grand, admittedly sometimes, blurry vision.[41]

KANT'S THEORY OF HUMAN AND RACIAL NATURE BASED ON HIS READING OF ROUSSEAU

Kant succinctly defined "nature" as "the existence of things under law."[42] In the announcement of his anthropology lectures for the academic year 1765–1766, he stated that he would set forth a new method for the study of "men," based not simply on observation of human beings in historical and contingent forms, but also on that which is fixed and permanent in their nature.[43] Though this announcement did not mention Rousseau by name, in the comments on the lecture notes Kant described the method he would use as a "brilliant discovery of our time,"[44] and stated that "Rousseau was the very first to discover beneath the varying forms which human nature assumes the deeply concealed nature of man."[45] Rousseau's influential writings were already published before the 1770s when Kant was grappling with the problem of necessary foundations for metaphysics and morality. *Discourse on the Arts and Sciences* was published in 1750, *Discourse on the Origin of Inequality among Men* appeared in 1758, and *New Hélöise* 1761. The most famous, *Of the Social Contract, or Principles of Political Right* appeared in 1762, the same year as *Émile*, a book on education. These books contain Rousseau's extensive speculations on human nature, and evidence abounds that they inspired Kant and influenced his own philosophical development. Kant biographers, such as Cassirer, record that in Kant's spartan study, there was only one ornament on the wall: a portrait of Rousseau. It is also reported that Kant, the model of punctuality in his daily promenade, became engrossed in *Émile* when it first appeared and forgot his daily walk.[46] One of Kant's students from 1762 to 1764, Gottfried Herder, also recorded:

> With the same spirit with which he examined Leibniz, Wolff, Baumgarten, Crusius and Hume, and analysed the laws of nature expounded by the physicists Kepler and Newton, he appraised currently appearing writings of Rousseau, his *Émile* and his *Hélöise*, as he did every fresh discovery in natural science which came to his notice, estimated their value and returned, as always, to an unbiased *knowledge of nature and of the moral worth of man*.[47]

To understand what Kant considered human nature, one must examine his reading of Rousseau. Kant worked out, through the writings of the romantic, what he believed to be "the moral worth of man."

In *Essay on the Origin of Language,* Rousseau wrote that speech "distinguishes man among animals," and then linked the origin of language to that of society; language is therefore "the first social institution."[48] Language and society are inseparable because "as soon as one man was recognized by another as [a] sentient, thinking being similar to himself, the desire or need to communicate his feelings and thoughts made him seek the means to do so."[49] In Rousseau's view, however, both language and society are human inventions and therefore not "natural." Language and society are results of the fact that a pure state of nature has been breached and a radically new dispensation—the state of *human* nature—inaugurated. For Rousseau, the state of nature, the condition of *l'homme naturel*, is different from conventional human nature which is the condition of civil, socialized *l'homme de l'homme*.

Although speech and society may be artificial, Rousseau nevertheless admitted that it is conceptually impossible to grasp the origins and evolution of the transition to civilized humanity—from inarticulate speech (gestures, hollering) to articulate speech (languages, symbols), for example. Since we cannot obtain factual information about this, Rousseau proposed that we imagine such steps, as a hypothesis through which current civilization can be explained and criticized. "We will suppose that this . . . difficulty [of explaining origin] is obviated. Let us for a moment then take ourselves as being on this vast space which must lie between a pure state of nature and that in which languages had become necessary."[50] When he located himself in this "vast space" between the state of nature and the state of civilization, Rousseau imagined the moment when society was constituted, and postulated that from one side of the divide to the other there was "a multitude of centuries," marked by distinct stages. Again one cannot factually ascertain the specifics of these stages.[51] Both in *Origin of Language* and in *Origin of Inequality*, Rousseau suggests that a stage which existed somewhere between the state of nature and civilization should be called the "Age of Huts." The Age of Huts was primitive, with "sparse human population [and] no more social structure than the family, no laws but those of nature, no language but that of gesture and some inarticulate sounds."[52] Beyond this primitive stage, communication grew from gesture to language, and community from family to civil society, giving rise to morality, laws, and the state.

In his anti-Enlightenment writings, Rousseau longed for an imagined, lost period of close-knit life based solely on family ties and emotional bonds, and blamed civilization—in particular, modern arts and sciences—for the evils he attributed to the cold and mechanistic modern form of life. A commentator accurately observed that, ideologically, Rousseau

> opposed the French Enlightenment's rarefied deism, its predilection for a mechanistic materialism, its denigration of emotive values, its dogmatic belief in inevitable progress, the elitism embodied in its adherence to the values and customs of an aristocratic culture and paternalistic government. . . . Championing the essential goodness and moral worth of the common man, the primacy of freedom and its requisite degrees of equality, man's oneness with nature and the consequent conviction that education should liberate natural potentialities instead of suppressing them, Rousseau set himself on a collision course with the "enlightened" views of his time.[53]

This general characterization of Rousseau is somewhat blunt, and perhaps particularly reductionistic (it could be argued that Rousseau is a much more complex thinker). But the description provides a typical example of a popular—and not altogether unjustified—image of Rousseau's thought, an image that Kant would both need and reject in the process of elaborating his thoughts about the essential nature of "man."

Kant distanced himself from the popular image of Rousseau because he wished to offer a different account of humanity and its prospects. Against modern values (which he believed corrupted morals by repressing man's innocence and goodness), Rousseau had been assumed to be an advocate of "ignorance," innocence, and even poverty—all in opposition to the modern pursuit of knowledge at the expense of morality, and progress at the expense of goodness. By some interpretations of the *Origin of Inequality* and in some explicit passages of the *Social Contract*, Rousseau seems to counter the claim that modernity represented the flowering of freedom, by asserting: "Man is born free; and everywhere he is in chains."[54] This argument would suggest that in the state of nature, humans were uninhibited, independent, innocent, and honest—in short, good; but under laws made by a few, modern society and its norms have put the majority in bondage, both economic and social, leaving the majority dependent and oppressed.

Rousseau developed this manner of arguing about modernity in the *Discourse on the Arts*, written at the urging of his friend Diderot, for an Academy of Dijon competition on "whether the progress of the arts and the sciences has tended to the purification or the corruption of morality."[55] The essay won first prize. Using a hypothetical and ideal image of *natural*, Rousseau claimed to have unmasked the disfigurements modernity has inflicted on human nature. He wrote: "Deep in the heart of the forest . . . I sought and found the vision of those primeval ages whose history I barely sketched. I denied myself all the easy deceits to which men are prone. I dared to unveil human nature and to look upon it in its nakedness, to trace the course of times and of events which have disfigured man. . . . I pointed out the true source of our misery in our pretended perfection."[56]

Whereas these aspects of Rousseau's writings seem to advocate a rejection of modern civilization and a return to a better state claimed to be more natural, others (such as those found in the main arguments of the *Social Contract*) refuse a wholesale rejection of modernity and the civil society, and attempt to justify the transition from nature to culture and society; they also inquire into what kinds of social structures would be appropriate to develop, rather than corrupt, human freedom and goodness.[57] For example, if civilization corrupts the natural state, in what, precisely, consists the original good in this state? How could the goodness be cultivated rather than suppressed in civil society?

Rousseau's work challenged Kant's modern bias and allegiances, and convinced him that science and mechanics—the domain of pure reason which dominated modern thinking and social attitudes—had little or nothing to contribute to the moral improvement of humanity. Responding to Rousseau's ideas about the "moral worth of the [supposedly unscientific and socially uncivilized] common man," Kant, in the *Fragments*, noted: "I am myself by inclination a seeker after truth. I feel a consuming thirst for knowledge and a restless passion to advance in it, as well as satisfaction in every forward step. There was a time when I thought that this alone could constitute the honor of mankind [but] Rousseau set me right . . . I learned to respect human nature."[58] Kant, however, dissented from Rousseau's claim that it is in the state of nature that human essential goodness may be found. In Kant's reading of *Origin of Inequality*, for example, the nature to which humans must return is not some supposedly better premodern condition, but a genuine cultivation of those human capacities that are considered of a "higher" level—and specific only to history and to modernity. In his interpretations of *Émile*, Kant did not think that Rousseau intended to alienate individuals from modern civilization. And in the *Anthropology*, he explained why:

> One certainly need not accept the ill-tempered picture which Rousseau paints of the human species. It is not his real opinion when he speaks of the human species as daring to leave its natural condition, and when he propagates a reversal and a return into the woods. Rousseau only wanted to express our species' difficulty in walking the path of continuous progress toward our destiny.[59]

Kant thus regarded Rousseau's contribution as only a critique of unqualified modern optimism with regard to Europe's moral progress.

In fact, after summarizing three of Rousseau's major works (*Discourse on the Arts and the Sciences*, *Origins of Inequality*, and *Julie*) and summarizing their intent as lamenting, respectively, "the damage done to our species by (1) our departure from nature into culture, which weakened our strength; (2) civilization, which resulted in inequality and mutual oppression; and (3) presumed moralization, which caused unnatural education and distorted thinking,"[60] Kant deflects any positive, self-sustaining meaning that one might attribute to these three texts and their claims. In Kant's reading, these books are merely a prepadeutic to Rousseau's later works, which give more positive characterization and value to modern society and culture. The above "three works which present the state of Nature as a state of innocence . . . should serve only as preludes to his *Social Contract*, his *Émile*, and his *Savoyard Vicar* so that we can find our way out of the labyrinth of evil into which our specie has wandered through its own fault."[61] Obviously assuming that the state of nature is also a realm of evil, Kant interpreted the thrust of Rousseau's body of work as showing not that one must return to a pure, innocent human state of nature but, rather, that the state of nature is a reason to *make* humanity out of oneself. Again, for Kant, "Rousseau did not really want that man should go back to the state of nature, but that he should rather look back at it from the stage he has now attained."[62] If the state of nature is a state of evil, it is human nature, as moral nature, that offers the possibility of overcoming this state; hence, "What is characteristic of the human specie in comparison with the idea of other possible rational beings on earth is this: Nature implanted in them the seed of *discord* (evil) and willed that from it their own reason would bring *concord* (good)."[63]

Likewise, if human nature, unlike the natural state, has a moral foundation, Kant—in qualified sympathy with Rousseau but certainly contrary to those who advocated a mechanistic view of human beings—disagreed with the idea that theoretical intelligence alone is sufficient to realize humanity. In the state of nature, humans are, simply, *animale rationabile*; they have to make of themselves *animale rationale*. The effort of making humanity and goodness out of oneself, a moral process, requires a capacity to respond to the needs of action through choices directed toward self-perfectibility. The individual, Kant emphasized, "has a character which he himself creates, because he is capable of perfecting himself according to the purposes which he himself adopts."[64] The purpose of the individual and civil society is therefore tied to what Kant considered the destiny of the specie as a whole: "to affect the perfection of man through cultural progress."[65] Kant not only suspected that the natural state might be evil but also that humanity must have "wandered" into this state of evil through "its own fault."[66]

Kant's peculiar appropriation of Rousseau was controversial—and still is.[67] The critic Paul De Man, for example, remarked: "It is as if the conspiracy that Rousseau's paranoia imagined during his lifetime came into being after his death, uniting friend and foe alike in a concerted effort to misrepresent his thought." Critics—Kant included—according to De Man, proceed with "an overtone of intellectual and moral superiority," as if they know "exactly what ails Rousseau and can therefore observe, judge, and assist him from a position of unchallenged authority, like an ethnocentric anthropologist observing a native or a doctor advising a patient."[68] Kant's Rousseau was clearly not the one promoting the idea of the "noble savage," or of passion over reason, or the hero of the *Stürm und Drang*. Instead, Kant found in Rousseau an agent and restorer of the rights of modernity and its version of humanity. Kant believed that his ethics was the crowning of this justification of history and modernity. "Man," according to him,

> on account of his reason, is destined to live in a society of other people, and in this society he has to cultivate himself, civilize himself, and apply himself to a moral purpose by the arts and the sciences. No matter how great his animalistic inclination may be to abandon himself passively to the enticements of ease and comfort, which he calls happiness, he is still destined to make himself worthy of humanity by actively struggling with the obstacles that cling to him because of the crudity of his nature.[69]

Humanity, in short, must construct in freedom its own culture, its own state.

Radical autonomy defines the worth, the dignity, and, for Kant, the essential nature of humanity, and pragmatic anthropology was designed to provide a description of this structure of the human, "the destination of man and the characteristic of his development."[70] In an earlier distinction between inner and outer human nature, for example, Kant, like Linnaeus, tried to show how humans are unique, and found it in the idea of character. Character has three dimensions: natural disposition, temperament, and morality. The first two refer to humans in their passive embodiment—passive because subject to physical laws or "what can be done to man"; the last component refers to a "rational creature who has acquired freedom," fashioning and refashioning oneself through categorical self-regulation.[71] It is character, then, that makes humans "rational" and morally "higher" than other biological beings. Exploiting once again his disagreements with Rousseau, Kant asked: "The question arises . . . whether man is good by nature or bad by nature. . . . A being endowed with the faculty of practical reason and with consciousness [must be] subject to a moral law and to the feeling (which is then called moral feeling). [This] is the intelligible character of humanity as such, and thus far man is good (by nature)."[72] However:

> Experience also shows that in man there is an inclination to desire actively what is unlawful. This is the inclination to evil which arises as unavoidably and as soon as man begins to make use of his freedom. Consequently the inclination to evil can be regarded as innate. Hence, according to his sensible character, man must be judged as being evil (by nature). This is not contradictory when we are talking about the character of the species because it can be assumed that the species' *natural destiny* consists in continual progress toward the better.[73]

The human project, therefore, is to overcome some ontological state of strife, to overcome a ceaseless state of evil with continual progress toward good. Kant implied, however, that in this work of overcoming evil, history is already on the side of humanity, for humans are the only animals whose state of nature implies history—already a moral outcome.

It is crucial however to note—and this is the racial equation in Kant's metaphysics of "man"—that his redescription of Rousseau's idea of humanity and modernity operates in the following, by now familiar, pattern: there is a distinction between the "phenomenal" (the domain of theoretical reason) and the "ideal" (the domain of practical reason). This in turn leads to the split in the reception of Rousseau: one Rousseau is "historical," and the other is "hypothetical." Rousseau's glorification of the primitive origins of human nature, for example, was interpreted by Kant as useful only as a functional critique of civil society's and modernity's self-conceit (the historical project); hypothetically, however, in order to fulfill the requirements of their position in this equation of moral and historical conflict, Kant's "primitives" must conceptually and categorically remain outside of history. What one may fail to notice—this shall become even clearer when we discuss Kant's categories of racial types—is that Kant conflated Rousseau's *hypothetical* assumptions as to the origin and direction of *European* civilization into a general statement about possible histories of *all* peoples, humanity in general. This conflation—or, in fact, confusion—of the particular and the universal may look like a small oversight on Kant's part, but it has serious consequences when we think of it, as Kant did, as a conceptual paradigm for historical analysis. This mistake allowed Kant to theorize, dialectically, the progress and promise of Europe as a racially "white" civilization confronting premodern, savage, "evil" racial empires: the "black," the "red," and the "yellow." The historicity of Europe, in this regard, is juxtaposed and comprehends itself in relation to its supposedly ahistorical opposites—and opponents. One consequence is that when peoples and cultures who are not European and white resist Europeanization and assert racial and historical autonomy from Europeanization and from cultural whiteness, they can automatically be looked at as evil monsters and traitors to humanity's best interests and the moral progress of history.

KANT'S IDEA OF RACE: THE TAXONOMY

In *Observations on the Feeling of the Beautiful and the Sublime*, Kant outlines a geographical as well as psychological classification of humans. In the same way that other animals are divided into types—domestic or wild; inhabiting land, air, or water—human races are classified as manifesting original and distinct classes, geographically distributed. Taking skin color as evidence of a racial class, Kant divided humans into "white" (Europeans), "yellow" (Asians), "black" (Africans), and "red" (American Indians). The "moral" interest of geography is to study the customs and mores held collectively and unreflectively by each of these racial groups, and Kant carried out such studies. His effort led to a catalog of racial attributes, some of them exotic and flamboyant but still intellectually influential, a fact that contributes to the current embarrassment that many feel in regard to what are now called Kant's "noncritical" writings. For example, Kant theorized that it was customary to permit theft in Africa, to desert children in China, to bury them alive in Brazil, and to strangle them in Alaska.[74] Kant believed that it was the task of practical philosophy (ethics) to demonstrate that such actions are immoral because based on natural impulses ("the inclination to evil," which, as I said earlier, Kant's theory of human nature automatically attributed to nonwhite peoples),[75] and on unreflective "commands of authority."[76] The interrelation between Kant's geography and ethics, his race theory and metaphysics of morals, are well established in this nexus. As we shall see, the examples of unreflective mores and customs listed are entirely supposed to be afflictions of nonwhites.

Within Kant's elaborations, the races that inhabit America, Africa, Asia, and "the Hindustan" (in fact, the Jews) are incapable of moral maturity because they lack *talent*—a "gift" of nature. After stating that "the difference in natural gifts between the various nations cannot be completely explained by means of casual causes," Kant looked for the explanation in psychology, in the "nature of Man himself."[77] Using the concept of ability or inability to be educated as criterion, he wrote: "When a people does not perfect itself in any way over the space of centuries, so it is to be assumed that there exists a certain natural pre-disposition (*Anlage*) that the people cannot transcend."[78] Thus, Americans are wholly uneducable because they lack "affect and passion"; and Africans, who do not lack affect and passion, can only be "trained" as slaves and servants. Kant explained: "The *race* of the American cannot be educated. It has no motivating force, for it lacks affect and passion. They are not in love, thus they are also not afraid. They hardly speak, do not caress each other, care about nothing and are lazy."[79] However,

The *race* of the Negroes, one could say, is completely the oppo-

site of the Americans; they are full of affect and passion, very
lively, talkative and vain. They can be educated but only as servants (slaves), that is if they allow themselves to be trained. They
have many motivating forces, are also sensitive, are afraid of
blows and do much out of a sense of honor.[80]

The distinction between capacity to be "educated" (or to educate oneself) and capacity to be "trained" can be deduced from the practical situations. Training consists of pure physical coercion and punishment, as we see
in Kant's other writings where he gives advice about how to effectively flog
the African servant. A critic notes that Kant "advises us to use a split bam-
boo cane instead of a whip, so that the Negro will suffer a great deal of pain
(because of the Negro's 'thick skin,' he would not be racked with sufficient
agonies through a whip) but without dying."[81] To beat the Negro efficiently
requires "a split cane rather than a whip, because the blood needs to find a
way out of the Negro's thick skin to avoid festering."[82]

The Negro needs this kind of training because Africans as a race are
supposed to be "exclusively idle," lazy, and prone to hesitation and jealousy.
For climatic (geographic) and psychological (ethical) reasons, every person
who belongs to this race is presumed incapable of self-cultivation and moral
perfection. "All inhabitants of the hottest zones," Kant claims, "are, without
exceptions, idle. With some, this laziness is offset by government and force.
. . . The aroused power of imagination has the effect that he often attempts
to do something; but the heat soon passes and reluctance soon assumes its
old position."[83] Did Kant hold these views because, given transatlantic slavery, Africans in Europe could be bought, sold, and routinely "trained"? In
Kant's writings, however, this historical question is totally absent; the
Negro's condition in Europe was for him only a metaphysical problem.

When he wrote about Asians, a category he made certain to include
and highlight the stereotype of the Jew, Kant stated:

The Hindus . . . do have motivating forces but they have a strong
degree of passivity (*Gelassenheit*) and all look like philosophers.
Nevertheless they incline greatly towards anger and love. They
thus can be educated to the highest degree but only in the arts

and not in the sciences. They can never achieve the level of abstract concepts. A great Hindustani man is one who has gone far in the art of deception and has much money. The Hindus always stay the way they are, they can never advance, although they began their education much earlier. [84]

In the classic tradition of what has come to be rightly known as Orientalism, the reader is reminded by Kant that "the Hindus, Persians, Chinese, Turks and actually all oriental peoples belong" to this description.[85]

The only race, then, that Kant recognizes as not only educable but capable of progress in arts and sciences is the white. In a single sentence, we are told that "The white race possesses *all* motivating forces and talents"[86]—and thus represents everything that is good and smart and beautiful—all the nice things nature had supposedly denied all the other races.

Kant's position on the evil psychological and moral status of non-European races is consistent with the explicitly color-coded classification of peoples in his geographical writing. The ultimate scientific evidence for racial groups, as species classes, is obtained externally, on the basis of skin color; hence, physical geography is "classifying things, grouping their external attributes, and describing what they are in their present state."[87] In "On the Varieties of Different Races of Man," a variation is given to the racial tableau that was already presented in the *Observations*. This time, the geographic factor of climate is more explicitly stated, even as color remained the dominant variable.

> STEM GENUS: *white brunette*
> First race, very blond (northern Europe), of damp cold.
> Second race, Copper-Red (America), of dry cold.
> Third race, Black (Senegambia), of dry heat.
> Fourth race, Olive-Yellow (Indians), of dry heat.[88]

This order precisely presumes that the ideal skin color is white, and that the others are superior or inferior to this as they approximate whiteness. Indeed, other skin colors are *degenerate,* ugly variants—reflecting the morally "fallen" and inferior mental status of their carriers—of the white original.

Kant could have gotten the idea for this order of skin colors and the implied notion of degeneration from Johann Friedrich Blumenbach (1752–1840), to whose work on race Kant referred in the *Anthropology*.[89] In *On the Natural Variety of Mankind*, Blumenbach regarded skin color as the highest mark of racial category, so that whereas there are five races, only three are basic. The "Caucasian" is the "most beautiful . . . to which the pre-eminence belongs"; the "Mongolian" and the "Ethiopian" are "extreme degenerations of the human species." The remaining two, the "American" and the "Malay," are degenerations from the white to, respectively, the Mongolian and the Ethiopian.[90] That Kant took these speculations seriously may be seen in a story he told about the process through which he believed the white skin turns black: at birth, the skin color of every baby of every race is white but gradually, over a few weeks, the white baby's body turns black (or red or yellow). "The Negroes," Kant claimed, "are born white, apart from their genitals and a ring around the navel, which are black. During the first month blackness spreads across the whole body from these parts."[91] The Negro genitalia, then, could be made the one original source of the "white" problem?

When Kant tried to become more scientific, he switched from this to other theories: in 1775, he thought that red, black, and yellow skin colors are caused by the presence of a mineral iron at the subcutaneous level of the body. "For good reason," he wrote, "one now ascribes the different colour of plants to the differing amounts of iron precipitated by various fluids. As all animal blood contains iron, nothing prevents us from ascribing to the different colors of the human races the same cause. In this way the base acid, or phosphoric acid . . . react[s] strongly with the iron particles and turn[s] red or black or yellow."[92] In 1785, he believed that an inflammable substance, phlogiston, existed in the African's blood and made the skin color dark. Phlogiston also accounted for the colors of other nonwhite skins:

> The purpose (of race) is nowhere more noticeable in the characteristics of race than in the Negro; merely the example that can be taken from it alone justifies us also in the supposition of seeing an analogy in this race to the others. Namely, it is now known that human blood becomes black, merely by deint of the fact that

> it is loaded with phlogiston. . . . the strong stench of the Negro
> which cannot be removed through any amount of washing, gives
> us reason to suppose that their skin removes a great deal of phlo-
> giston from the blood and that nature must have organized this
> skin in such a way that the blood can be dephlogistonized to a
> much greater degree than is the case with us.[93]

In the *Anthropology*, Kant also spoke of "innate, natural character which, so to speak, lies in the composition of the person's blood."[94] But to whatever cause he attributed differences in skin color, and thus racial differences, Kant managed to maintain throughout a hierarchical moral interpretation of these color-coded differences, grounding them not only in geography but also in morality and metaphysics. He also continued to attribute the presumed grades of superiority or inferiority of a race to the presence or absence of "talent." Thus, "in the hot countries the human being matures earlier in all ways but does not reach the perfection of the temperate zones. Humanity exists in its greatest perfection in the white race."[95]

The moral quality *Talent*, as elusive as phlogiston, is what Kant believed guarantees for the white race a superior position, metaphysically and ethically, in the racial order. White skin, it seems, is only the concrete, physical evidence of this racial superiority; skin color reveals race as species class (*Klassenunterschied*)[96] and, morally, as "difference in character" ("Verschiedenheit des Naturcharakters").[97] Skin color is therefore not only a code for, but proof of, rational superiority or inferiority; this assumption renders intelligible statements such as this, from Kant: "This fellow was quite black from head to foot, a clear proof that what he said was stupid."[98]

RACE: A TRANSCENDENTAL?

Kant's work on race situates itself within prior Enlightenment racial classificatory programs, such as those established by Buffon, Linnaeus, and the French doctor François Bernier. Buffon, for example, classified races geographically, using principally physical characteristics as indices.[99] But since he believed that there was a common, homogeneous human origin,

Buffon attributed the differences in bodily characteristics to environmental factors. The concepts of "species" and "genre," as may be applied to racial classifications, are, for Buffon, artificial; races as *classes* simply have no natural existence: "In reality," Buffon wrote, "only *individuals* exist in nature."[100] Although Kant accepted Buffon's geographical classification, he rejected the idea that races are not classes. For Kant the geographical distribution of races is a fact, and the differences among them are permanent, fixed, and transcendent of environmental factors; the differences, he argued, are founded in an immutable natural germ (*Keime*).[101] This explains why Kant believed that the mixing of races is a contravention of the law of nature: "Instead of assimilation, which was intended by the melting together of the various races, Nature has here made a law of just the opposite."[102]

Kant's position follows more closely Linnaeus's table of the races. By 1735, Linnaeus had inventoried "the universe"—planets, atmosphere, minerals, and vegetables, and at the summit of the pyramid he placed *homo*. Kant's analysis reproduced Linnaeus's division of humans—physical, cultural, geographical, and temperamental (melancholic, sanguine, choleric, and phlegmatic)—but situated them transcendentally on an axis that, as we have seen, permanently links moral character to racial classes. In a number of references to *Systema Naturae*, Kant evinced Linnaeus's passion for carefully composed taxonomy, but did not hesitate to criticize the Swede's system as a mere "aggregate," one without a philosophical, transcendental, grounding. Kant argued:

> One should call the system of nature created up to now more correctly an aggregate of nature, because a system presupposes the idea (*Idee*) of a whole out of which the manifold character of things is being derived. We do not have as yet a system of nature. In the existing so-called system of this type, the objects are merely put beside each other and ordered in sequence one after another. . . . True philosophy, however, has to follow the diversity and the manifoldness of matter *through all time*.[103]

In short, Linnaeus's system—because of its environmentalism—was considered by Kant as transcendentally deficient. In Kant's view, scientific knowledge must secure for itself grounds of logical necessity, for this is what confers upon knowledge the status of universality and permanence. Linnaeus's system, including the racial hierarchies, needed to be provided with a necessary reason. Cassirer thinks that in the *Critique of Judgment* Kant tried to supply precisely what he thought was lacking in Linnaeus: a philosophical foundation for natural and racial kinds.[104]

Beyond Buffon and Linnaeus, then, Kant practiced a transcendental philosophy of race. In the *Critique of Pure Reason* Kant had described ways of orienting oneself geographically in space, mathematically in space and time, and logically in the construction of both categories into other forms of knowledge of consistent entities. In the *Observations*, an aesthetic and anthropological work, Kant deployed the transcendentalism of the *Critique of Pure Reason* in order to establish ways in which moral feelings apply to humans *generally*,[105] how the feeling differs between men and women, and among the races (hence, the title of section 4 of the *Observations*: "Of *National* Characteristics, So Far as They Depend upon the Distinct Feeling of the Beautiful and the Sublime"). Forest Williams argued, regarding the *Critique of Judgment*, that Kant conceptualized reflective judgment as constituting and expressing a structure of properly universal human feeling, rather than merely postulating a regulative idea for knowledge. The position that the reflective expression of judgment is constitutive of feeling, Williams explained, "is tantamount to introducing an anthropological postulate, for a constitutive feeling which is universal implies a *depth-structure of humanity*."[106] Now whether this depth-structure of humanity is understood as already given or potential, it is obvious that the notion derives from Kant's appropriation and interpretation of Rousseau, for whom there is a "hidden" nature of man.

What can we conclude from these? First, that as with his geography and anthropology, Kant's aesthetics, both in *Observations* and in *Critique of Judgment*, harbor an implicit foundation in philosophical anthropology and, in light of our study, in raciology as well.[107] The themes Kant presented in these books—feeling, taste, genius, art, the agreeable, the beautiful, and so forth—give synthesis to the principles and practices he philosophically defined as immanent to humans, but only to white human nature. When he associated feeling with character, Kant wrote: "I hope that I express this completely when I say that it [the feeling of the sublime] is the feeling of the beauty and worth of human nature."[108] And then about the African he asserted: "The African has no feeling beyond the trifling." What authority justifies this claim? Hume.

> Mr. Hume challenges anyone to cite a simple example in which a Negro has shown talents, and asserts that among the hundreds of thousands of blacks who are transported elsewhere from their countries, although many of them have been set free, still not a single one was ever found who presented anything great in art or science or any other praiseworthy quality, even among the whites some continually rise aloft from the lowest rabble, and through superior gifts earn respect in the world. So fundamental is the difference between the two races of man, and it appears to be as great in regard to mental capacities as in color.[109]

The inferiority of the Negro, as proposed by Hume, is now in Kant successfully grounded in transcendental philosophy.

The fact that Kant insisted so much on the transcendentality of "feeling" as measurement of moral humanity and racial perfection is, in its historical contexts, not at all surprising. In the 1740s, Johann Jakob Breitinger, for example, emphasized the theoretical primacy of the *effect* of a work of art on the audience; and in the 1750s, Christian Furchtegott Gellert and Friedrich Gottlieb Klopstock believed that the poet was "an agent working on the *feeling*s of the audience"; while in 1766, Gotthold Ephraim Lessing's *Laocoön*, though intended to prove a distinction between poetry and painting, was committed to understanding the relationship between the two by reducing the source of all art to "feeling."[110] Kant took up these notions of art and psychology but, as was his habit, sought to ground them transcendentally. He philosophically advanced an accepted understanding that feeling, in certain spheres, is of ultimate value as a special mode of knowledge, surpassing the theoretic-scientific—or at least venturing beyond it. By additionally racializing this transcendental structure of feeling, however, Kant apparently secured the objectivity of his earlier anthropological and geographical description (distinction, classification, hierarchies, etc.) of humanity, by conferring upon the arbitrary description the status of an immutable rational law. In an academic-political sense, this transcendental move also justified Kant's newly introduced courses—anthropology and it its twin, geography; now he could argue that they are real and true "sciences," as required by the university and by King Frederick.[111] Moreover, he could rest content in the knowledge that his racial system was philosophically superior to Linnaeus's and Buffon's.

NOTES

The epigraph is from Vol. 20, p. 45, of *Gesammelte Schriften* (*GS*), 24 vols., Berlin: Königlich Preussische Akademie der Wissenschaften [Deutschen Academie der Wissenschaften zur Berlin], 1900–1966.

1. Immanuel Kant, "Review of Herder's *Ideas for a Philosophy of the History of Mankind*," in *Kant on History*, ed. Lewis White Beck, New York: Macmillan, 1963, pp. 50–51.
2. Immanuel Kant, "Perpetual Peace," in *Kant on History*, pp. 103–104.
3. Ibid., p. 92, n. 1.
4. See Isaiah Berlin, *The Sense of Reality: Studies in Ideas and Their History*, ed. Henry Hardy, New York: Farrar, Straus and Giroux, 1996, pp. 232–233.
5. Ibid.
6. Ibid.
7. See Kant, "On the Different Races of Man," in *Race and the Enlightenment: A Reader*, ed. Emmanuel Eze, Oxford: Blackwell, 1997, pp. 38–48.
8. Isaiah Berlin, *The Sense of Reality*, p. 233.
9. Kant, *Anthropology from a Pragmatic Point of View*, trans. Mary J. Gregor, The Hague: Martinus Nijhoff, 1974, p. 177.
10. Sander L. Gilman, *On Blackness without Blacks: Essays on the Image of the Black in Germany*, Boston: G. K. Hall, 1982, p. 33.
11. Ibid.
12. Kant, *Observations on the Feeling of the Beautiful and the Sublime* (*Observations*) [1764], trans. John T. Goldthwait, Berkeley: University of California Press, 1960, p. 110.
13. Immanuel Kant, *Sämmtliche Werke*, ed. G. Hartenstein, Leipzig: L. Voss, 1867, Vol. 5, pp. 241–242.
14. Earl W. Count, *This Is Race: An Anthology Selected from the International Literature on the Races of Man*, New York: Henry Schuman, 1950, p. 704.
15. Paul Gedan, notes to *Physische Geographie*, in Rich Adickes, *Kant als Naturforscher*, 2 vols., p. 388.
16. Immanuel Kant, *Anthropology from a Pragmatic Point of View* (*Anthropology*), trans. Victor Dowdell, Carbondale and Edwardsville: Southern Illinois University Press, 1978, p. 6n.
17. See, for example, the arguments of Frederick van de Pitte, *Kant as Philosophical Anthropologist* (*KPA*), The Hague: Martinus Nijhoff, 1991.
18. Kant, "Perpetual Peace," in *Kant on History*, p. 121; Kant's emphases.

19. Ernst Cassirer, *Rousseau, Kant and Goethe* (*RKG*), New York: Harper Touchbooks, 1963, p. 25.
20. J. A. May, *Kant's Concept of Geography and Its Relation to Recent Geographical Thought*, Toronto: University of Toronto Press, 1970, p. 4.
21. Only the introduction is available in English, as Appendix A, in May, *Kant's Concept of Geography*.
22. Reprinted in Kant's *Philosophische Anthropologie. Nach Handschriftlichen Vorlesungen*, ed. Friedrich Christian Starke, Leipzig, 1831.
23. Translated by Earl W. Count, in Count, *This Is Race*, pp. 16–24.
24. Others are Max Scheller, *Formalism in Ethics and Non-Ethics of Value*, trans. Manfred S. Frings and Roger Funk, Evanston, IL: Northwestern University Press, 1973; Martin Heidegger, *Kant and the Problem of Metaphysics* (*KPM*), trans. Richard Taft, Bloomington: Indiana University Press, 1990; Ernst Cassirer, *Kant's Life and Thought*, trans. James Haden, New Haven, CT: Yale University Press, 1981; Frederick van de Pitte, *Kant as Philosophical Anthropologist*, The Hague: Martinus Nijhoff, 1991.
25. See, for example, James Miller, *The Passion of Michel Foucault*, New York: Anchor, 1993; and Didier Eribon, *Michel Foucault*, trans. Betsy Wing, Cambridge, MA: Harvard University Press, 1991.
26. Michel Foucault, introduction to George Canguilhem, *The Normal and the Pathological*, New York: Zone Books, 1991, pp. 7–24. This interest in Kant is also evident in Foucault's review of Cassirer's work on Kant and the Enlightenment movement, in *La Quinzaine Littéraire* 8 (July 1, 1966), "Une histoire restée muette."
27. Martin Heidegger, *Kant and the Problem of Metaphysics* (*KPM*), "Preface to the Fourth Edition," p. xvi.
28. Cassirer, *Kant's Life and Thought*, p. 408.
29. Heidegger, "Preface to the Second Edition," *KPM*, p. xvii.
30. Heidegger, *KPM*, p. 1.
31. Martin Heidegger, *Being and Time*, trans. J. Macquire and E. Robinson, New York: Harper and Row, 1962, p. 44.
32. Kant's *Anthropology* is currently cataloged by most libraries under the heading "Psychology."
33. Katherine Faull, *Anthropology and the German Enlightenment*, London: Associated and Bucknell University Presses, 1994, p. 13.
34. Kant, *Entwurf und Ankündiung eines Collegii der physischen Geographie* (1757) (*GS*), Vol. 3. The section on man runs from pages 311 to 320.
35. Linnaeus, *Systema Naturae*, in Eze, *Race and the Enlightenment*, p. 16.
36. Carl von Linnaeus, "Hommo," *Systema Naturae*, in Eze, *Race and the Enlightenment*, chapter 1.
37. Ibid., p. 9.
38. Ibid., p. 3.
39. Ibid., p. 5.
40. Immanuel Kant, *GS*, Vol. 20, p. 45.
41. The grounding of moral philosophy in anthropology suggests that Kant's interests in the latter were not peripheral to the critical projects. Kant frequently summarized his philosophy as the attempt to understand "two things that fill the mind with ever new and increasing admiration and awe," namely, "the starry heavens above and the moral law within." While the "starry heavens above" refers to physical nature under causal law (as

studied by physics and described in *Critique of Pure Reason*), "the moral law within" is the domain of freedom of individuals or racial groups as moral beings. For Kant, Newton in physics had achieved success in understanding the deterministic laws of nature, but philosophy has been unable to establish an equivalent necessary basis for morality. Kant was also aware of the problems presented within philosophy by the metaphysical dogmatism of the rationalists (Descartes, Spinoza, Leibniz) and the skepticism of Hume's empiricism. Against the rationalists, he argued that the mathematical model they proposed as ideal for metaphysics and moral inquiry was unachievable, for whereas mathematics studies ideal entities, moving from definitions by purely rational arguments to apodictic conclusions, metaphysics must proceed analytically rather than dogmatically, in order to clarify what is given indistinctly in empirical experience. "[The] true method of metaphysics," Kant concluded, "is basically the same as that introduced by Newton into natural science and which had such useful consequences in that field" (Kant, *GS*, Vol. 2, p. 286).

42. Kant, *Critique of Practical Reason*, pp. 153–154.
43. Kant, *GS*, Vol. 2, p. 311.
44. Ibid., p. 312.
45. Ibid., Vol. 20, p. 58.
46. Cassirer, *RKG*, pp. 1–2
47. Gottfried Herder, *Letters on the Advancement of Humanity* (1793–97), nd.; my emphasis.
48. Jean-Jacques Rousseau, *Essay on the Origin of Language* (*OL*), trans. John H. Moran and Alexander Gode, Chicago: University of Chicago Press, 1986.
49. Ibid., p. 5.
50. Ibid., p. 15. On the problem of determining the exact relationship between language and society, speech, and community, Rousseau wrote: "For myself, I am so aghast at the increasing difficulties which present themselves, and so well convinced of the almost demonstrable impossibility that languages should owe their original institution to merely human means . . . I leave to any one who will undertake it the discussion of the difficult problem, which was most necessary, the existence of society to the invention of language, or the invention of language to the establishment of society." He criticized writers, such as Condillac, who believed that they could answer this question. Such authors, he said, merely project into unknown primordial past "ideas taken from society."
51. The thoroughly "thought-experiment" nature of Rousseau's views on this matter merits emphasis because Kant, in his anthropological discussion of the "primitive" races, would ignore the tentative nature of Rousseau's musings. Extended study of Rousseau's hypothesis about the stages of civilization may be found in Robert Derathé, *Rousseau et la science politique de son temps*.
52. Discrepancies on this topic abound between these texts. Jacques Derrida makes sport of this in Part 2 of *Of Grammatology*, trans. Gayatri Spivak, Baltimore and London: Johns Hopkins University Press, 1976.
53. Jean-Jacques Rousseau, *Of the Social Contract, or Principles of Political Right*, trans. Charles Shrover, New York, Harper and Row, 1978. Quote from translator's introduction, p. xiv.
54. Ibid., p. 4.
55. See Frederick Copleston, *A History of Philosophy*, Vol. 6, Westminster: Newman Press, 1964, p. 69.
56. Rousseau, *The Confessions*, trans. W. Conyngham Mallory, New York: Bretano, 1928, p. viii.
57. The subtitle of the *Social Contract*, "Principles of Political Right," points to this goal of for-

mulating normative principles through which one can distinguish between a free and therefore legitimate society and a repressive one. Rousseau's influence on Kant on this score is indisputable, and can be easily noticed in Kant's ethical concepts, for example, in the relationship between the universal "goodwill" and the "categorical imperative," which are, in fact, transcendental versions of Rousseau's *principes du droit politique*. Cassirer goes as far as to argue that "Rousseau not only influenced the content and systematic development of Kant's foundation of ethics [but also] formed its language and style" (*RKG*, p. 32).

58. Kant, *GS*, Vol. 7, p. 624.

59. Kant, *Anthropology*, p. 243.

60. Ibid., pp. 243–244.

61. Ibid.

62. Ibid., p. 244.

63. Ibid., p. 322.

64. Ibid., p. 238.

65. Ibid.

66. Kant, *Kant on History*, ed. L. W. Beck, New York: Library of the Liberal Arts, 1963, pp. 53–68.

67. See, for example, Peter Gay's preface to Cassirer, *RKG*.

68. See P. N. Furbank, introduction to Rousseau, *The Confessions* [anon. trans., 1904], London: David Campell, 1992, p. xvii.

69. Kant, *Anthropology*, pp. 241–242.

70. Ibid., p. 241.

71. Kant, *Anthropology*, p. 3. See also Kant, *GS*, Vol. 7, p. 265.

72. Ibid., p. 240.

73. Ibid., pp. 240–241; emphasis added.

74. Kant, *GS*, Vol. 8, "Bestimmung des Begriffs einer Menschenrasse," p. 93; or see Fritz Schultze, *Kant und Darwin: Ein Beitrag zur Geschichte der Entwicklungslehre*, Jena: Hermann Dufft, 1875.

75. Kant, *Anthropology*, p. 241.

76. Kant, *Lectures on Ethics* (1765–66).

77. See Kant, *Kants philosophische Anthropologie*, ed. Friedrich Christian Starke, Leipzig, 1831.

78. Ibid., p. 352. "Wenn sich ein Volk auf keine Weise in Jahrhunderten vervollkommnet, so ist anzunehmen, daß es schon in ihm eine gewisse Naturanlege geibt, welche zu übersteigen es nicht fäahig ist."

79. Ibid., p. 353. "Das Volk der Amerilaner nimmt keine Bildung an. Es hat keine Triebfedern, denn es fehlen ihm Affect un Leidenschaft. Sie sind nicht verliebt, daher sind auch nicht furchtbar. Sie sprechen fast nichts, liebkosen einmander nicht, sorgen auch für nichts, und sind faul."

80. Ibid. "Die race der Neger, Könnte man sagen, ist ganz das Gegenteil von den Amerikanern; sie sind voll Affect und Leidenschaft, sehre lebhaft, schwatzhaft und eitel. Sie nehmen Bildung an, aber nur eine Bildung der Knechte, d.h. sie lassen sich abrichten. Sie haben viele triebfedern, sind auch empfindlich, fürchten sich vor Schlägen und thun auch viel aus Ehre."

81. Christian Neugebauer interpreting parts of *Physische Geographie* in his revealing essay "The Racism of Kant and Hegel," in Odera Oruka, *Sage Philosophy*, New York: E. J. Brill, 1990, p. 264.

82. "Die Mohren . . . haben eine dicke Haut, wie man sie denn auch nicht mit Ruthen, son-

dern gespaltenen Rihren peitscht, wenn mann sie zughtigt, damit das Blut einen Ausgang finde, und nicht unter der haut eitere." If the passage just quoted by Neugebauer (n. 81) was drawn from the same source as mine, rather than from a combination of references, his interpretation would be understandable from this perspective.

83. Kant, *Physische Geographie*, Zweiter Band, 1. Abs. 3 (IX 195); Kant, *Philosophischen Bibliothek*, Herg.: K. Vorlander, Leipzig, 1920, pp. 15, 16–17. "Alle Bewohner der heißesten Zonen sind ausnehmendtrage. Bey einigen wird diese Faulheit noch etwas durch die Regierung und Zwang germa igt. . . . Die aufgeweckte Einbildungskraft macht aber auch, de er oft etwas wagt: aber die Hitze is bald voruber, und die Zaghaftigkeit nimmt . . . ihren alten Platz ein."

84. Kant, *Kants philosophische*, pp. 352 and 353. "Die Hindus haben zwar Triebfedern, aber sie haben einen starken Grad von Gelassenheit, und sehen alle wie Philosophen aus. Demohngeachtet sind doch zum Zorne und zur Liebe sehr geneit. Sie nehmen daher Bildung im höchsten grade an, aber nur zu Künsten und nicht zu Wiseenchaften. Sie bringen es niemals bis zu abstrakten Begriffen. Ein hindostanischer großer Mann ist der, der es recht weit in der Betrügerei gebracht und viel Geld hat. Die Hindus bleiben immer wie sind, weiter bringen sie es neimals. . . . Dahin gehören die Hindus, die Perser, der Chisen, die Türken, überhaupt alle orientalischen Völker."

85. Ibid.

86. Ibid., p. 353. "Die Race der Weißen enthält alle Triebfedern und Talente in sich; daher erden wir sie etwas genauer betrachten müssen."

87. Kuno Fisher, *A Critique of Kant*, trans. W. S. Hough, London: Swan, Sonnenschein, and Lowrey, 1888, pp. 67–68.

88. Count, *This Is Race*, p. 23.

89. Kant, *Anthropology*, p. 211.

90. Johann Friedrich Blumenbach, *On the Natural Variety of Mankind* [1775], London: Longman, Green & Co., 1865, pp. x–xi.

91. "Die Neger werden wei geboren, au er ihren Aeugungsgliedern und einen Ring um den Nabel, die schwarz sind. Von diesen Teilen aus zieht sich die Schwarze im ersten Monat uben den ganzen Korper" (Kant, *Physische Geographie*, quoted in Neugebauer, "The Racism of Kant and Hegel," p. 265). Neugebauer points out what V. Y. Mudimbe had noticed (*The Invention of Africa* [Bloomington: Indiana University Press, 1988, p. 48]): in 1648, a Giovanni F. Romano, an Italian missionary, wrote about the origin of black skin: "I natural del Congo sono tutti di color negre chi pui, e chi meno; . . . Quando nascendo, non sonso negri ma bianchi, e poi a poco a poco si vanno fecendo negri").

92. Kant, *Von den verschiedenen Racen der Menschen: Zur Ankündigung der Vorlesungen der physischen Geographie im Sommerhalbjahr 1775*, reprinted in Fritz Schultze, *Kant und Darwin*, pp. 58–79). "Man schreibt jetzt mit gutem Grunde die verscheidenene Farben der Gewächse dem durch unterschieldliche Säfte gefällten Eisen zu. Da alles Thierblut Eisen anthält, so hindert uns nichts, die verschiede Farbe fieser Menschenracen ebenderselben Ursache beizumessen. Auf diese Art würde etwa das Satzäure, oder das phosphorisch Säure, oder . . . die Eisentheilchen im Reichtum roth oder schwarz oder gelb wiederschlagen."

93. Ibid., 150. "Nun ist dieses Zwekmäßige zwar an der Eigenthümlichkeit keiner Race so deutkich zu beweisen möglich, als an der Negerrace; allen das Beispiel, das von dieser allein hergenommen worden, berechtigt uns auch, nach der Analogie eben dergleichen von den übrigen wenigstens zu vermuthen. Man weiß nämlich jetzt, daß das

Menschenblut, bloß dadurch, daß phlogiston überladen wird, schwarz werde. . . . Nun giebt schon der starke und durch keine Reinlichkeit zu vermeidende Geruch der Neger Anlaß, zu vermuthen, daß ihre Haut sehr viel Phlosgiston aus Blute wegschaffe, und daß die Natur diese Haut so organisiert haben müsse, daß das Blut sich bei ihen in weit größerem Maße durch si dephlogistiren könne, als es bei uns geschieht." Today, most reference dictionaries define "phlogiston" as "the hypothetical principle of fire regarded formerly as a material substance."

94. Kant, *Anthropology*, p. 235.

95. Kant, *Physische Geographie*, quoted in Neugebauer, "The Racism of Kant and Hegel," p. 264." In den heißen Läandern reift der Mensch in allen Stücken früher, erreicht aber nicht die Vollkommenheit temperierter Zonen. Die Menschheit is in ihrer großten Vollkommenheit in der Rasse der Weißen. Die gelben Inder haben schon geringeres Talent. Die Neger sind tiefer, und am tiefsten steht ein Teil amerikanishen Völkerschaften."

96. Kant, "Bestimmung des Begriffs einer Menschenrassce" (1785), in Schultze, *Kant und Darwin*, p. 136.

97. Ibid., p. 138.

98. Kant, *Observations*, p. 113.

99. Buffon, *Histoire Naturelle* (1758–1769).

100. Ibid.

101. Kant, "Bestimmung des Begriffs einer Menschenrasse," p. 98.

102. Kant, *Anthropology*, p. 236.

103. Kant, *Physische Geographie*, p. 160; also in May, *Kant's Concept of Geography*, pp. 260–261.

104. Cassirer, *The Problem of Knowledge*, p. 127; for Cassirer, Kant, in the *Critique of Judgment*, was playing the role of "logician to Linnaeus' descriptive science."

105. Kant, *Observations*, p. 1.

106. Forest Williams, "Anthropology and the Critique of Aesthetic Judgement," *Kant Studien* 46, 1954–1955: 173.

107. For extended examination of the interrelations between anthropology, race, and aesthetic theory in eighteenth-century German thought, see Peter Martin, *Schwarze Teufel, edle Mohren: Afrikaner in Bewus-tsein und Geschte der Deutschen*, Hamburg: Janus, 1993.

108. Kant, *GS*, Vol. 20, pp. 46–47; or *Observations*, p. 51.

109. Kant, *Observations*, pp. 110–111.

110. Nicholas Boyle, *Goethe: The Poet and the Age, Vol. 1, The Poetics of Desire*, Oxford: Clarendon Press, 1991, pp. 27–31.

111. Kant had to be given special permission by the minister of education to teach anthropology and geography from private notes, without a "compendium."

PART II

———

THIS PAST MUST ADDRESS ITS FUTURE

CHAPTER 4

NÉGRITUDE: DER HUMANISMUS DER ANDEREN MENSCHEN

When you removed the gag that was keeping these black mouths shut, what were you hoping for? That they would sing your praises? Did you think that when they raised themselves up, you would read adoration in the eyes of these heads that our fathers had forced to bend down to the very ground? Here are black men standing, looking at us, and I hope that you—like me—will feel the shock of being seen.

—Jean-Paul Sartre, "Black Orpheus"

BACKGROUND TO THE GREAT REFUSAL

The intellectual and cultural movement known as Négritude flourished during the first half of the twentieth century. Though its sources of inspiration included the pre–World War II black literary developments in the United States (the Harlem Renaissance in particular), Négritude as an ideology was launched by black students in Paris in the early 1930s. Although Aimé Césaire and Léopold Sédar Senghor would become the best-known advocates of Négritude, others, mostly French West Indians, including Jules Monnerot, René Ménil, and Etienne Lérot, became the earliest champions of the black student protest that was the direct ancestor of Négritude when they launched, in June 1932, the journal *Légitime Défense*. This journal claimed, mysteriously, to be dedicated to "African love of life . . . African joy of love and African dream of death"; it wished to combat what it called the "shame" of blackness as well as the sources of the shame—which, according to the editors, was the trinity colonialism, capitalism, and Christianity.[1]

Given its ambitions, it is not surprising that *Légitime Défense* ran only one issue. But two years later Léon Damas, Aimé Césaire, and Léopold Sédar Senghor launched a successor, *L'Etudiant Noir*. More constructive in outlook and exhibiting a greater interest in, even when not a greater knowledge of, Africa itself, *L'Etudiant Noir* presented a more consistent and a more mature literary and artistic vision. When asked how the word "Négritude" first became a theme in the journal, Césaire explained: "It was an elementary semantic step; [we] simply transformed the French adjective for black . . . *nègre*, into a noun by adding a suffix, -*itude*. . . . Antilleans were ashamed of being Negroes, they searched for all sorts of euphemism for Negro: they would say a man of color, a dark-complexioned man. . . . We adopted the word *nègre* as a term of defiance. . . . We found a violent affirmation in the word *Négritude*."[2] The "violence," of course, is in the reversal of an earlier refusal: the affirmation of blackness and Africa was a defiance of whiteness and Europe—a defiance in particular of the official colonial policy of assimilation. This French policy was aimed at turning Africans into Frenchmen and Frenchwomen—or caricatures of these; instead, Négritude wished to translate Africanity into a cultural presence in modernity and in France. Both the assimilation and the reversal logically entail each other, because, as Césaire asserted, "Europe despised everything about Africa, and in France people spoke of a civilized world and a barbarian world. The barbarian world was Africa, and the civilized world was Europe."[3]

Beyond the semantics, then, Négritude was a cultural program. Following the initial declarations in *L'Etudiat noir*, a series of highly creative works followed: Césaire published his influential poem, "Cahier d'un retour au pays natal" (1939), and Senghor the "Chant d'ombre" (1945) and "Hosties noires" (1948). Then in 1947, through collaboration with Allioune Diop, as well as the supports of Sartre and Picasso, the publishing house Présence Africaine and a journal of the same name were founded. The aim of both press and journal was, unambiguously, to "explain the originality of Africa and hasten its appearance in the modern world."[4]

At that time only the black movements in the United States seemed to provide an existing model of Africa's "appearance in the modern world." As Abiola Irele, a student of the black literature of the period, remarked: in Harlem there existed "a tradition of black protest writing which expressed the psychological tensions and social aspirations of black people," and an essential aspect of this protest was the dramatization of black alienation in the West and a corresponding quest for a modern black cultural and spiritual identity.[5] Specific contacts between African Americans and Africans and Afro-Caribbeans in Paris were frequent. The Caribbean, in fact, formed the vehicle of many of the black cultural transactions, and the agents included Jean Price-Mars, whose *Ainsi parla l'Oncle* played a role in Haiti similar to Du Bois's sociological studies of African Americans; others were Léon Laleau, Jacques Stephen Alexis, Jean Brière, René Belance, and Jacques Roumain. These writers and artists constituted what was known as the Haitian Renaissance, which also may be considered an immediate antecedent to Négritude.[6]

But in Paris Négritude did not simply mimic the Haitian or American experience. It actively sought to recover new uses and evaluations of African cultures, through new anthropological works that were conducted by the likes of Leo Frobenius, Melville Herskovits, and Placide Tempels, the author of *La Philosophie bantoue*. The development of African anthropology from the perspective of cultural pluralism promoted by these anthropologists created new modes of thinking about Africa, leading to an emergence of a changed self-awareness among black intellectuals. According to Irele, "The notion of the inherent superiority of the white race was undermined by the growth of a 'relativist' attitude toward the study of culture, which showed non-Western cultures to be functional within their own settings. This attitude encouraged a new appraisal of African societies, values and arts, and a new understanding of African people."[7]

Frobenius's *History of African Civilization*, for example, translated into French as early as 1936, was widely read. Senghor, speaking of his education in Paris, noted that he read "everything . . . that appeared, from Proust to Virginia Woolf, from Rilke to Supervielle . . . all the books about Africa, starting from Frobenius's great work, and the poems of American Negroes."[8] Senghor also described the Paris of the time "the greatest museum of Negro-African art, nowhere else has Negro art been so well understood, commented on, exalted, assimilated." Paris, Senghor concluded, "by revealing to me the values of my ancestral civilization . . . forced me to adopt them and make them bear fruit. Not only me, but a whole generation of Negro students, West Indians as well as Africans."[9]

It did not go unnoticed that Picasso and Modigliani fraternized with the African students and poets, and frequented the Musée de l'Homme where "primitive" arts of Africa were often on display. The impact of African arts and culture in twentieth-century Europe's artistic consciousness produced transformations that were significant enough for some critics to refer to the period as the "Négritude period" of modern art. Césaire, for example, claims that "Negroes were made fashionable in France by Picasso, Vlaminck, Braque, etc."[10]

In light of these multiple sources of inspiration, it is no wonder that Négritude's philosophical self-understanding was variously presented even among the best of its proponents. Senghor wrote that Négritude is "the manner of self-expression of the black character, the black world, black civilization."[11] For Césaire, however, "Négritude is simply recognition of the fact of being black, and the acceptance of that fact . . . of our history and our culture."[12] What unites the competing visions of Négritude is the need to assert African humanity—a humanity whose denial was evident in the institutions of racism in Europe and the United States and in the colonialism in Africa.

To affirm blackness or Africa under these circumstances was indeed a refusal of an original negation, even if its intent was more than this protest element. On the one hand, Négritude was an emergence of embodied and institutionalized critique of colonial Reason; on the other hand, it was a philosophical affirmation of Africanity. Césaire's and Senghor's works best represent this dual aspects of Négritude, and so we shall devote the rest of this chapter to a closer analysis of their most important writings.

AIMÉ CÉSAIRE

Césaire's declaration that Négritude was "the acceptance of . . . our destiny of being black"[13] must have appeared scandalous—at a time when European discourse featured blacks as irrational, evil, and ugly. As Sandra Harding recently explained, "Africans were 'not European'; they were what Europeans rejected in their own lives."[14] But Césaire's Négritude reversed this system of value.

> We lived in an atmosphere of rejection, and we developed an inferiority complex. I have always thought that the black man was searching for his [modern] identity, and it has seemed to me that if what we want is to establish this identity, then we must have a concrete consciousness of what we are—that is, of the first facts of our lives: that we are black; that we were black and have a history.[15]

Affirming black consciousness involved coming to terms with black history (even as it has been constructed by whiteness), taking pride in it, and making it functional in the development of a distinctively black modernity. Césaire explained:

> We affirmed that we were Negroes and that we were proud of it, and that we thought that Africa was not some sort of black page in the history of humanity; in sum, we asserted that our Negro heritage was worthy of respect, and that this heritage was not relegated to the past, that its values were values that could still make important contributions to the world.[16]

But in affirming blackness and Africa, what does one do with the stereotypes that were intended to degrade, and the black misery? First, one must reverse them. In "Cahier," Césaire proclaims:

> Take me as I am!
> I accept. I accept . . . totally
> Without reserve.
> My race which no ablution of hyssop or mixed lilies
> could purify

My race eaten by macula
My race ripe grape for drunken feet
My queen of spittle and lepers
My queen of whips and scrofula
My queen of squarms and chloasms . . .
I accept, I accept. . . .
The flogged nigger who says: Forgive me, master,
And the twenty-nine legal blows of the whip,
And the spiked iron collar,
And the hamstrings cut for my runaway audacity,
And the fleur-de-lys streaming from the brand iron
On my shoulder.
Look, am I humble enough?
. . . .
Hooray to those who have invented neither powder nor
          the compass
Those who have tamed neither gas nor electricity
Those who have explored neither the seas nor the
          skies. . . .
My Négritude is not rock, its deafness hurled against
          the clamor of day;
My Négritude is not a thing of dead water or the dead
          eye of the earth;
My Négritude is neither a tower nor a cathedral;
It plunges into the red flesh of the earth,
It plunges into the red flesh of the sky,
It perforates opaque dejection with its upright patience.
Hooray to the royal *Kailcédrat*!
Hooray to those who have invented nothing,
To those who have explored nothing,
To those who have conquered nothing,
But abandoned themselves to the grip of the essence of
          all things.[17]

The rest of this poem increasingly asserted Africa against Europe, pro-claiming a "black" emergence:

> We are standing now, my country and I, hair in the wind, my
> little hand now in its enormous fists, and the strength is
> not in us but above us, in a
> voice that pierces the night, and the audience like the sting of an
> apocalyptic hornet. And the voice proclaims that Europe for
> centuries
> has stuffed us with lies and bloated us with pestilence,
> For it is not true that the work of man is finished,
> That there is nothing for us to do in the world,
> But the work of man has only just begun,
> And it is up to man to vanquish all deprivations immobilized in
> the corners of his fervor,
> And no race has the monopoly on beauty, intelligence, or
> strength.[18]

The audience for these declamations included African nationalists and avant-garde artists, especially those who were critical of what they saw as the sterile rationalism and mechanistic degradation of both humans and culture by Europe's version of modernity. In the neo-African cultures the critics of European modernity found inspiration and a new vitality, and Césaire's work found new strength in the opposition between "artificial" modernity and idealized images of a "natural" Africa. Unlike Europe, he claimed, Africa, was

> Ignorant of surfaces, caught by emotion of all things,
> Indifferent to conquering but playing the game of the world,
> Truly the eldest sons of the world,
> Porous to all the breathing of the world,
> Fraternal space for all the breathing of the world,
> Spark of the sacred fire of the world,
> Flesh of the world's flesh palpating with the very movement of
> the world. Tepid dawning of ancestral virtues.

> Blood! Blood! all our blood roused by the virile heart of the sun!
> Those who know the oily body of womanly moon,
> The healing exaltation of antelope and star,
> whose survival advances in the germination of the grass.
> Hail for the perfect circle of the world, enclosed concordance![19]

These qualities were precisely those in the names of which Europeans had despised Africa: nontechnological, insufficiently differentiated relationship to nature, animistic, and so forth. For Césaire, Europe, not Africa, is the truly naive and savage:

> Horribly weary from its enormous effort,
> Its rebellious joints crack beneath hard stars.
> Its rigid, blue steel penetrates the mystic flesh;
> Hear its traitorous victories trumpet its defeats;
> Hear the grandiose alibis for its sorry stumbling,
> Pity for our conquerors, omniscient and naïve![20]

In fact, Europe's naivete was matched only by its moral turpitude: "From the hold I hear the curses of the chained, the coughs of the dying, the sound of someone thrown into the sea . . . the howling of a woman in labor . . . the scrape of fingernails in search of throats . . . the snigger of the whip . . . the scampering of vermin in the eeriness."[21] If this is what modern reason is about, Césaire declared, then: "Reason, I sacrifice you to the evening breeze"; the black slave would rather affirm "the madness that remembers, the madness that roars, the madness that sees, the madness that breaks loose."[22]

In exposing the true nature of colonial Reason or the reason of capitalist slavery, the "madness" affirmed is, of course, ironic: it is the "madness" that breaks out as freedom. It is the "madness" that the artists of Surrealism also glorified. In 1941 André Breton wrote that Césaire's "Cahier" was "nothing less than the greatest lyric monument of our time"; he in fact considered Césaire a renovator of Surrealism.[23] Hubert Huin, however, thought that the same work "made surrealism ineffective, completed it by destroying it, enriched it by engulfing it."[24] While welcoming these critical receptions, Césaire maintained that Négritude was not an African version of Surrealism. "I was ready to accept surrealism," he said, "because I already had advanced on my own. In it I had found more of a confirmation than a revelation."[25] But it is Sartre who might have best captured the symbiosis and the distance that existed between Négritude and Surrealism. He noted that whereas "the purpose of Surrealism is to rediscover—beyond race and condition, beyond class, behind the fire of language—dazzling silent darknesses which are no longer opposed to anything, not even day, because day and night and all opposites are blended in them and suppressed," Césaire's work, "on the contrary, bursts and wheels around like a rocket; suns turning and exploding into new suns come out of it: it is a perpetual going-beyond. It is not a question of the poem's becoming part of the calm opposites, but rather making *one* of the opposites in the "black-white" couple expand like a phallus in its opposition to the other." Négritude, Sartre insisted, was "*against* Europe and colonization. What Césaire destroys is not *all* culture but rather *white* culture; what he brings to light is not desire for *everything* but rather the revolutionary aspirations of the oppressed Negro."[26] The "madness" championed by Césaire is therefore quite different from Surrealism's cult of unreason. As Renate Zahar remarked: "Irrationality expressed in the exaltation of the metaphysical values like the 'black Soul' and a mystical communion with nature should not blind us to its inherent rational elements which are a manifestation of the revolt against the fake rationality of capitalism."[27]

In *Discourse on Colonialism* Césaire's attacks on Europe's "hypocrisy" became more blunt. The argument that "the West invented science. That the West alone knows how to think; that at the borders of the Western world there begins the shadowy realm of primitive thinking . . . faulty thinking"—all these charges, he claimed, were merely excuses.[28] He accordingly condemns

> the psychologists, sociologists *et al.*, their views on "primitivism," their rigged investigations, their self-serving generalizations, their tendentious speculations, their insistence on the marginal, "separate" character of the non-whites. . . . Each of these gentlemen, in order to impugn on higher authority the weakness of primitive thought, claims that his own is based on the firmest rationalism.[29]

These philosophies and "sciences" of the African, Césaire believed, were produced "for the sake of the colonial cause."[30]

LÉOPOLD SÉDAR SENGHOR

> [N]égritude shows that pride and dignity have been recovered in the face of the European claim to "lay down the law." But it does more, and this explains its generosity. It wants to offer a truth which has been forgotten by modern societies, mechanized and encumbered with artifice as they are.
>
> —Georges Balandier, *Ambiguous Africa*

More so than Césaire, Senghor is the "metaphysician" of Négritude. While Césaire's concerns were largely framed in political terms (what he called "concrete consciousness"), Senghor promoted Négritude as a form of racial metaphysics—a metaphysics of blackness. If, epistemologically speaking, Césaire is the black Hume, Senghor is Africa's Kant. Senghor wanted to establish the racial elements that he considered to be the "common denominator of all Negro Africans."[31] In poems, essays, and political tracts, he propounded theories in which the "African personality," essential and universal, received theoretical elaborations.

Some have argued that the key to understanding Senghor's theory of blackness lies in his personal experience—the experience of being "blackened" in France. Senghor's best biographer, Janet Vaillant, thinks that he early drew "the conclusion that there must be an objective cause for [his experience of racism], some important reason why he had tried, as he put it, to suppress his ancestor, why Du Bois had felt an ever-present sense of twoness, why Césaire also felt uneasy and confused about his true self." Vaillant therefore thinks that Négritude was for Senghor a way to "understand these forces and put his ancestor in a new light. He had to find a way to heal his inner division, to be whole."[32]

When Senghor arrived at the conclusion that "whatever blackness entailed, it was not just a matter for Africans alone but for black men throughout the world,"[33] he felt obliged to educate both Africans and Europeans about Africa and the role of Negro cultures in world civilization. He did this by producing theories about the uniqueness of a glorious African "soul," in contrast to a parallel but less noble white soul. In the poem "To New York," for example, the city is described as consisting of two racial and opposed parts, one white (Manhattan) and the other black (Harlem). Of white New York:

> At first I was bewildered by your beauty,
> Those huge, long-legged, golden girls.
> So shy, at first, before your blue metallic eyes and icy smile . . .
> And full of despair at the end of the skyscraper streets . . .
> Your light is sulfurous against the pale towers
> whose heads strike lightning into the sky,
> Skyscrapers defying storms with their steel shoulders
> And weathered skin of stone. . . .
> No laugh from a growing child, his hand in my cool hand.
> No mother's breast, but nylon legs . . .
> No tender word, and no lips,
> Only artificial hearts paid for in cold cash.[34]

Harlem, by contrast, is presented as full of "soul," warmth, and the spirituality of black love:

> I saw the festival of Night begin at the retreat of day.
> And I proclaim Night more truthful than day.
> It is the pure hour when God brings forth
> Life immemorial in the streets,
> All the amphibious elements shining like suns.
> Harlem, Harlem! Now I've seen Harlem, Harlem!
> A green breeze of corn rising from the pavements
> Plowed by Dan dancers' bare feet,
> Hips rippling like silk and spearhead breasts,
> Ballets of water lilies and fabulous masks
> And mangoes and love rolling from the low houses.[35]

The contrasts between the races could not be more extremely stated: the dry, icy, and joyless Manhattan in competition with the gaiety, laughter, and tenderness of Harlem's Dan. Or "life" of God itself pouring forth into Harlem streets in contrast to the artificial hearts paid for in cold cash in

Manhattan. Senghor however believed that a marriage of the two cities was possible: "Listen . . . let black blood flow into your steel joints," he admonished Manhattan; let the "oil of life flow," and "give your bridges the curve of hips and supple vines."[36]

This, then, is an outline of Senghor's philosophy of Négritude: blacks and whites are racial opposites, although a "universal" synthesis may be possible—if the whites do not, in their emotional coldness and moral indifference, first annihilate everyone. Janice Spleth, in her biography of Senghor, writes that "an outstanding characteristic of Senghor's poetry is its coherent and unifying substructure. . . . Every poem, either in its theme or form, illustrates some aspect of the poet's concept of Négritude."[37] Senghor's poetic vision of black and white, of Africa and Europe, as opposites (though potentially reconcilable), and his constant efforts to explain in what the racial differences consist, are very explicit in his critical works.

In "African-Negro Aesthetics"[38] and "On Negrohood: Psychology of the African Negro,"[39] the major elements in Senghor's racial theories are in full display. Other works with similar contents include *Les Fondements de l'Africanité ou Négritude et Arabité*, *Négritude et civilisation de l'universel*, *On African Socialism*, and *Négritude et humanisme*. "African-Negro Aesthetics," despite its title, may be considered a classic treatise on epistemology and metaphysics. It sketches out the "physiopsychology" of the Negro-African— a term the author curiously uses to describe the physical and psychological structures of perception he claims are peculiar to the Negro. Senghor believes, for example, that there are unique ways of perception that ultimately account for racial differences. Assuming that culture is a result of interactions of humans with nature, Senghor claims that the tropical sun is responsible for conditioning the Negro's structure of feeling and perception. Borrowing from the racial theories of Joseph Arthur Comte de Gobineau, Senghor thinks that the sun infuses the black body with a high voltage of emotional energy, so that "Emotion is Negro as Reason is Greek." The emotivism of the Negro predisposes the Negro to a level of capacity for sympathy, which in turn accounts for the Negro's deeper facility in establishing and maintaining social bonds. The Negro's higher capacity to "participate" in communal life therefore constitutes the essence of Negro intelligence and reason.

The Negro's "participant reason" conditions the Negro's attitude not just toward other humans but also toward nature. In his or her relationship to the natural world, Senghor claims, the Negro does not seek mastery over, but symbiosis with nature. Whereas the white mind is detached, analytical, and nonparticipatory—sundering the self from the Other, subject from object, the observer from the observed—the African mind, by contrast, "is synthetic." This is a non-antagonistic, sympathetic reason. It is, claimed Senghor, "another path to knowledge" because whereas "white reason is analytical through use, Negro reason is intuitive through participation."[40]

In *Les Fondements de l'Africanité ou Négritude et Arabité*, Senghor already knows that critics—mainly African critics—have condemned his theory of the Negro mind, but he reaffirms his position. He insists:

> Voici donc le fluctuant, arabo-berbère or négro-africain, soutendu par l'emotivité, relié sur soi, sentant d'abord soi-même et ne sentant les autre qu'à travers soi. . . . Ce n'est pas que l'object ne soit pas senti; il l'est même rapidement et violemment. Mais, précisément, parce qu'il en est ainsi, l'image qui naît de cette *réaction* participe beaucoup plus du sujet que de l'object. En d'autres termes, l'object est beaucoup plus senti que pensé: beaucoup plus imaginé que défini, plus assimilé qu'analysé.[41]

Though he maintains that European philosophers and anthropologists who say that the African is irrational or "devoid of reason" are mistaken, Senghor reproaches them only for failing to see that the Negro's intuitive or emotive reason is a *different form* of reason, not an inferior one—let alone an absence. In fact, Senghor suggests in several places that white reason is a "superficial" and inferior form of reason; only the black relational reason attains participatory union with the truth of the real. He supported this claim of the superiority of black reason in part by appealing to the judgments of surrealists, existentialists, and even physicists. For example, in quoting Sartre that emotion is "the descent of consciousness into the magic world,"[42] Senghor redefined "magic" to mean "spirituality"—as in African animistic spirituality. He also appealed to Albert Einstein, who remarked that "the mystical emotion" is the true source of all great knowledge and art.[43] Senghor contended that statements such as these supported his claim that African and black (participatory, magical, animist, and mystical) epistemology is superior to white mechanistic reason.

It is therefore ultimately in the distinction between spirituality and mechanics, soul and machine, and love and cash, or gift and exchange that Senghor rested his theory of black and white racial difference. To justify his thinking that blacks are evolutionarily more rational and more morally mature than whites, Senghor explained:

> European Whites themselves—artists, philosophers, even scientists—[are] going to the school of participant reason. We are witnessing a true revolution in European epistemology, which has been taking place since the turn of the century. . . . The new method, and hence the new theory of knowledge arose out of the latest scientific discoveries: relativity, wave mechanics, quantum mechanics, non-Euclidean geometries. And also out of new philosophical theories: phenomenology, existentialism . . . it was a response to the need to outgrow the scientific positivism of the nineteenth century. . . . Nowadays, whether we look at science, philosophy or art, we find discontinuity and indeterminism at the bottom of everything, of the mind as well as the real.[44]

Naturally, these revolutions in white European science and philosophy were interpreted by Senghor to mean that Europe finally was catching up with Africa—perhaps a beginning of the possibility that the universal racial and cultural synthesis hoped for might be around the corner.

Against nineteenth-century objectivism, Senghor noted: now "we find the researcher implicated in his own research," and "the light of knowledge is no longer that unchanging clarity which would light on the object without touching it and being touched by it";[45] once again life and thought are no longer walled off one from another. But it is the black race that stands to gain—by regaining its superiority and saving humankind as a whole from what could only have been impending moral disaster: "Je n'aurai que l'apparence," Senghor accepted, "de développer un paradoxe en essayant de montrer que la Négritude, par son ontologie, sa morale et son esthétique, répond à l'humanisme contemporain, tel que l'ont préparé les philosophes et savants européens depuis la fin du XIXe siècle."[46]

Senghor's African participant reason in short goes beyond concepts and categories "to plunge into primordial chaos," in order to impose wisdom and reality on experience "not yet shaped by discursive reason." This type of black thought allows knowledge to "coincide [. . .] with the *essence* of a thing in its innate and original reality."[47] In fact, this type of knowledge is thoroughly authentic and generates "no artificial product of discursive reason made to cover up reality; it discovers truth through the power of mystical emotion." It is the type of essential knowledge that "re-discovers" and rerepresents beings in their ontological authenticity; "knowledge coincides here with the *being* of the object in its originating and original reality, in its discontinuity and indeterminacy: in its life."[48]

Senghor ultimately presents his essentialist epistemology of the emotion in apparent antagonism to Descartes. In lieu of "I think, therefore I am," Senghor says "I dance the Other, therefore I am."[49] And dance, Senghor insisted, ought to be understood literally, although he only *likened* the Negro to "one of those Third Day Worms, a pure field of sensation. Subjectively, at the tips of his sensory organs, his insect antennas, he discovered the Other. Immediately he is moved, going centrifugally from the subject to object on the waves of the Other."[50] The Negro, it seems, "feels" objects and acquires knowledge by means of feeling alone; reality, too, has an "essence" hidden from its appearance—an essence to which the Negro has some direct, dynamic access.

The black, in Senghor's account, by virtue of a physiologically conditioned Afro-tropical sensibility, is therefore "naturally" predisposed to attain deeper insights into reality and so has little need for "cold," "superficial" logic that touches only the appearance of reality. What is paramount in this black mode of knowing should not be confused with Kant's type of transcendental idealism, for example. Senghor claims that faced with something to be known—God, human being, animal, tree, natural or social event—"the Negro African does not draw a line between himself and the object; he does not hold it at a distance, nor does he merely look at it and analyze it."[51] He or she "plunges" into them, and experiences—in the blind embrace, as it were—mystical and revealed truths. The Cartesian ego has simply taken leave.[52] Senghor admonishes that African "reason is not the *visualizing* reason of the European White, but a kind of *embracing* reason which has more in common with *logos* than with *ratio*. For *ratio* is compass, T-square and sextant; it is measure and weight. *Logos* on the other hand was the living word."[53] The "living word" had earlier been characterized as life, love, play, dance, and lyrical poetry. Négritude, for Senghor, was a movement to promote this "Negro-African method of knowledge and comprehension,"[54] an agenda that many Afrocentrists are today advancing with equal vigor.[55]

In the second essay, "On Negrohood: Psychology of the African Negro," Senghor extended his doctrine about the African's mind to the analysis of organization of work and society in Africa. Like Buffon, he emphasizes the importance of the environment: the "black soul" was forged under the influence of Africa's tropical climate, and in an agricultural and pastoral world. Black culture is therefore a consequence of the African's adaptation to the geographical environment as a farmer, who lives "off the land and with the land."[56] Because of this agrarian background, the African is extremely sensitive to nature; and, much more than in a temperate climate, nature generously responds to the needs of humans and to the labor of the farmer.

By living close to nature and being most sensitive to it, the African perceives and understands the world differently from those who live in highly technologized societies of modern Europe. Senghor created what he himself acknowledged is a simplified dichotomy between the "black farmer" and the "white technician," between the feeling-reason of the farmer and the eye-reason of the engineer. Yet, he continued to refer to this contrast as that between racial black and racial white. In "On Negrohood," Senghor analyzed white and black societies in order to show their innate racial differences.

Whereas the European white takes an essentially pragmatic attitude toward nature and the world and uses (Senghor's choice of word, interestingly, was—as the French did the Senegalese—"assimilates") them for his own end, the African, being more sensitive to the world, seeks actively to be assimilated by nature. This fundamental differences in white and black attitudes determines the difference between black and white (a) ontology, (b) organization of society and labor, and (c) ethics and aesthetics.

Ontologically, it is the idea of *harmony* that drives the African view of life, an idea that expresses itself as a relationship of "participation" between male and female, humans and nature, and, eventually, the black and white races. Senghor designates this primordial harmony "love," and explains his meaning in quite original ways. Drawing from Pierre Teilhard de Chardin's theodicy,[57] Tempels's Bantu philosophy, and Ogotomeli's Dogon cosmology as reported by Marcel Griaule,[58] Senghor explains:

> The importance of love as an essential energy, the stuff of life, is at the heart of *Négritude*, underlying the black man's ontology. Everywhere the couple—male-female—translates the integrity of the being. To be sure, procreation as the means of perpetuating the family and species occupies an important place in Negro-African society. But let us not be deceived: Beyond the embrace of the bodies is the complementary union of souls. . . . In Negro-African mythology, the combination *Word-and-Music* stands at the origin of creation. By uttering this formula, God created all beings, for it is at the same time feeling, thought, and action. This creative energy is love.[59]

This pan-lovism assumes the existence of a single life force that manifests itself in a wide variety of ways. All objects are considered to possess a spiritual force—a force of unity of all things, or love. This force confers unity on all matter, and always seeks to enhance the vitality of even the littlest unit of matter. Without this energy and its augmentation, nothing can exist and no moral progress can be made. In fact, Senghor believed that it is only the African's force of love that will eventually save the world: "Because the Negro Africans have kept a sense of brotherhood and dialogue, because they are inspired by religions that preach love and, above all, because they live those religions, they can propose positive solutions for the construction of the international as the national community."

But everything visible and invisible in the world, from a grain of sand to animals to humans, and ancestors, and, finally, God itself subsists as love:

> The Bantu speak of God himself as "the Strong One," he who possesses Force in himself. He is also the source of the Force of every creature. God is the "Dijina dikatampe": the great name, because he is the great Force, the "mukomo," as our Baluba have it. . . . In the minds of the Bantu, all beings in the universe possess vital force of their own: human, animal, vegetable, or inanimate. Each being has been endowed by God with a certain force, capable of strengthening the vital energy of the strongest being of all creation: man.[60]

The vital energy of the blacks will pull all things into what I must now call a Moral Whole, but since this Whole can only be experienced through the various forms of its dependent plurality, humans must feel morally responsible for all of nature, and Africans are showing the way along this path of cosmic responsibility. With their ontological knowledge, Senghor's Negro-Africans are careful to harm nothing and no one—in order to preserve the ontological equilibrium of the Whole. Every individual has a duty to preserve and strengthen the life force of the other, and maintain in balance the life chain upon which all depends, for one's own good and for the good of others. This is why the African's most profound prayer is to live in harmony with differences, including racial differences.

Senghor's idea of white European ontology, predictably, is the opposite of the black African. Because the whites rely upon analytical reason, their cultures use reason to separate humans from each other and, collectively, humans from nature, so that the whites are incapable of experiencing the Whole. White Europeans analyze an object by breaking it into constituent parts, isolating the parts one from the other, and mastering and conquering the Whole. Thus, to understand something, the white European kills it, and in the process deforms himself or herself by separating instead of mystically uniting the knower and the known. This "divisive" white epistemology and ontology renders nature meaningful only to the extent that nature is useful to human designs; this is a fact of white attitude that Senghor believes predates modernity. "For two thousand years, the Middle Ages excepted," he wrote, "the Western European has mutilated Man, opposing reason to imagination, discursive to intuitive knowledge, science to art."[61] The African, on the other hand, has always known that to try to master nature is arrogant and foolish—and dangerous. Senghor reported an interesting observation by one of the elders in his village, who was, unsurprisingly, terrified about the arrival of the whites: "They do not realize, those Whites, that life is not to be domesticated, and especially not God who is the source of all life and in whom all life resides. It is life that humanizes, not death. I am afraid all will turn out badly. The Whites in their destructive madness will end up bringing us misfortune."[62]

Senghor thinks that African metaphysics and epistemology automatically make one an animist, who feels linked to all beings, animate and inanimate. The animist takes care to adapt to nature so that all life—present, past, and future—is reverentially treated, and this is the key to understanding the social organization of African societies. Senghor writes that the African places the highest social value on family and family ties, and he contrasts the nuclear family in Europe with the extended family in Africa. The African family includes both the living, the dead, and unborn; the dead and the unborn are literally incorporated into the family as totemic elements, which can be living animals, carved woods, or even a plant. A clan may consider an animal or a tree as one of its members, and thereby admits and respects the reality that humans are related and connected to other forms of life. And since a family's vital force depends on the number and prosperity of family members, the totemic dead and children born and unborn occupy a place of special importance in the survival and maintenance of existence for the family.

Senghor also made the controversial claim that in most African cultures, the oldest male in the family is, by reason of age and gender, the most respected and, barring incompetence, also the leader. Age is important because, in addition to the recognition of experience, wisdom, and mastery of the tradition, the oldest is also considered the most effective mediator between the living and the dead, the most vital constituents of the community. The head may also serve as the family or village priest, and, as Senghor explains it, this sort of family or clan regime is not at all a despotism because the individual does not act on matters of importance without proper consultation with a council of elders. Such a council is automatically composed of representatives from all strata of the clan: delegates from the women's caucus, the age groups, trade unions, and so forth. The aim of council deliberations is always the achievement of consensus, even if debates—or "palaver"—should last for several days. In this way, every adult participates in the political decision-making processes, either directly by self-representation or indirectly through the delegates from the social unit, or units, to which the individual belongs. Membership in these social units also serves definite moral functions: they integrate individuals into society, and enable one to build a sense of identity and belonging. Senghor, as usual, contrasted this ideal of African society with what he experienced as the harsh individualism of modern white European societies.

When he turned to consider the principles of organization of labor in Africa, Senghor found affinities between African labor practices and the socialist forms advocated by Karl Marx. Because the typical African society posits social harmony as a goal, labor relations are marked by cooperation rather than competition. For example, Senghor thinks that in most traditional African societies, private ownership of land is prohibited. Instead, there are systems of communal land tenure whereby the right to use of land is acquired only by families and towns. The head of the family or the chief is therefore responsible for parceling out the land to individual farmers for use at each planting season. In this way it is labor, not capital, that conveys rights of ownership; labor has priority over capital.

In terms that echo Marx, Senghor argues that work in traditional African society is not alienated, for in and through work it is the accord of "man and the universe" that is realized, so that work liberates rather than enslaves.[63] What the African worker knows, according to Senghor, is that achievement of personality lies less in the quest for singularity and more in the development of one's potential through participation in a community. By contrast the white European worker, because of his or her dependence on the capitalist, must approach not only nature but also fellow humans manipulatively, with intent to exploit for private advantage. This, as Senghor saw it, is a predatory relationship with nature and other humans, and can be attributed to the white lack of participant reason.

In *On African Socialism*, in discussing the meaning of work in modern European culture, an analysis drawn even more directly from Marx, Senghor argued:

> No longer is it the creative labor of the worker realizing his aim freely, in body and consciousness, by "fulfilling himself." Now it is work on the assembly line, imposed from the outside by the employer. [There is] alienation as well in product. With the division of labor and the relative abundance of products, the latter are no longer the "fruits of labor," possessed in common by the community. They have become *merchandise*, possessed individually by the employer and put up for sale. An *exchange-value* has been substituted for their *use-value*; and we have passed from a community economy to a mercantile, capitalist economy. . . . As labor and the products of labor escape the worker and turn against him to dominate him, he loses his spirit. His only preoccupation now becomes the satisfaction of his material, biological, animal needs. He mistakes this satisfaction for life, for end, whereas it is only the means.[64]

Modern capitalism indeed appeared to be very far removed from the Negro African's sensibility, as Senghor portrayed it. This explains, at least in part, Senghor's search, as president of Senegal in the 1960s, for an *African* version of socialism, based on African reason and African understanding of labor.

Unlike the African, the white reason knows only how to objectify and to subdue, to "master" and conquer; by "focusing its energy completely on this task" of domination, the typical European economy has "achieved remarkable technological advance and improved the material well-being of [its] peoples" but, Senghor believes, "at a great cost":

> The European conception of what is real and important has directed Europe's energy away from seeking to understand the ultimate reality that binds the world together. Instead of trying to understand and live in harmony with nature, the white European has ruthlessly bent nature to serve his immediate needs.[65]

Because an attitude of subdue-and-master informs white social relations, the white, instead of seeking balance and harmony in community, believes that "man is to man a wolf"; rather than cooperation in community, the white selfishly seeks to survive in a competition of all against all; instead of anticipating society as an arena of belonging, whites seek to defend themselves against it by carving out exclusive and private spaces. In short, the white person

> has sought to escape human community rather than to create it, because he sees community participation as a possible limit on his individual freedom, rather than as a necessity for personal fulfillment. For the European, freedom is the right to be left alone. One therefore sets up barriers to defend oneself from the claims of others.[66]

This is only negative "freedom"—but Senghor thinks that this is all the white European is capable of, and that the white lack of a positive idea of freedom produces loneliness and isolation. And because social isolation impoverishes the individual by preventing key personal growths that are possible only through relationships of trust, Senghor concludes that the capitalist white European culture stifles not only emotional but also spiritual and moral maturity.

Finally, Senghor contrasts the communitarian ethic of the Negro with white modern relations that are based on contract. He writes that, by nature, whites can create community only through formal codes of law—and by force. Because white reasoning about right and wrong can only be formal and legalistic, ethics is inevitably reduced to a don't-get-caught mentality. This, of course, is just the opposite of the rich ethical life of the African presented by Senghor: work, honor, piety, and generosity toward others. Compared to African mores, white ethical codes are merely abstract ideas that one may learn by rote but is unlikely to live by.[67]

Logically, black art mirrors black sensibility, as white art mirrors white sensibility. What is considered "beautiful" in Europe, for example, is the singular or the unique, not the profound. This allows shallowness to pass as improvement in style. By contrast, African art always reveals a profound process of realization of self, a gift to the community. Since the Negro believes that what is most profoundly human about oneself is that which one shares with others, Negro art becomes another vehicle for articulating the common effort to realize communal human potentials. Because the principal purpose of art is creation and achievement of social harmony and moral consensus, what is stylistically "beautiful" for the Negro must necessarily exhibit rhythm and relational imagery, in other words, life and community.[68]

CRITIQUE OF NÉGRITUDE

Senghor believed that Négritude was an effort to "assimilate, not be assimilated" by Europe. "Like Arab socialists," he wrote, "we shall integrate the contributions of European socialism with our nationalism, with the values of *Négritude*, defined as the common denominator of all Negro Africans."[69] Critical literature assessing both Senghor's theory and practice of Négritude abounds, and ranges from the hagiographic to the dismissive.[70] More recently, however, a few new themes have been developed, and they are these new themes that I shall examine here.

First, it has been suggested that Négritude's critique of modern European reason is "postmodern," albeit *avant la lèttre*. It is proposed that, much like the "existentialist" Kierkegaard or Nietzsche, Césaire and Senghor noticed, both conceptually and concretely in the history of blacks in the modern world, the cost to Africa of Europe's modernity and its philosophic, scientific, and economic projects—the capitalism-animated projects of Reason and Progress.[71] By rebelling against this Reason and its idea of Progress, Senghor's theories and cultural politics are said to constitute a powerful if romantic anticolonial resistance. This, for example, was Tsenay Serequeberhan's position in *The Hermeneutics of African Philosophy*.[72]

One should ask, however, whether Négritude must be tied to postmodernism in order to appreciate its anticolonial force. Senghor's Négritude, clearly, has more in common with Rousseau and German romanticism, including Göethe and the *Sturm und Drang* movement, for example, than with Derrida, Feyerband, or Deleuze. To the extent that antiblack racism and colonialism could be identified as historically connected to a capitalist European modernity, the critique of this modernity is most evident in Césaire, not Senghor.

Césaire's "Cahier" and the *Discourse on Colonialism* consistently maintained that racism and colonialism were animated by forms of irrationality and "madness." When Senghor proposes the superiority of African or black "participant reason," for example, is he merely trying to supplant what he considered irrationality and madness by "feeling" and "sympathy"—in effect, new forms of reasoning and reasonableness that, apparently, dominant and conquering modern reason had sought to banish? In "Qu'est-ce que la Négritude," Senghor argued that "Au demeurant, cette lutte culturelle se doublait, d'une lutte politique: la Négritude était également arme de combat pour la *décolonisation*"[73]; and when he was accused of advocating inverted racism in the assertion of black superiority, he retorted: "Négritude . . . is not racism, but culture; it is *a situation understood and overcome* in order to integrate and harmonize with the cosmos. As symbiosis of determining factors—geographical and ethical—Négritude becomes rooted in the factors by taking on an original color, but historically it does so to transcend them."[74] This passage can be interpreted in many ways, but to the extent that Négritude was understood by Senghor as aimed at "deconstructing" colonial Reason, it is anticolonial but not necessarily antireason.

If modern philosophical Reason was implicated in historical projects that devalued black existence, Négritude's assertion of African freedom and a "higher reason" is hardly to be considered a romantic cult of the irrational (or the unconscious, as the Surrealists wrongly believed), or a promotion of the mystical (as advocates of African animist spirituality would pretend). When Négritude is understood as Senghor wished—as "symbiosis of geographical and ethical factors . . . rooted in an original color . . . but historically transcending that color"—then not even Hountondji's notorious attack and veiled mockery, in *African Philosophy: Myth and Reality*, takes away from Négritude's recognized historical significance. Those who today easily recruit Hountondji's "professional" philosophy to attack Négritude must recall Hountondji's observation that "there was . . . a time . . . when what we badly needed, in the face of colonial power and its positive attempts to depersonalize us, was the restoration of self-confidence and the reaffirmation of our creativity. In those circumstances ethnophilosophy [including Senghor's racial metaphysics and epistemology of blackness] could appear . . . as a form of discourse that could be profitably taken over and developed by colonial peoples for their liberation."[75] In light of everything we know of the image of the black in modern Western thought, it seems to me that Négritude discharged this historical duty with a measurable success.

But Négritude also displays unfathomable weaknesses. Beyond the ethical protests encoded in the emotional exhibition of Africa's and black suffering, how does one justify Négritude's claims to exclusivist cultural and racial standards or reason? There are three possible paths to examining this claim: one could assert—dogmatically—that a "feeling-based" way of knowing and being in the world is the best of all possible epistemological and existential attitudes. Senghor did not seem to hesitate to express this point of view; in fact, he believed that the best civilizations were built by this African form of reason—civilizations that were destroyed by modern white barbarism: "We proclaimed ourselves, with the poet Aimé Césaire, the 'Elder Children of the Earth.' Did we not dominate the world up to Neolithic times, fertilize the civilizations of the Nile and Euphrates before they later became the innocent victims of white barbarians"?

Négritude could also, however, be seen as advocating a relativistic claim that there are a plurality of epistemologies and moral practices, and that the emotive or "sympathetic" variety is just as valid as any other. In a recent study of the literature of Négritude, Donald R. Wehrs thinks that Négritude "presents Western colonialism as the means by which an hegemonic, monological culture of imperialism displaces traditional cultures characterized by religions and rituals that recognize through polytheism a plurality of truths."[76] The argument, then, is that whereas African reason asserted a relativistic or pluralistic conception of truth and reality, the modern white reason was universalistic, monological, and imperialistic. Notable African writers, including Chinua Achebe, actually believe that these are cultural facts and have written extensively about it.[77]

Finally, Négritude could be said to have thought of itself as neither dogmatic nor relativistic, but simply as asserting black reason as one among multiple forms of reason, and as engaging in a conversation that is at least implicitly universal. In a passage quite revealing in this regard, Senghor gave a report of a conference in Rome between the European Society of Culture and the African Society of Culture, where "civilization was the crucial point of the debate." He remarked that at the meeting,

> Europeans claimed to be the only ones who had envisaged culture in its universal dimensions. From there it was only a step, which had already been taken years earlier, to maintain that European civilization was identified with the Civilization of the Universal and thus should be adopted as *the* Universal Civilization. We had little difficulty in demonstrating that each "exotic civilization" had also thought in terms of universality, that Europe's only merit in this regard had been to diffuse *her* civilization throughout the world, thanks to her conquest and techniques.[78]

Each culture, each civilization, then, might in fact think of itself as universal, despite Western culture's actual or imagined global reach—by force. But this is not a conception of cultures that rules out the possibility of a genuinely universal culture, or *Civilization de l'universel*; in fact, it seems to invite it.

But the dominant tendency in Senghor's theory of Négritude remained stuck in a position between the second and third theoretical sketches just presented. Like Césaire, Senghor recognized that Négritude is, historically, a *j'accepte* addressed to a particular situation of the black, a situation of exclusion and oppression. But it is an acceptance offered in an effort to negate and transcend this situation (hence, "a situation understood and overcome"). The problem might be that it is not clear how, having rooted Négritude in African geography and a "black" ethics, as Senghor preferred, one could still successfully affirm *and* transcend not only Africa but also the "blackness" of this ethics. Another way of rephrasing the problem: Where lies what Georges Balandier called Négritude's "generosity"?

NOTES

1. For more on the history of this journal, see O. R. Dathorne, *African Literature in the Twentieth Century*, Minneapolis: University of Minnesota Press, 1975, beginning from p. 220.

2. Aimé Césaire, "Interview with René Depestre," in *Discourse on Colonialism (Discourse)*, New York: Monthly Review Press, 1972, pp. 73–74; see also Janet G. Vaillant, *Black, French, and African: A Life of Léopold Sédar Senghor (BFA)*, Cambridge, MA: Harvard University Press, 1990, p. 244.

3. Ibid.

4. Alioune Diop, *Présence Africaine* 1 (November–December 1947): 1.

5. Abiola Irele, ed., *Selected Poems of Léopold Sédar Senghor*, Cambridge: Cambridge University Press, 1977, p. 6.

6. Ibid., pp. 6–7.

7. Ibid., p. 8.

8. Ibid.

9. Quoted by Mercer Cook his introduction to Léopold Sédar Senghor's *On African Socialism*, pp. xii–xiii.

10. Césaire, "Interview with Réne Depestre," in Césaire, *Discourse on Colonialism*, trans. Joan Pinkham, New York: Monthly Review Press, 1972, p. 74.

11. Léopold Sédar Senghor, "Problematique de la Négritude," *Liberté 3: Négritude et civilisation de l'universel*, Paris: Seuil, 1977, pp. 269–270.

12. Aimé Césaire, quoted in Senghor, "Problematique de la Négritude," ibid., p. 270.

13. Ibid.

14. "The Curious Coincidence between African and Feminist Moralities," in Eze, ed., *African Philosophy: An Anthology*, Masden, MA: Blackwell, 1998, p. 308.

15. Césaire, *Discourse*, p. 76.

16. Aimé Césaire, "Notes of the Return of the Native Son," in *The Négritude Poets: an Anthology of Translations from the French*, ed. and trans. Ellen Kennedy, New York: Thunder Mouth Press, 1998; pp. 75-76.

17. Ibid.

18. Ibid., pp. 79–81.

19. Ibid.

20. Ibid.

21. Ibid.

22. Ibid., pp. 49.

23. Quoted in Ellen Conroy Kennedy, ed., *The Négritude Poets: An Anthology of Translations from the French*, New York: Thunder Mouth Press, 1998, p. 64.

24. Further discussion of the symbiotic relationship that existed between Négritude and Surrealism may be found in Jahn Jahneiz, *Muntu*, New York: Grove Press, 1961; and Michael Fabre, *From Harlem to Paris: Black American Writers in France, 1840–1980*, Chicago: University of Illinois Press, 1991.

25. Césaire, *Discourse*, p. 67.

26. Sartre, Jean-Paul, "Black Orpheus," *What Is Literature and Other Essays*, Cambridge, MA: Harvard University Press, 1998, p. 311.

27. Renate Zahar, *Frantz Fanon: Colonialism and Alienation*, New York: Monthly Review Press, 1974, pp. 61–62.

28. Césaire, *Discourse*, p. 51.

29. Ibid., p. 35.
30. Ibid.
31. Léopold Sédar Senghor, *Liberté 1: Negritude et humanisme*, Paris: Seuil, 1964, p. 9.
32. Vaillant, *Black, French, and African*, p. 245.
33. Ibid.
34. Léopold Sédar Senghor, *The Collected Poetry*, trans. Melvin Dixon, Charlottesville: University Press of Virginia, 1991, pp. 369–371; see also pp. 87–89. (I introduced minor changes in the translation to match more closely, more literally, the original.)

> New York! D'abord j'ai été confondu par ta beauté, ces grandes filles d'or
> > aux jambes longues.
> Si timide d'abord devant tes yeux de métal bleu, ton sourire de givre
> Si timide. Et l'angoisse au fond des rues à gratte-ciel
> Levant des yeux de chouette parmi l'éclipse du soleil.
> Sulfureuse ta lumière et les fût livides, dont les têtes foudroient le ciel
> Les gratte-ciel qui défient les cyclones sur leurs muscles d'acier et leur
> > peau patinée de pierres . . .
> Pas un rire d'enfant en fleur, sa main dans man main fraîche
> Pas un sein maternel, des jambes de nylon . . .
> Pas un mot tendre en l'absence de lèvres, rien que des coeurs artificiels
> > payés en monnaie forte.

35. Ibid.

> J'ai vu dans Harlem bourdonnant de bruits de couleurs . . .
> C'est l'heure du thé chez le livreur-en-produits-pharmaceutiques
> J'ai vu se préparer la fête de la Nuit à la fuite du joir. Je proclame la Nuit
> > plus véridique que le jour.
> C'est l'heure pure où dans les rues, Dieu fait germer la vie d'avant mémoire
> Tous les éléments amphibies rayonnants comme des soleils.
> Harlem, Harlem! voici ce que j'ai vu Harlem, Harlem! Une brise verte
> > de blés sourdre des pavés labourés par les pieds nous de dansers
> > Dans
> Croupe ondes de soie et seins de fers de lance, ballets de nénuphares et
> > de masques fabuleux
> Aux pieds des chevaux de police, les mangues de l'amour rouler des
> > maisons basses.

36. Ibid.

> Qu'il donne à tes ponts la courbe des croupes et la souplesse des lianes.
> Voici revoir les temps très anciens . . .
> Mais il suffit d'ouvrir les yeux à l'arc-en-ciel d'Avril
> Et les oreilles . . . à Dieu qui d'un rire de saxophone créa le ciel et la
> terre en six jours. Et le septième jour, il dormait du grand sommeil
> nègre.

37. Janice Spleth, *Léopold Sédar Senghor (LSS)*, Boston: Twayne Publishers, 1985, p. 20.
38. Léopold Sédar Senghor, "African-Negro Aesthetics," *Diogene* 16 (Winter 1956): 23–38.
39. Léopold Sédar Senghor, "On Negrohood: Psychology of the African-Negro," *Diogene* 37, (Spring 1962): 1–15.
40. Senghor, "African-Negro Aesthetics," *Diogene* 16, (Winter 1956): 24.

41. Léopold Sédar Senghor, *Les Fondements de l'Africanité ou Négritude et Arabité*, in *Liberté, Vol. 3: Négritude et civilisation de l'universel*," 105–150; italics in original.

42. Jean-Paul Sartre, preface to *Anthologie*, ed. Senghor, p. 41.

43. Einstein did write, "The most beautiful thing we can experience is the mystical [mysterious?]. It is the source of all true art and science. He to whom this emotion is a stranger . . . is as good as dead." See Einstein's: "Strange Is Our Situation Here upon Earth," in *Modern Religious Thought*, ed. J. Pelikan, Boston: Little, Brown, 1990, p. 204.

44. Senghor, "African-Negro Aesthetics," p. 8. See also Senghor, "Négritude: A Humanism of the Twentieth Century," in *Post-colonial Discourse and Postcolonial Theory: A Reader*, ed. Patrick Williams and Laura Chrisman, New York: Columbia University Press, 1994.

45. Ibid.

46. Senghor, *Liberté 3: Négritude et civilisation de l'universel*, pp. 69–79; 72.

47. Léopold Sédar Senghor, "African Road to Socialism," in *On African Socialism*, trans. Mercer Cook, New York: Praeger, 1964, p. 71.

48. Ibid.

49. Ibid.

50. Ibid., p. 72.

51. Ibid.

52. For a contemporary and quite systematic defense of Senghorian psychology and epistemology—without the label "Senghorian" but clearly in the same spirit of assertion of African or Afro uniqueness and exceptionalism, see Paget Henry, *Caliban's Reason: Introducing Afro-Caribbean Philosophy* (New York: Routledge, 2000).

53. Senghor, "On Negrohood," p. 7.

54. Ibid.

55. Stephen Howe's *Afrocentrism* is in many respects a rigorous attack on several brands of epistemological and political Afrocentrism, some of which advocate what may be called Senghor-type black emotive reason, also in the name of black difference. But Senghor's animist metaphysics and emotive epistemology are far more forgivable than anything of their kind that I have read in Afrocentrism proper, so that even Senghor's essentialism and obscurantism easily resist comparison to the far more esoteric epistemological Africology agitated for by some ardent promoters of Afrocentrism. Unlike the small subset of Afrocentrists that I have in mind, Senghor is always careful to note that Africa's "sympathetic reason" is "more closely related to *logos* . . . . For *logos*, before Aristotle, meant both reason and the word." Then he would add: "At any rate, Negro-African speech does not mold the object into rigid categories and concepts without touching it; it polishes things and restores their original color, with their texture, sound, and perfume; it perforates them with its luminous rays to reach the essential surreality in its innate humidity" (Senghor, "The African Road to Socialism," p. 74). Senghor may be accused of sensualizing processes of knowledge much more that they actually are, or of romanticizing—even eroticizing—epistemology. But this sort of anthropomorphism is hardly unique to Senghor, or confined to the discipline of philosophy and poetry. Feminist and anthropological critiques of scientific language show that even the—how else shall we put it—"hard" sciences are not immune from the use of revealing metaphors to describe both known and unknown phenomena of nature. Senghor, it seems to me, mistakenly thought that this way of "embracing" real and imagined aspects of nature is somehow an exclusively African trait. Of course, he would be correct if it is proven that all the races of peoples are descended from Africa.

56. Senghor, *Liberté 1: Négritude et humanisme*, p. 255.

57. See Pierre de Chardin's *L'Apparition de l'homme*, Paris: Seuil, 1956. Senghor wrote a book called *Pierre Teilhard de Chardin et le politique africaine*, Paris: Seuil, 1962.

58. Placide Tempels, *Bantu Philosophy*, Paris: Présence Africaine, 1959; Marcel Griaule, *Dieu d'eau, entreties avec Ogotemmeli*, Paris: Fayard, 1966.

59. Senghor, *On African Socialism*, pp. 147–148.

60. Tempels, *Bantu Philosophy*, p. 46.

61. See Vaillant, *BFA*, p. 254.

62. Senghor, "Elément Constitutif," in *Liberté Vol. 1: Négritude et humanisme*, Paris: Seuil, 1964, pp. 258–259; See also Vaillant, *BFA*, pp. 254–55.

63. "Elément Constitutif," pp. 275–276; see also *On African Socialism*, pp. 93–94.

64. Senghor, *On African Socialism*, p. 165.

65. Vaillant, *BFA*, p. 257.

66. Ibid.

67. Ibid.

68. As president of Senegal, Senghor was instrumental in organizing the First All-African Festival of Arts and Culture, FESTAC, in Dakar, in 1967.

69. Senghor, *On African Socialism*, p. 133. See also pp. 132, 165.

70. Useful examples covering the spectrum include: Sylvia Washington Ba, *The Concept of Negritude in the Poetry of Léopold Sédar Senghor*, Princeton: Princeton University Press, 1973; Irving Leonard Markovitz, *Léopold Sédar Senghor and the Politics of Négritude*, New York: Atheneum, 1969; Louis-Vincent Thomas, "Panorama de la Négritude," in *Langages et Littératures* (Dakar) 14, 1965: 45–101; Cheikh Anta Diop, *Nation nègre et cultures*, Paris: Présence Africaine, 1955; Graziano Benelli, *La necessità della parola: Léopold Sédar Senghor*, Ravenna: Longo, 1982; Gisela Bonn, *Léopold Sédar Senghor: Wegbereiter der Culture Universelle*, Dusseldorf: Econ, 1968; Irmgard Hanf, *Léopold Sédar Senghor: Ein afrikanscher Dichter französischer Prägung*, Munich: Fink, 1972; Lylian Kesteloot, *Les Ecrivains noirs de langue française: Naissance d'une littérature*, Bruxelles; edition de l'Institut de Sociologie de l'Universitié Libre de Bruxelles, 1965; Okechukwu Mezu, *Léopold Sédar Senghor et la defense et illustration de la civilisation noires*, Paris: Librairie Marcel Didier, 1968; Stanislas Adotevi, *Négritude et Négrologues*, Paris: Union Génerale d'Editions, 1972; and Marcien Towa, *L. S. Senghor, Négritude ou Servitude*, Yaoundé: Editions CLE, 1971. There exist, for example, four bibliographies on Senghor: Moustapha Tambadou, "Bibliographie de la Léopold Sédar Senghor," in *Ethiopiques* 3, 1–2, 1985: 203–216; Collete Michael, *Negritude: An Annotated Bibliography*, Cornwall, CT: Locust Hill, 1988; Bureau de Documentation de la Présence de la République, *Léopold Sédar Senghor: Bibliographie*, 2nd ed., Dakar: Fondation Léopold Sédar Senghor, 1982; and Gail Kostinko, *Léopold Sédar Senghor: A Selected Bibliography*, Washington, D.C.: Moorland Spingarn Research Center, Howard University, 1974.

71. See, for example, entries on "francophone, African philosophy" in the recent *Routledge Encyclopedia of Philosophy*, ed. Edward Craig, New York: Routledge, 1998.

72. Tsenay Serequeberhan, *The Hermeneutics of African Philosophy*, New York: Routledge, 1992.

73. Senghor, "Qu'est-ce que la Négritude," in *Liberté 3: Négritude et civilisation de l'universel*, p. 91, emphasis in the original.

74. Senghor, *Pierre Teilhard de Chardin et la politique africaine*, p. 20. See also Mercer Cook's,

introduction to Senghor, *On African Socialism*.

75. Paulin Hountondji, postscript *African Philosophy: Myth and Reality*, Bloomington: Indiana University Press, 1983, pp. 170–71.

76. Donald R. Wehrs, "Colonialism, Polyvocality, and Islam in *l'aventure ambigüe* and *Le devoir de violence*," in *MLN* 107, 5, John Hopkins University Press, December 1992: 28.

77. See, for example, Chinua Achebe, *Hopes and Impediments: Selected Essays*, New York: Doubleday, 1989; and *Morning Yet on Creation Day: Essays*, Garden City, NY: Anchor Books, 1976.

78. Senghor, *On African Socialism*, pp. 67–103.

CHAPTER 5

NÉGRITUDE AND MODERN AFRICANA PHILOSOPHY: BLACK IS, BLACK AIN'T

AFRICAN PHILOSOPHY AS COUNTERMODERN ANTHROPOLOGICAL DISCOURSE

Conceptually, Négritude was a multifaceted high-wire intellectual and political act negotiating, on the one hand, doctrines of racial relativism and, on the other, an ambiguous longing for a multiracial universalism. Négritude wanted to affirm an African and black racial particularity even as it showed, in its theories and practices, a remarkable willingness to engage in critical dialogue with modern Western thought from—in the case of Senghor, for example—Marx and Hegel through Pierre de Chardin to Sartre. Césaire and Senghor selectively appropriated resources from modern Western traditions, but for the purposes of asserting the difference and the uniqueness of an African and black world; they staged their arguments as determinate demands requiring that Europeans understand and respect the "dignity" of Africans (Césaire)[1] in the name of a "universal brotherhood" (Senghor).[2] Key questions, however, remained: If Négritude offered itself as an "Africanist" or black critique of racial whiteness and capitalist exploitation in European modernity, if Négritude presented itself as an alternative mode of conversation about the anthropology of blackness and whiteness, should we not ask if this Négritude, through these questions and its cultural politics, also succeeded in transforming not only its condition of subjection but also the Euro-American objects of its critiques? If Négritude failed in this transformative mission, why? If it succeeded, what is left, today, for a successor philosophy of Africa or of black race and cultures? What determinate "black" or "Afro" projects could an African or black philosophy inherit from Négritude? What connects today's African or black philosophy to its Négritude prehistory?

It is very difficult to think, certainly, of African philosophy as a *racial* philosophy (for example, as the philosophy of only the philosophers who have African or black racial origins). There are many productive specialists in African and black philosophy who have no, as W. E. B. Du Bois would have said, African or black "blood" in their veins.[3] What we can claim is that Afrophilosophy refers to philosophies which are about African or black experiences. What makes this characterization useful is that whereas it includes the racial experience, it avoids reducing all African or black experiences—or the history of African or black philosophy—to the racial question. And it does not suggest that only Africans or black philosophers can practice Afrophilosophy, or that philosophies categorized as "African" or "black" must belong to only this category.

Without the constraints imposed by some of Négritude's claims, one can therefore establish a working definition of Afrophilosophy that needs no racial essence in order to exist or to legitimize itself, or to find for itself useful projects. But as with Négritude it is unimaginable—to me at least—to think of a modern philosophy that could claim to be about Africa or Africans or African-descended peoples and yet express no interest in the racial experiences of African and black people throughout the world. Race, for some, remains what Du Bois called it: the problem of the twentieth century—but a problem whose seeds, as I have tried to show, go beyond the nineteenth century to which Du Bois had attributed them.[4] Race problems shadow the twentieth century and beyond. The race question therefore need not be peripheral to the problems of modern—or postmodern—philosophies, African or otherwise; for "race" itself is a modern invention.

Négritude, I think, failed the interests of modern African philosophy when it opposed a supposedly European technical "eye-reason" (instrumental rationality) to an African "feeling-reason" ("participant" rationality). Obscured by this mechanical binary is perhaps the most interesting of all philosophical questions: What is reason? What is thinking? In the *Dialectic of Enlightenment* Theodor Adorno and Max Horkheimer argued that in thought, humans necessarily "move away from nature and put her at arms length *as something to be dominated.*" Against Senghor one could argue with Adorno and Horkheimer that thinking "is suffused with illusion if it insists on denying its vital function of separation, dissection and objectification." When Césaire or Senghor boasts about the wholeness and, I assume, holiness of Africa's animist "reason-embrace" as a form of rationality that "kills" and "subdues" nothing while intuitively embracing everything, a form of reason that "caresses" instead of judging and so forth, one must think of the counter-argument advocated by Adorno and Horkheimer, that any form of reason that remains stuck at a level of "mystical union" with objects is "a mirage, an impotent, interiorized trace of a revolution betrayed."[5] The African or black mind—if there is ever such a thing as a "racial" mind—regardless of what Césaire and Senghor made of it, is not without a "revolutionary" character. One only has to think about, for example, the qualities embodied by the Yoruba god Ogun or the Igbo god Agwu, paradigms of the rebellious seeker of knowledge, the Promethean instinct in humans, as understood not just by Yoruba or Igbo writers but in most other cultures of Africa.

Senghor failed, I think, to recognize the intrinsically alienated character of the human condition, in the midst of the rest of nature, as understood even in "traditional" African cultures. Alfred Jospe, who wrote about the Jewish culture from a tradition, you might argue, not without similarities to Senghor's background, is quite enlightening when he describes "chutzpah" as what most characterizes rational reflection. Thought, Jospe argues, entails a "rejection of peace between man and nature." This rejection occurs because humans desire "to touch, to build, to transform, to change the physical world as well as man's inner world"; reason, therefore, whether traditional and "participant" or modern and "instrumental," Jospe implies, entails as a matter of course "a spirit of defiance which refuses to acquiesce in the status quo . . . ready to defy the forces of man, of nature, of history—yes, even God—in order to reach for something better, more complete, closer to the realization of hope and ideal."[6] It is this Promethean instinct that is fully on display in the legends of Africa's Ogun or Agwu.[7]

Senghor's archetypal framing of the "black" and the "white" in ahistorical stereotypes presents characteristics of each that defy all known histories of peoples in either Europe or Africa. What even critics of modernity Adorno and Horkheimer recognized, and Jospe and Wole Soyinka advocate, cannot be called "Eurocentric" or un-African. One must affirm, again with Adorno and Horkheimer—critics of the instrumental rationality that animated most of Europe's capitalist projects—that "by the fact that enlightenment is proved right in its conflict with hypostatized utopias and boldly proclaims the principle of combination through disunion, the rupture between subject and object which it declines to conceal becomes the index of the latter's untruth and of truth itself."[8] Senghor's "African" utopia and the hypostatized opposite whiteness do not allow for explanations of how thought could be at once subjective and objective, harmonious and disharmonious, conciliatory yet warring with traditions, nature, or the gods.

The consequences of Négritude's theoretical neglect of these more general issues about reason carry over into Senghor's descriptive anthropological works: by the time he completed the long list of the presumed differences between "black" African and "white" European mentality, we had abstract models of two types of human species: one type is black and employs all her senses, intuition, and empathy to understand the world and to create communities that enhance moral development and harmony with the environment, and the other is white, a tribe of disharmonious individuals, each restlessly searching for unlimited material satisfaction in power over others and nature. In this harsh opposition the white technical, material, and amoral civilization threatens to destroy the African and black humane civilization, the only modern custodian of true reason, morality, and emotional and spiritual maturity. Nothing bridges the chasm between the white and the black except Senghor's *civilisation de l'universel*, a grand bazaar of cultures where, in a *rendezvous de donner et de reçevoir*, blacks and whites must barter cultures like goods: you give what you have and receive what you don't have, so that humanity, through this commerce, is rendered whole and without racial antagonisms. In the grand exchange of stock the black mind, like dough, shall be "leavened" by the white technical reason; but like a rusted steel, the creaking white technical reason shall be "oiled" to suppleness by African and black music and poetry.

When he correlated agrarian environment with culture and personality, Senghor, if his black-white, Africa-Europe dichotomy would hold, must ignore the varieties within Africa's geography and the cultural differences among its peoples. Much of what he understood as unique to African humanity, but which he also attributed to specific forms of relationship to the land, could be observed in any agrarian society—in Europe or Africa, among whites as among blacks. It is impossible therefore not to suspect that the significance accorded to "white" and "black" (on the grounds of "race") by Senghor are superficial and fabricated: if one ascribed to the European culture rationalism, materialism, and individualism, and to the African intuitive reason, empathy, and spiritual values, we must explain the fact that when Karl Marx and Max Weber critiqued capitalism and industrialism, they attributed to precapitalist and preindustrial conditions those qualities that Senghor attributed to Africa's racial difference. What Senghor ascribed to "white" racial culture were for Marx strictly characteristics of capitalist social and economic systems; and the qualities Senghor called exclusively "African" or "black," were for Marx, again quite narrowly, identified with a prospective communism. Weber, on the other hand, was interested in describing the differences between industrial and preindustrial Western societies, and saw Europe as headed toward over-rationalization, overmechanicanization, and, above all, what he regretfully called cultural and spiritual "disenchantment." In a language that echoes the Senegalese sage whose warnings against the danger of "white" mechanical "madness" Senghor would report, Weber expressed the pain and loss to be suffered in modern industrial society: "Not summer's bloom lies ahead of us . . . but rather a polar night of icy darkness."[9]

The similarities between the romantic critiques of modern European society by Marx and Weber on the one hand, and Senghor on the other, highlight the reductionist tendencies in Senghor's understanding of the differences he observed between Africa and Europe.[10] Was Senghor repeating—in reverse—the classical procedures of European anthropology, whereby in the attempt to establish that form of rationality which one claims is properly African, one must depend, negatively, upon stereotypical images of European societies and cultures? In the same way anthropologists (and philosophers who depend on them for "empirical" illustrations of theories of rationality) take recourse to descriptions of "*the* primitives" in order to set off, as in a mirror, the assumed virtues of modern Western reason and culture, Senghor, it seems, makes unreserved appeal to abstract constructions of "the European worldview," "the European mentality," or "the white reason," each of which serves as a foil for thematizing claims about, at best, idealized African reason and cultures. Is it possible, then, that in "Othering" Europe, Senghor was paying the classical modern anthropologist a familiar compliment?

RETURN TO THE SOURCE

In *Myth, Literature, and the African World*, Wole Soyinka defends what he calls an "accommodationist" concept of African (or, more strictly, Yoruba) mode of reasoning. The accommodationist reason is a form of rationality in which thought does not compartmentalize knowledge or truths into either the purely instrumental or purely contemplative, the purely technical or purely artistic. It is a form of reason that challenges not only Senghor's partisanship with "intuitive" participatory rationality but also Adorno's and Horkheimer's assumptions about the processes of objectification of nature—which they saw as necessarily an activity of "domination." Are there not, Soyinka might ask, nondominating forms of objectivity?

While showing that the ideological vision of Négritude "should never be underestimated or belittled," Soyinka nonetheless insists that this vision went wrong when it was pursued by oversimplification of Africa's modern racial problems. Négritude, he explained, wanted to reestablish black values, but its effort was not led "by any profound effort to enter into this African system of values." Instead, Négritude "extolled the apparent," and took "its reference points . . . far too much . . . from European ideas even while its Messiahs pronounced themselves fanatically African." These missteps—in Soyinka's view, strategic ones—resulted in an unacceptable situation:

> In attempting to refute the evaluation to which black reality had
> been subjected, Négritude adopted the Manichean tradition of

European thought and inflicted it on a culture which is most radically anti-Manichean. It not only accepted the dialectical structure of European ideological confrontations but borrowed from
the very components of its racist syllogism.[11]

The "Manichean tradition" refers, certainly, to the facile opposition of the
black/white, intuition/analysis, technology/humanism, and so forth around
which early Césaire and clearly Senghor sought to construct the differences
between African and European cultures.

While correctly affirming the existence and uniqueness of an African
world, Négritude, Soyinka argued, was incapable of thematizing the nature
of this world because its methods were too determined by the terms dic-
tated by that Other culture, the European, considered opposite, and against
which Négritude must then assert itself. The "racist syllogism" that
Négritude was forced to adopt was also European in origin: "analytical
thought is a mark of high human development; the European employs analytical thought; therefore the European is highly developed." Or: "analytical thought is a mark of high human development; the African is incapable
of analytical thought; therefore the African is not highly developed."
Soyinka thinks that it was an error for Négritude not to have challenged the
first conclusion ("the European is highly developed"), implicitly accepting
all its premises. Both the premises and the conclusions were "the battle-
ground [established] by Eurocentric prejudices and racial chauvinism."
Instead of attacking the prejudices and the chauvinism, however, Négritude
merely proceeded to rearrange the racist syllogism in a different fashion:
"intuitive understanding is *also* a mark of human development; the African
employs intuitive understanding; therefore the African is highly developed." By opposing reason to emotion, analysis to understanding, and so
forth on *racial* grounds, Senghor left himself vulnerable to a question that
the Ghanaian philosopher W. E. Abraham would hurl at him: "When
Senghor says that the African is non-intellectual—that reason is Greek and
feeling African, that the African knows things by his nose—that is sheer
nonsense! What does he think I have above my nose?" Abraham went as far
as to suspect that "there is nothing particularly African about [Senghor's]
poetry," and that Senghor was "an apologist of France speaking to Africa."[12]

Soyinka was part of a chorus of this and similar African criticisms of Senghor; he lamented the "truncation" of the African mind that occurs when Négritude poetry accepts

> the most commonplace blasphemies of racism, that the black man has nothing between his ears, and proceeded to subvert the power of poetry to glorify this fabricated justification of European cultural domination. Suddenly, we were exhorted to give a cheer for those who never invented anything, cheer for those who never explored the oceans. The truth, however, is that there isn't any such creature.[13]

To Senghor's consternation, African secondary schools and universities sponsored essay and poetry competitions aimed at denouncing what were widely perceived as his blasphemies against Africa and the black race.[14]

It is noteworthy that the arguments between Senghor and the African critics paralleled the encounter between Sartre and Fanon, also about the philosophical but above all political implications of Négritude aesthetics. In the preface to the first edition of Senghor's *Anthologie de la Poésie nègre et malgache*,[15] Sartre provided a sustained examination of the ideological intentions of Négritude poetry in ways that greatly influenced later critical receptions. In words that echoed the Surrealists' point of view, Sartre wrote that Négritude poetry was "committed, even directed automatic writing [écriture automatique engagée, et même dirigée]—not because there is intervention of reflection, but because the words and the images are constantly translating the same torrid obsession." The Negro poet is depicted as one possessed: "falling into trances, thrashing about on the ground like one possessed, singing his wrath, his pain, his revulsion, displaying his wounds, his life torn between 'civilization' and his black heritage, in brief: behaving lyrically to the highest degree."[16] Indeed, Sartre saw in the African poetry only evidence that "the Black man attests to a natural Eros"; his poetry lacking "artificial" (rational) civilization, and flowing directly from unconscious and irrational forces. "For our black poets," Sartre impudently wrote,

> Being comes out of Nothingness like a penis becoming erect;
> Creation is an enormous perpetual delivery; the world is flesh and

the son of flesh; on the sea and in the sky, on the dunes, on the rock, in the wind, the Negro finds the softness of human skin; . . . he is both Nature's female and its male; and when he makes love with a woman of his race, the sexual act seems to him to be a celebration of the Mystery of Being. This spermatic religion is like the tension of a soul balancing between an erect phallus, and that more deaf, more feminine one being a growing plant.[17]

When he wanted to compare this supposedly special spermatic Negro quality to what he knows about France, Sartre, naturally, could find no examples. He therefore concluded: "only [D. H.] Lawrence seems to me to have had a cosmic feeling for sexuality," but even Lawrence's feeling, unlike Sartre's Negro, "remains very literary in his works." Sartre therefore quite happily took Senghor's initial thesis and extended it to the furthest miles: the "French language and thought are analytic . . . the black soul . . . synthetic?"[18]

After drowning Négritude poetry in the "natural" and the erotic, Sartre proceeded to subjectivize its racial claims to modernity, and relativize its political claims to history. Although he accepted Senghor's vague argument that Négritude was about "a certain quality common to the thought and conduct of blacks,"[19] Sartre drew a distinction between what he called the "subjective" and the "objective" dimensions of Négritude. Subjectively, Négritude is characterized as the black person's interior search for, and experience of, her "blackness," as a personal identity; objectively, it refers to black or African-inspired cultures and civilization. But from a Marxist perspective, Sartre further argues that in its subjectivity and objectivity, Négritude only confirms the observation that, for humans in general and not just blacks, consciousness is inextricable from one's existence—an existence structured in economic and social activities. But if existence determines consciousness, Négritude, as black consciousness, is necessarily linked to the economic and social conditions of the black race, and is totally accounted for by these conditions. Sartre therefore concluded that if modern capitalist relations between Africa and Europe and between white capital and black labor were transformed, Négritude's conditions of possibility would disappear, and with it, Négritude.

Emphasizing therefore this dialectic of the subjective and the objective, Sartre explains:

> It is only after [the African] has ceased to live unreflectively and totally within the world of objective Négritude that he feels the need to express his subjective Négritude. This is the irony of his history. The black poet writes an Orphic poetry because he must first desert his native land before he returns to it by descending into himself. For the black Diaspora, it is only by reentering Africa and coming into contact with the objective world of Négritude that subjective Négritude can be reawakened.[20]

The language and structure of this argument is clearly of Hegel: the African ceases to live unreflectively in the world of *objective* Négritude only when she feels the need to express her *subjective* Négritude, and only then does the possibility of black *history* start. In this regard, though, Sartre's is no different from the then-orthodox interpretations of Négritude even among its most vocal African critics. Soyinka, for example, contended that African poets who were born, educated, and lived on the continent wrote about Négritude out of "a totally artificial angst"; for them, being black was never an issue until "after Négritude revealed to them the very seductive notion that they had to commence a search for their Africanness. Until then they were never even aware that it was missing."[21] Christopher Miller saw a paradox in regard to the founding of both the journal and the publishing house Présence Africaine. He wrote:

> Created at the apogee of French colonial power, *Présence Africaine* was founded and remains in Paris, the center of the colonial empire, absent from the Africa whose presence it began to pursue, describe, and advocate. Nothing should be done about France without France: the most necessary condition for any anticolonial struggle that would transcend ethnic boundaries was the French language and its literacy. Without Paris, then, without the absence of Africa, there would also be no *Présence Africaine*.[22]

Négritude, in short, is a creation of those individuals who have been described as New World Africans. It has to have been this class of Africans who the most felt a need to search, recover, and affirm their "Africanity" in the face of its degradation by slavery in Europe, and colonization on the continent.

On these premises, Sartre argued that Négritude could not amount to more than the significance of its origins: as a reaction of alienated Africans to European racist and capitalist cultures. As such, Négritude is no more than a negative moment of a dialectic: the racism of white Europe is the thesis, Négritude is the antithesis; hence the famous phrase that Négritude is an "antiracist racism"—the implication being, of course, that both racisms should be transcended. But into what?

If, as Sartre thought, the "theoretical and practical assertion of the supremacy of the white man is its thesis," and "the position of Négritude as an antithetical value is the bottom of negativity," Négritude he believed must be a "minor term of a dialectical progression,"[23] bounded to its own subjectivity. Although the Negro protests his racial oppression, what the Negro really wants is, according to Sartre, "the abolition of *all* kinds of ethnic privileges." The Negro was ready to "assert his solidarity with the oppressed of every color," and "after that, the subjective, existential, ethnic notion of Négritude 'passes' . . . into that which one has of the proletariat: objective, positive, and precise."[24] What we have, then, is a forced conjunction, in fact disappearance, of race into class—the only way, it seems, that Négritude can become "historical."

The idea that the ethnic is opposed to the historical, and race to class, as the psychological is opposed to the political is, for Sartre, a given: "The first is concrete and particular, the second is universal and abstract; the one stems from what Jaspers calls understanding and the other from intellection; the first is the result of a psychobiological syncretism and the second is a methodical construction based on experience." Thus Négritude as a negative moment will never be "sufficient in itself"; it is only "preparing the synthesis or realization of the human being in a *raceless* society."[25] But curiously, Sartre also believed that "these black men who use it [i.e., Négritude] know this perfectly well"[26]—even when, as we shall see, most of the men referred to were actively protesting precisely this particular interpretation of their movement.

It is not that Sartre was insensitive to the "special" burden of being black in Europe: in fact, he writes about it. Comparing the (black) African in Europe to the (white) Jew, for example, he noted that "a Jew—a white man among white men—can deny that he is a Jew, can declare himself man among men." The Negro, on the other hand,

> cannot deny that he is Negro, nor can he claim that he is part of some abstract colorless humanity: he is black. Thus he has his back up against the wall of authenticity: having been insulted and formerly enslaved, he picks up the word "nigger" which was thrown at him like a stone, he draws himself erect and proudly proclaims himself a black man.[27]

Moreover, while he notes that the Negro is in actual fact "victim of the capitalist structure of our society," Sartre also acknowledges that the circumstances under which capitalist oppression occur "vary according to history and geographic conditions"; hence

> the black man is a victim of it *because he is a black man* and insofar as he is a colonized native or deported African. And since he is oppressed within the confines of his race and because of it, he must first of all become conscious of his race. He must oblige those who have vainly tried throughout the centuries to reduce him to the status of a beast, to recognize that he is a man. On this point there is no means of evasion.[28]

If all this is true, why then seek to reduce the "fact of blackness" (as Fanon would call it) to only a negative moment in, supposedly, a progressive dialectic of "history"? If the black cannot get out of, so to speak, the black skin, if race would thus always be a factor in the "white" perception of the black African, why must one hope that Négritude is nothing but a preparation to its own historical suicide? And if, as Sartre says, "the selfish scorn that the white men display for black men . . . has no equivalent in the attitude of the bourgeois toward the working class,"[29] why should we think that only the same cure for the class problem must be recommended for the race problem? If racism must be opposed "with a more exact view of black subjectivity," and "race consciousness" must therefore be "based first of all on the black soul," as it is in the white soul, how is the class-economic answer totally appropriate to what is, therefore, a disease of the soul?

A CRITIQUE OF SARTRE

Although he thought that the unity which will be achieved, "bringing all oppressed peoples together in the same struggle, must be preceded in the colonies by . . . the moment of separation or negativity," it was precisely this negativity that Sartre designated by the name "antiracist racism" and wished that the sooner it disappeared the quicker would come the universal liberation of "man"—the "abolition of racial differences."[30] It is, however, inexplicably expected that only the "black man" can—or will—bring about this universal outcome. Sartre argues:

> Previously, a black man claimed his place in the sun in the name
> of *ethnic* qualities; now, he establishes his right to life on his mis-
> sion; and this mission, like the proletariat's, comes to him from
> his historical position: because he has suffered from capitalistic
> exploitation more than all the others, he has acquired a sense of
> revolt and a love of liberty more than all the others. And because
> he is most oppressed, he necessarily pursues the liberation of all,
> when he works for his own deliverance. . . . But, after that, can
> we still believe in the interior homogeneousness of Négritude?
> And how can one say that it exists?[31]

Is this a too optimistic view of the outcomes of prior histories of antagonistic race relations? Or is this a too pessimistic view of the future of noninvidious racial identities—identities often won and defended by groups at great price? How would the utopian raceless future come about? Is Sartre's explanation sufficient?

Sartre *knew* that there has never been an interior—nor exterior—homogeneity to Négritude.[32] But the question—Will Négritude's reasons cease to exist?—was a pretext for another. If, as he argues, Négritude "is the root of its own destruction," "a means and not an ultimate end," a "crossing to" and not "an arrival at,"[33] shall one not simply wait for "these black men" to realize that they must make a "strange and decisive turn"—a turn in which "race is transmuted into historicity"? "The black Present," Sartre thought, must be exploded and temporalized, so that "Négritude—with its Past and its Future—is inserted into Universal History." This insertion will ensure that Négritude "is no longer a *state*, nor even an existential attitude," but a "Becoming." For Sartre, it is only in such a historical "disappearance" that the black contribution to the evolution of humanity would no longer be mere "savor, taste, rhythm, authenticity, a bouquet of primitive instincts"—the "natural" elements to which, precisely, he had previously reduced Négritude poetry.[34]

An interesting thing is that Sartre appears to have actually believed that the "History" and "Humanity" to which the black is invited, like a praying mantis, to "insert" its phallus and die is actually color-blind, "raceless." He also presumes that in "race"—and, one must note, the specifically black race—there is no history, only "instinct" and primitivity. Finally, Sartre thought that the advocates of Négritude shared his belief and presumption. But did they? Did Césaire or Senghor, for example, think that the racial situations of blacks were, as Sartre thought, merely "a special case of the general exploitation of man by man that marks the bourgeois epoch"?[35]

Césaire, for one, protested this interpretation. For example, whereas Sartre thought that in Césaire's poetry "'White' symbolizes capital, just as 'Negro' symbolizes work," or that when Césaire writes "about the black men of his race, he is writing about the worldwide proletarian struggle,"[36] Césaire's position, as stated by himself, was much clearer:

> There are people, even today, who thought and still think that it is all simply a matter of the left taking power in France, that with a change in the economic conditions the black question will disappear. I have never agreed with that at all. I think that the economic question is important, but it is not the only thing.[37]

In *Black Skin, White Mask,* Frantz Fanon observes that "Orphée noir"—the preface to Senghor's *Anthologie* that we have been discussing—was a remarkable example of a European effort to explain away black existence; it was an "intellectualization of the *experience* of being black."[38] Fanon remarked how Sartre "summoned up the negative side, but he forgot that this negativity draws its worth from an almost substantive absoluteness";[39] besides, this absoluteness results from the fact that the African's "challenge to the colonial world is not a . . . treatise on the universal, but the untidy affirmation of an original idea propounded as an absolute."[40] For Fanon, "black consciousness is immanent in its own eyes. I am not a potentiality of something, I am wholly what I am. . . . My Negro consciousness does not hold itself out as a lack. It *is.*"[41]

Or perhaps it is *also* a lack (African identity, Achebe reminded us, "is in the making").[42] But whereas Sartre wrote in anxious uncertainty about the future of Négritude, worrying whether the "poetic impulse" would coincide with his dream of revolution, Fanon was more concerned about the insinuation that "it is not I who make a meaning for myself, but it is the meaning that was already there, pre-existing, waiting for me. . . . Without a Negro past, without a Negro future, it [is] impossible for me to live by my Negrohood. Not yet white, no longer black, I was damned. Jean-Paul Sartre has forgotten that the Negro suffers in his body quite differently from the white man."[43] Fanon, following the examples of Césaire, understood that the colonial-racial situation required a more radical disruption—a disruption of the "white" world order more ferocious than proposed by Sartre's strategy of "assimilation."

Some critics have charged that Sartre, instead of making efforts to interpret Négritude as the promoters understood it, tried to co-opt the movement not just for Marxism in general but specifically for the domestic French political Left, where Négritude would function for the blacks in France as a minor version of Marxism, with black political energies in the metropolis and in the colonies directed accordingly toward the French communist positions. In fact, Sartre noticed—or wished?—that "it is certainly not just by accident that the most ardent cantors of Négritude are also militant Marxists."[44] The idea was that once a communist revolution succeeded, Négritude would have exhausted its usefulness and would disappear into a supposedly raceless French "universal" culture.[45] But it was precisely this sort of assimilationist melting pot, real or imagined, that Césaire and, to a point, Senghor had, in the first place, rejected. In fact, Senghor often described his Négritude position—unrealistic as it might have been given the brutality of colonialism—as "assimilate [France], not be assimilated [by it]." But neither for Senghor nor Césaire was Négritude a little term in a major European logic, framed by the French bourgeois society. Sartre's confidence and his exuberance are therefore inexplicable when he says that Négritude is "To French bourgeois racism . . . an anti-racist racism," or that "French racism is but a single strand in the complex web of the interrelated beliefs that make up [French] bourgeois ideology." He could therefore conclude: "Come the revolution, French bourgeois ideology and racism will disappear simultaneously"; and that "with the disappearance of French racism, its antithesis, Négritude, will also disappear."[46] The irony, of course, is that this theory and politics proposes self-immolation for a black racial project presented to Sartre to defend. We are not surprised then when Soyinka cried foul: Négritude, he wrote, was "stabbed in the back . . . from totally unexpected quarters."

By denying universal value to Négritude as an idea, and by framing it as a minor term in a "universal" dialectic of a French communist revolution, Sartre's Hegelian-Marxist analysis ended up abolishing the most basic premises of Négritude: négritude did not think of itself as "an absolute that knows it is transitory."[47] From a theoretical point of view, what was lacking in Sartre's dialectical reading of Négritude was the sense of a more radical ontology, with the accompanying political affirmation of radical difference—the *différance*, as Deleuze and Derrida would later develop this concept—also out of Hegel. It is clear that Sartre's reading of Hegel had not come under the influence of Jean Hyppolite, as did Deleuze's or Derrida's. Certainly after Kojève, whose seminars Sartre had attended along with Hyppolite, a less anthropological tradition of French Hegelianism developed around Hyppolite, and produced original readings of *The Phenomenology* and the master-slave dialectics in surprising ways that Sartre, it seems, could hardly have imagined.[48] In Sartre, Négritude was "really" nothing but an instance of Hegelian-Marxist dialectics which, following Kojève, was still framed in a view of consciousness, and therefore of history, as belonging to the Absolute. But this history and this Absolute, as Lacan would point out, still belonged to "those who know"—or those who claim to know.[49] Sartre had no doubt that Hegel and Marx provided the full answers to the black question—the question of "backward" national and racial atavism where, in "the end," race and nationalism would be seen to have never been the real issue.[50] On the other hand, when Hyppolyte—in a clear departure from Kojève—abandoned the idea of the reconciliation of Absolute consciousness as an anthropological project, it was only one step from there to the idea that the "difference" in Being is *différance*, an alterity that could never be (anthropologically or politically) surmounted. Compared to this insight, Sartre's analysis, unwittingly, remained stuck in a conservative philosophical framework that could not have suggested to him a stronger support for and justification of an idea intrinsic to a most responsible intention of Négritude. As a biographer of Senghor explained this intention: Négritude was founded precisely on the basis of opposition to the idea "that any black contribution can only be a minor one, a small contribution to the onward progress of France."[51]

THE RACIAL REMAINDER

Sartre, however, would not be the last to interpret the black experience of race in a strongly economistic manner. In the influential *Caste, Class, and Race*, published around the same time as Sartre's *Orphé noir*, Oliver Cox argued for a mode of analysis of race "that subordinated both race and nation to class," since, he argued, it was in the relations between exploiting and exploited classes that the dynamic of history was to be found. Specifically, Cox believed that at some ultimate point, "white workers and black workers would see through the rationalizations of the capitalist system and unite to overturn it."[52] Michael Banton, in this tradition, also argued that "the most effective examples of ethnic minority organization relate to minorities that find themselves occupying a lower position in the system of social stratification than their self-respect will tolerate," and that "so long as they feel unfairly placed they collaborate in the attempt to improve their position"; but once they attain a position of improved status, "the impulse to minority organization is gone and minority members disappear into the status structure of the majority."[53] Race, it seems, easily disappears into class. But Banton may be exaggerating here. For one thing, the full nature of this minority "emancipation" not made clear. To the extent that this thesis points only to the fact that when ethnic minorities assimilate into middle-class status, this transition and new status may dampen their zeal for racial or ethnic activism—as a result of complacency in success (as defined by the dominant class) or out of fear of loss of the newly acquired status—there is some truth in it. But it is another matter to argue from this observation that (a) the "real" problem of race is a class issue or that (b) socially and economically successful blacks and other minorities no longer suffer racial prejudice.

A useful exercise, however, is to determine when the purported "ultimate" occurs such that a racial minority "sees through" the supposed veneer of race into its "real" social class reality. The exercise could test whether or not Banton's "emancipated" minority, in their success, also thereby escapes being victims of racial prejudice and racial discrimination, and the social stratification that the prejudice and discrimination generate.

For reasons obvious in the title, we choose to look at Julius Wilson's *The Declining Significance of Race*,[54] an economic class analysis of how well blacks have improved their social conditions in the United States. The book's focus on measurable class progress, while it does not capture the total picture of all the range of black racial experiences, nonetheless allows one to determine in meaningful ways the declining impact of racism on opportunities for survival and prosperity that have been forged by African Americans. In a tone that suggested the increasing significance of class, Wilson explained: "I now feel that many important features of black and white relations in America are not captured when the issue is defined as majority versus minority and that a preoccupation with race and racial conflict obscures fundamental problems that derive from the intersection of class and race."[55]

But if class and class-related issues ought be given more prominence, how much significance, even if reduced, ought to be accorded to race per se? Wilson explicitly denies the view that race is no longer an issue: "I do not," he wrote, "subscribe to the view that racial problems are necessarily derived from the more fundamental economic class problems. The issues are far more complex than such an analysis would suggest." He is convinced that "When black and white relations are viewed from a broad historical perspective, a uniform reliance on class to explain all forms and degrees of racial conflict can be as misleading as a uniform reliance on race."[56] This, clearly, is a position different from Sartre's, and conforms rather closely to Césaire's "There are people . . . who thought . . . with a change in economic conditions the black question will disappear. I have never agreed with that at all"; or with C. L. R. James's observation that "The race question is subsidiary to the class question in politics. . . . But to neglect the racial factor as merely incidental [is] an error only less grave than to make it fundamental."[57]

If race is not a "transitory" factor in modern society's politics or economics, what then is its intrinsic status or value? From his earliest books, such as *Power, Racism, and Privilege*[58] through *The Declining Significance of Race* to the most recent *The Truly Disadvantaged*[59] or *When Work Disappears*,[60] Wilson shows no signs of abandoning the point of view that race matters. To show in what ways racism, for example, has simply mutated even during periods of black economic and social expansion, Wilson divided the history of race relations in the United into three stages, each embodying "a different form of racial stratification structured by the particular arrangement of both the economy and the polity." He explains:

> Stage one coincides with antebellum slavery and the early post-bellum era and may be designated the period of *plantation and racial-caste oppression*. Stage two begins in the last quarter of the nineteenth century and ends at roughly the New Deal era and may be identified as the period of *industrial expansion, class conflict, and racial oppression*. Finally, stage three is associated with the modern, industrial, post–World War II era, which really began to crystallize during the 1960s and 1970s, and may be characterized as the period of *progressive transition from racial inequalities to class inequalities*.[61]

The racial problem has remained center-stage, then, whether as consigning blacks to a "caste," "oppression," or "inequality."

Is there a chance that the race problem might transmute itself out of existence—or at least into social and political insignificance? Wilson thinks that whereas "In earlier years the systematic efforts of whites to suppress blacks were obvious to even the most insensitive observer," and "blacks were denied access to valued and scarce resources through various ingenious schemes of racial exploitation, discrimination, and segregation, schemes that were reinforced by elaborate ideologies of racism," the situation changed, in the second period, such that "however determinative [these earlier tactics] were for the previous efforts of the black population to achieve racial equality, and however significant they were in the creation of poverty-stricken ghettoes and a vast underclass of black proletarians . . . they do not provide a meaningful explanation of the life chances of black Americans today."[62] To explain the nature and the mechanisms of racism today, Wilson considered two related but competing theories.

The first is the classic Marxist position: race is "nothing more than the ideal expression of dominant material relationship."[63] The second is the "split labor-market theory," which is also, in the main, compatible with the first. While the first explanation asserts that racial prejudices and institutionalized segregation are "simply part of a superstructure determined and shaped by the particular arrangement of the class structure,"[64] the second tries to show how workers are managerially set up in racial antagonism: the (white) workers against the poor, unemployed, or poorly paid black labor which serves as a ready bargaining chip in the hands of the employer, against ambitious white workers who, for example, might seek higher wages or stronger unions. This explanation shows that, in the United States or South Africa, for example, when labor is segregated along the black (lower-paid) and the white (higher-paid), the dominant, geographically segregated white working class will constantly find racial reasons to fight competing, cheaper, black sources of labor. And where this physical exclusion through legal segregation or apartheid is impractical, there results a system of ethnic stratification which monopolizes for the whites skilled positions, and prevents the cheaper black labor from developing skills—technical and political—necessary to compete with higher-paid labor.[65]

However, these explanations, alone, according to Wilson, do not totally account for the persistence and the new dynamics of racism in the United States. He says: "As I examine the historical stages of race relations in the United States, I find that the patterns of black/white interaction do not consistently and sometimes do not conveniently conform to the propositions outlined in these explanations of racial antagonism. In some cases, the orthodox Marxian explanation seems more appropriate; in other instances, the split labor-market theory seems more appropriate; and in still others, neither theory can, in isolation, adequately explain black-white conflict."[66] The question therefore remains: What is an adequate theory? What accounts for the racial remainder which the economic and social class theory do not fully recover?

As in his previous books, Wilson in *The Declining Significance of Race* only alludes to "ideologies of racism," which he characterizes as "systems of belief." The systems of racial beliefs are not particularly class-specific, even as we should expect that they manifest themselves differently at different class strata. We may also understand that while the ideologies of racism do not work in isolation from economic and political forces, they have other cultural sources and psychological reasons for their persistence. This, you might say, would be the strictly noneconomic argument for racism that, following Kant and Rorty, I had proposed at the beginning. Wilson indeed laments situations where "the influence of racist norms on intergroup interaction both in and outside of industries has been dismissed as peripheral by the economic class theorists who tend to relegate racial belief systems to the ranks of the superstructure." He rejects this peripheralization of racism as "mere" belief systems because, in a repetition of John Rex's argument: "once a deterministic belief system is used to justify a particular stratification situation, that situation is itself changed thereby and the belief system may set in motion wholly new social processes." What we have is a situation where an established racial order connotes, for example, not only "a prolonged period of interaction between specific racial groups in a society in which inequality is institutionalized along racial lines," but also one in which "the system of inequality is reinforced and directed by entrenched social norms, norms that define and prescribe subordinate positions for designated racial groups."[67]

CONCLUSION

We do not, in short, have enough reasons to expect that once everyone is rich and educated, antiblack racism will disappear. From reading Wilson, what we are entitled to affirm, about a United States or a South Africa, for example, is that owing to increased "black political resources that made the government more sensitive to Negro demands," and because a newly "segmented labor structure in which blacks are either isolated in the relatively unionized, low-paying, basically undesirable jobs of the non-corporate sector, or occupy the higher-paying corporate and government industry positions in which job competition is either controlled by powerful unions or restricted to the highly trained and educated, regardless of race," economic and social conflicts may no longer have race as their main catalyst.[68] But race remains an issue.

In a little noticed-passage, Sartre recognized the difficulty, and perhaps sheer impossibility, within specific frameworks of "white" discourses, of affirming African or black life and culture as good, beautiful, and worthy. He wrote that the modern problem of race is

> nowhere more manifest than in the use of two connected terms, "white" and "black." . . . But it is a connection based on a hierarchical system: by giving the Negro this term, the teacher also gives him a hundred language habits which consecrate the white man's rights over the black man. The Negro learns to say "white as snow" to signify innocence, and to speak of the blackness of a look, of a soul, of a deed. As soon as he opens his mouth, he is accusing himself. . . . Imagine how strange such phrases would sound to us as the "blackness of innocence" or the "shadow of virtue."[69]

To demonstrate the poetic "strangeness" of such understanding of the black in European languages, Sartre mentions Grabbe's *Duke Theodore of Gothland*,[70] where the "black," Finnish general, Bedoa, describes his African lover to Gustav, the son of the duke.

> Bedoa: "Never, Ella! shall I forget thee, thou purest of African women; how noble was her heart! How woolly was her hair! Two feet long her bossom! And oh she was so black, as black as innocence!"
> Gustav: "What? Is innocence black?"
> Bedoa: "Well, we Negroes have a different taste from yours: for us the beautiful is black, but the devils are white!"[71]

Grabbe's piece was, of course, considered by the audience a "horror" drama.

Sartre was left to conclude that, in the European languages at least, "The black man must find death in white culture in order to be reborn with a black soul, like the Platonic philosopher whose body embraces death in order to be reborn in truth."[72] It is this "death," I think, that most black intellectuals—"caught" as they are even in a modernity whose terms are predominantly shaped by European languages and discourse—have consistently resisted. Not death as such, but the death sentence imposed by white supremacy. From Fanon's questions ("The white man is not only the Other but also the master, whether real or imagined")[73] to Soyinka's metaphysical assertion of "African world," where there is a "sudden awakening of a new generation of writers to threats to their self-apprehension," black intellectuals do not seem to mind death, but they don't want to die white. As Achebe bluntly put it: "Most African writers write out of an African experience and of commitment to an African destiny. For them that destiny does not include a future European identity for which the present is but an apprenticeship."[74]

I draw, therefore, several lessons work for Africana philosophy from its Négritude prehistory, especially from Sartre's interventions from a position of "Otherness." First, although Sartre's interests in Négritude fit into his Marxist theory of history, and perhaps the domestic French politics, his analysis of the movement provided a perspective that successfully highlighted its most basic contradictions—some of which were unproductive. Although he applauded the protest elements, Sartre also brought to light the impossibility, and perhaps the undesirability, of turning Négritude into an essentialist, race—rather than primarily cultural and political—theory. Since Europeans proclaimed that the African had no culture, it was no surprise that the African felt it was one's duty to show that the white was wrong. "Négritude," Fanon recognized, "grew out of the cultural necessity to . . . produce an antithesis to European hegemony."[75] That Sartre recognized this protest element in Négritude—and fanned it in France and among European intellectuals—was, as Fanon also recognized, "normal"; the normality drew its legitimacy "from the lies propagated by men of Western culture."[76]

But it would have been to ask for uncritical support, nay, a blind approval of the movement, to expect Sartre not to point out—regardless of whether one "needed to know"—the quite glaring theoretical if not practical constraints of any purely racial protest. In fact Senghor himself later acknowledged that Sartre's characterization of Négritude as "anti-racist racism" was not entirely without merit.[77] If colonialism despised the colonized for belonging to another race, Négritude was compelled, it seemed, to radicalize its counterclaims. Race and skin color, in the process, were extolled and elevated to the status of essential and autonomous values. But precisely because of this, one could say that Négritude, even in its rebellious stance, "remained entirely within the pale of existing [racist] modes of thought and expression."[78]

Whether the situation could have been otherwise for Négritude is, I think, an interesting question. For example, given the destructive aspects of "whiteness" (slavery, Jim Crow, colonial conquests, apartheid, etc.), could Africans and blacks, on the continent and in Europe or the Americas, have been expected to develop a nonracialized rhetoric of liberation? Are there historical bases in fact to suppose that modern Europe or the United States—or even contemporary South Africa—in their economic organizations and in their intoxicating white language of race, could have redeemed themselves as they did if blacks had promoted a purely "universal" rhetoric of liberation? After all, as Charles Mills reminded us, "Westerners *created* race in the first place by demarcating themselves from other 'races,' bringing into existence a world with two poles."[79]

Second, we need not be forced into a position where we must *either* reject Sartre's observations about the negativity of Négritude *or* uncritically affirm Négritude's essentialist quest for a primordial African or black "authenticity." For those who need it, Soyinka's work, for example, is full of alternative "ideological and social visions" in which, like Sartre, he recognized the transitory status of Négritude but, unlike Sartre, denied that this transition was a preparation for some colorless "universal." The "negative" aspects of Négritude, for Soyinka, lie squarely on an *African* path to recovery from, and positive self-apprehension after, European racist and colonial impositions. Although he has been criticized for suggesting that there exists "a cultural entity which we define as *the* African world,"[80] this criticism does not detract from the meaning of the program. It is quite all right to recognize that Soyinka's idea of Africa may be a fiction—*his* fiction. What is important, I think, is the formal claim to return, as Soyinka has consciously attempted, to an African culture and literary tradition—a tradition that he wishes to show is as universal as any other.[81]

Whatever Négritude's many failings might have been (e.g.: on the continent, in the reactionary "political Négritude" of independent Senegal as in the Négritude-inspired movement of *authenticité* in Mobutu's Zaire), the movement was undoubtedly a success not only at its birthplace, France, but also in other parts of Europe and the United States where dreadful and virulent racism was damaging the lives of African-descended peoples. A measure of Négritude's success was evident in the examples of its symbiotic relationships with Surrealism, Marxism, and Existentialism. Where it did not succeed as "philosophy," Négritude succeeded as thought-for-action. Although it failed to provide satisfactory resolutions to its many performative contradictory epistemological claims, Négritude did not lose the irreducible character of its ethical voices, maintaining these as a series of stands against suffering and denigration of black humanity, as it sought to protest injustice and inspire new forms of resistance.

NOTES

1. See Aimé Césaire, "Le Cahier d'un retours au pays natal."
2. For Senghor's arguments in favor of *la civilization de l'universel*, see, for example, *Négritude*

et Arabité. In 1937 in Dakar, Senghor wrote that every "creative civilization" takes "nourishment from without," and that "no culture or race that tried to exclude all others could flourish." Cultural synthesis, *métissage*, then, was Senghor's recommendation for not only the European but the African as well.

3. In our time, in the United States alone, among the living, we can mention Barry Hallen, Bruce Janz, Julie Maybee, Gail Presby—and occasional contributors like Robert Bernasconi, Peter Amato, Sandra Harding, Richard Bell, and so forth.

4. Du Bois was correct to say that "the discovery of personal whiteness among the world's peoples is a very modern thing"; but he was wrong to confine race or modernity as only "a nineteenth and twentieth century matter." His reasoning was that "the ancient world would have laughed at such [racial] distinction. The Middle Ages regarded skin color with mild curiosity; and even up to the eighteenth century we were hammering our national manikins into one great, Universal Man, with fine frenzy that ignored color and race even more than birth. Today we have changed all that, and the world in a sudden, emotional conversion has discovered that it is white and by that token, wonderful!" (Du Bois, "The Souls of White Folk," in *W. E. B. Du Bois: A Reader*, ed. David Levering Lewis, New York: Henry Holt, 1995, pp. 453–465; 453). The nineteenth and the twentieth centuries certainly saw the flourishing of racialism in theory and in practical life, but the seeds of these conceptions, at least among the philosophers we have studied, were already there in the eighteenth.

5. *The Dialectic of Enlightenment*, New York: Continuum, 1983; see the chapter "The Concept of Enlightenment."

6. See Alfred Jospe, "The Threefold Rebellion," in *Tradition and Contemporary Experience: Essays on Jewish Thought and Life*, ed. Alfred Jospe, New York: Schocken, 1970, p. 149.

7. See, for example, Wole Soyinka's *Idanre and Other Poems*, New York: Hill and Wang, 1992.

8. Jospe, "The Threefold Rebellion," p. 149.

9. Max Weber, "Politics as a Vocation," *From Max Weber: Essays in Sociology*, ed. and trans. H. H. Gerth and C. Wright Mill, New York: Oxford University Press, 1958, p. 128; Weber, "Science as a Vocation," *From Max Weber*, p. 155; Weber, *The Protestant Ethic*, New York: Scribner's, 1958, pp. 180–183; Janet Vaillant, *Black, French, and African*, Cambridge: Harvard University Press, 1990, p. 259.

10. Sandra Harding's "The Curious Coincidence between African and Feminist Moralities" (Emmanuel Eze, *African Philosophy: An Anthology*, Masden: Blackwell, 1998, chapter 41) is an attempt to find new ways of describing historical forms of reason in nonessentialist gender or race terms. (See also Harding, "Postcolonial Studies of Science," in *Routledge Encyclopedia of Philosophy*, New York: Routledge, 1998; and "Is Modern Science an Ethnoscience? Rethinking Epistemological Assumptions," in *Postcolonial African Philosophy*, ed. Emmanuel Eze, Oxford: Blackwell, 1997, pp. 45–70).

11. Wole Soyinka, *Myth, Literature, and the African World*, Cambridge: Cambridge University Press, 1972, p. 127.

12. W. E. Abraham, televised interview, National Education Television, Ghana; quoted in O. R. Dathorne, *African Literature in the Twentieth Century*, Minneapolis: University of Minnesota Press, 1975, p. 218.

13. Ibid., p. 129.

14. Senghor recounts some of these criticisms in many places, including the essay "Négritude: A Humanism of the Twentieth Century," in *Postcolonial Discourse and Post-Colonial Theory: A Reader*, ed. Patrick Williams and Laura Chrisman, New York: Columbia University Press, 1994, pp. 27–35.

15. Jean-Paul Sartre, "Orphée noir," in *Anthologie de la nouvelle poésie nègre et malgache de la langue française*, ed. Léopold Sédar Senghor, Paris: Presses Universitaires de France, 1948, 1969, pp. ix–xliv.

16. Sartre in Senghor, *Anthology de la nouvelle poésie negre et malgache*, Paris, 1948, p. xxvii. "descente inlassablement en soi-meme . . . un bonheur poétique exceptionel: en s'abandonnant aux trances, en se roulant par terre comme un possédé en proie de soi-meme, en chantant ses colères, ses regrets, ou ses détestations, en exhibant ses plaies, sa vie déchirée entre la 'civilization' et le vieux fond noir, bref en se montrant le plus lyrique."

17. "Black Orpheus," 318, 319. To understand how easily—even today—African arts are grossly misunderstood when their reflectiveness is reduced to the "simple" characterizations of "primitive" art, see the chapter "Africa's Art of Resistance" in Manthia Diawara, *In Search of Africa*, Cambridge, MA: Harvard University Press, 1998.

18. Sartre, "Orphée noir," pp. xlff.

19. Ibid., p. xv.

20. Vaillant, *Black, French, and African*, p. 250.

21. Soyinka, *Myth, Literature, and the African World*, p. 104.

22. Christopher Miller, "Alioune Diop and the Unfinished Temple of Knowledge," in *The Surreptitious Speech*, ed. V. Y. Mudimbe, Chicago: University of Chicago Press, 1992, pp. 427–434; 427.

23. Sartre, "Black Orpheus," pp. 319–321.

24. Sartre, "Black Orpheus," p. 326.

25. Ibid.

26. Ibid.

27. Ibid., p. 296.

28. Ibid., pp. 295–96.

29. Ibid., p. 297.

30. Ibid., p. 296.

31. Ibid., p. 325.

32. Elsewhere he had asked: "Does the poet who would be the Prophet for his colored brothers invite them to *become* more Negro, or does he disclose to them what they *are*, by a sort of poetic psychoanalysis? Is Négritude necessity or liberty? For the authentic Negro, is it a matter of conduct deriving from essences, as consequences derive from a principle, or is one a Negro in the way that the religious faithful are believers, that is to say, in fear and trembling, in anguish, in perpetual remorse for never sufficiently being what one would like to be? Is it a given fact or a value? The object of empirical intuition or a moral concept? Is it a conquest of meditation? Or does meditation poison it? Is it never authentic except when unmeditated and in the immediate? Is it a systematic *explanation* of the black soul, or a Platonic Archetype which one can approach indefinitely without ever attaining it? Is it, for black men, like our engineer's common sense, the most widely shared thing in the world? or do some have it, like grace; and if so, does it have its chosen one? One will undoubtedly answer this question by saying that it is all of these at once, and still other things. And I agree: like all anthropological notions, Négritude is a shimmer of being and of needing-to-be; it makes you and you make it: both oath and passion" ("Black Orpheus," p. 326).

33. Sartre, *Orphée noir*, pp. xlff.

34. Sartre, "Black Orpheus," p. 325.

35. Sartre continued: "It is a special case because the black man, unlike the white proletarian, cannot understand his place in society simply by considering society's economic structure. He must first recognize that race is the primary factor in his oppression. Consciousness of his Négritude is the black man's first step toward understanding the basic dynamic of his place in capitalist society."

36. Sartre, "Black Orpheus," p. 326.

37. Césaire, *Discourse on Colonialism*, 78.

38. Ibid.

39. Fanon, *Black Skin, White Mask*, p. 134

40. Ibid., p. 133

41. Ibid., p. 135

42. Chinua Achebe, interview with Anthony Appiah; quoted in *In My Father's House: Africa in the Philosophy of Culture*, New York: Oxford Universtiy Press, 1992, pp. 74–75.

43. Fanon, *Black Skin, White Mask*, pp. 134, 138.

44. Sartre, "Black Orpheus," p. 326.

45. See Sartre, "Black Orpheus," pp. 16–18.

46. Vaillant, *Black, French, and African*, p. 249.

47. Sartre, "Black Orpheus," p. 329.

48. See, for example, Jean Hyppolite, *Figures de la pensée philosophique*, 2 vols., Paris: Presses Universitaire de France, 1971, especially the chapters on Hegel, Marx, and Heidegger. Also of interest: Jean Hyppolite, *Logic and Existence*, trans. Leonard Lawler and Amit Sen, Albany: State University of New York Press, 1997.

49. See Jacques Lacan, *The Seminar of Jacques Lacan, Book II*, ed. Jacques-Alain Miller, New York: W.W. Norton, 1995, pp. 70–71.

50. Césaire's resignation from the French Communist Party, in the famous "Lèttre à Maurice Thorèz," had everything to do with his realization that the party, in its practices, was essentially implementing programs that, when it took account of the specificities of the black question, did so in ways that fulfilled expectations already bounded by Sartre's theoretical formulations.

51. Vaillant, *Black, French, and African*, p. 249.

52. Oliver Cox, *Caste, Class and Race: A Study in Social Dynamics*, New York: Monthly Review Press, 1948.

53. Michael Banton, *The Idea of Race*, Boulder, CO: Westview Press, 1997.

54. William Julius Wilson, *The Declining Significance of Race: Blacks and Changing American Institutions*, 2nd ed., Chicago: University of Chicago Press, 1980.

55. Ibid., p. ix.

56. Ibid.

57. C. L. R. James, *Black Jacobins*, New York: Vintage, 1963, p. 286.

58. William Julius Wilson, *Power, Racism, and Privilege*, New York: Macmillan and Company, 1973.

59. William Julius Wilson, *The Truly Disadvantaged*, Chicago: University of Chicago Press, 1987.

60. William Julius Wilson, *When Work Disappears*, New York: Knopf, 1996.

61. Wilson, *The Declining Significance of Race*, p. 2.

62. Ibid., p. 1.

63. See Karl Marx, *Karl Marx: Selected Writings in Sociology and Social Philosophy*, ed. T. B. Bottomore and Maximilian Rubel, Harmondsworth: Penguin, 1956, p. 93.

64. For this view Wilson cites, among others, Oliver Cox, *Caste, Class and Race: A Study in Social Dynamics* (Garden City, NY: Doubleday, 1948); Paul Baran and Paul M. Sweezy, *Monopoly Capital: An Essay on the American Economic and Social Order* (Harmondsworth: Penguin, 1966); Michael Reich, "The Economics of Racism," in *Problems of Political Economy*, ed. David M. Gordon (Lexington, MA: Heath, 1971).

65. Wilson, *The Declining Significance of Race*, p. 7. In *Rituals of Blood*, Orlando Patterson observes that "different classes of Euro-Americans supported lynching for different economic reasons. Lower class Euro-Americans were threatened by competition from cheap Afro-American labor, while the elite planters who desired such labor were threatened by any condition that promoted the solidarity of Afro-American and Euro-American labor. During periods of economic depression in the cotton industry, there was a lethal convergence of Euro-American hostility toward Afro-Americans, with the poor resenting and scapegoating Afro-American labor, and the elite finding inter-'racial' violence the best safeguard against the Afro-American and Euro-American poor uniting against them" (p. 181).

66. Wilson noted (*The Declining Significance of Race*, p. 11): "it is difficult to determine clearly the influence and strength of racial norms, even in established racial orders."

67. Wilson, *The Declining Significance of Race*, pp. 9, 11.

68. Ibid., p. 19.

69. Sartre, "Black Orpheus," p. 304.

70. Grabbe, *Duke Theodore of Gothland*, 1822.

71. Grabbe, "Herzog Theodore von Gothland," verse 3899ff. Quoted in Jahn Jahneiz, *Muntu*, p. 145.

72. Sartre, "Black Orpheus," p. 307.

73. Fanon, *Black Skin, White Mask*, p. 38.

74. Chinua Achebe, "Colonialist Criticism," *Morning Yet on Creation Day*, Ibadan: Heinemann, 1977; pp. 3–18; 7.

75. Fanon, *Black Skin, White Mask*, pp. 173–174.

76. Ibid.

77. Vaillant, *Black, French, and African*, p. 175.

78. Renate Zahar, *Frantz Fanon: Colonialism and Alienation*, p. 44.

79. Mills, *The Racial Contract: Blackness Visible: Essays on Philosophy and Race*, Ithaca, NY: Cornell University Press, 1998, xv.

80. See Appiah, "The Myth of an African World," in Appiah, *In My Father's House*. In the course of his arguments, which remained faithful throughout to the problematics captured in the title of the chapter, we encounter passages such as: "I think we should ask what leads Soyinka astray when it comes to his accounting for his cultural situation. And part of the answer must be that he is answering the wrong question. For what he needs to do is not to take an *African* worldview for granted but to take for granted his own culture—to speak freely not as an African but as a Yoruba and a Nigeria. The right question, then, is not 'Why Africa shouldn't take its traditions for granted?' but 'Why I shouldn't take mine?' The reason that Africa cannot take an African cultural or political or intellectual life for granted is there is no such thing: there are only so many traditions with their complex relationships—and, as often, their lack of relationship—to each other" (pp. 79–80).

81. See Soyinka, "The Fourth Stage through the Mysteries of Ogun to the Origin of Yoruba Tragedy," in Eze, ed., *African Philosophy: An Anthology*, Masden, MA: Blackwell, 1998, pp. 438–446. It starts: "The persistent search for the meaning of tragedy, for a re-definition in

terms of cultural or private experience is, at the least, man's recognition of certain areas of depth-experience which are not satisfactorily explained by general aesthetic theories; and, of all the subjective unease that is aroused by man's creative insights, that wrench within the human psyche which we vaguely define as 'tragedy' is the most insistent voice that bids us return to our own sources" (p. 438).

CHAPTER 6

Achieving Our Humanity

Introduction

In June 1863, July 1884, and May 1886, Frederick Douglass published three essays entitled, respectively, "The Present and the Future of the Colored Race in America," "The Future of the Negro," and "The Future of the Colored Race." The middle essay was written about two decades after the Dred Scott decision in the United States, and a few months before the continent of Africa was permanently carved up in Berlin among competing European powers. Yet the first paragraph starts in this tentative, cautious tone:

> It would require the ken of a statesman and the vision of a prophet combined to tell with certainty what will be the ultimate future of the colored people of the United States, and to neither of these qualifications can I lay claim. We have known the colored man long as a slave, but we have not known him long as a freeman and as an American citizen. One thing, however, may safely be laid down as probable, and that is that the Negro, in one form and complexion or another, may be counted upon as a permanent element of the population of the United States.[1]

One hundred years after this was written, the Negro in the United States had become known as a freeman, a freewoman, and a citizen. History and sociology document the trajectories of the Afro-American's political, economic, and cultural struggles to attain this freedom and citizenship. The lessons also show, perhaps beyond what Douglass was able to imagine in 1884, how in the struggles for freedom and citizenship the Afro-American has transformed the very meaning of what it is to be American.[2]

Now let us fast-forward to 1996, to a book entitled *The Future of the Race* by Henry Louis Gates, Jr., and Cornel West. The authors use Du Bois's trope of "The Talented Tenth" to rearticulate their expectations for continued racial progress not just for African Americans but for all Americans. They reaffirm their commitments to Du Bois's vision of the responsibility of the most educated and high-achieving African Americans to lead others on this path of progress. The book inventories the achievements (political, cultural, and economic) of African Americans in the United States since the civil rights movement of the 1960s. It is also a portrait of the long journey ahead for both "the race" of the book's title and for the country as a whole: "If it is the best of times for the black middle class . . . it is the worst of times for an equally large segment of our community"; and "Dr. King did not die so that *half* of us would 'make it,' and half of us perish, forever tarnishing two centuries of struggle and agitation for our equal rights." The authors believe that one "must accept King's credo that none of us is free until each of us is free." As it was for King, the "us" is not restricted to the black haves or have-nots, and West and Gates explicitly state, "All of us are brothers and sisters, in spirit—white and black, brown, red, and yellow, rich and poor black, Protestant and Catholic, Gentile, Jew, and Muslim, gay and straight—even if—to paraphrase Du Bois—we are not brothers- or sisters-in-law." They emphasize that "what is at stake is nothing less than the survival of our country, *and* the African American people."[3]

The questions animating my work naturally derive from the tensions implicit both in Douglass's reading of his present and the future of the enslaved and disenfranchised Africans in America, and in Gates's and West's own readings of the future of free and entitled Afro-Americans. What Douglass could only *hope* for, Gates and West *assume*. Douglass's future is Gates's and West's present. Douglass, for example, did *not* "think that the Negro will become more distinct as a class."

Ignorant, degraded, and repulsive as he was during his two hundred years of slavery, he was sufficiently attractive to make possible an intermediate race of a million, more or less. If this has taken place in the face of those odious barriers, what is likely to occur when the colored man puts away his ignorance and degradation and becomes educated and prosperous? The tendency of the age is unification, not isolation; not to clans and classes, but to human brotherhood.[4]

What was only a tendency in Douglass's age has become the history of our time. What was to Douglass an unfamiliar and imagined "future" of the race is, from our standpoint, familiar, near, and known.

What is not known in *The Future of the Race* is the future of "race" in general. There is a tension—a productive one, for sure, but with consequences far from unambiguous—between a defense of the future of the race and the desire for a future without racial discrimination (where all are brothers and sisters, even if not in-laws). Are racial bonds stronger than brotherly and sisterly bonds of love? Doesn't racial discrimination thrive on our tendency to treat others as nonbrothers and nonsisters, as outsiders, as Others?

This attitude of morally and lovelessly Othering individuals and groups happens both by omission and by commission. It is by omission if through "default" one loves and cares only for one's own—an "own" whose boundaries are made possible by attributing, often inattentively, negative social significance to those who lie "outside" one's default boundaries. It is by commission when one actively seeks to exclude others from one's "inner circle" of those to love or care about on the basis of "race." Racism or racial discrimination manifests itself as a refusal to love others—those who are considered, literally or metaphorically, nonbrothers and nonsisters.

Here is a question: If we achieve the goal of concern and care and love for all—"white and black, brown, red, and yellow, rich and poor black, Protestant and Catholic, Gentile, Jew, and Muslim, gay and straight," of what *future* social significance is race, religion, or sexual orientation to us? Should we harbor the suspicion that love may not be sufficient for us? If love knows no boundaries, racial or otherwise, of what use are these boundaries when love triumphs? On the other hand, is this a defense of "the race" which is not necessarily a defense of race? If yes, what then is the future of race? What are the future consequences of the current defense of "the race" in a world in which race has no socially significant future?

West in *The Future of the Race* speaks about his concern for the "ethical content" of our racialized "ethnic identities." A talented and prodigious philosopher, West knows well that there can be no ethnically tribalized or racialized morality or "ethics" suitable for a nation like Nigeria, or the United States, or even a cosmopolitan city. In a world such as ours only the ethics of the universal will do. In fact, nobody has explored the practical consequences of these tensions between the tribal or racial and the universal better than West, in his study of the arguments generated in Afro-American communities during the Senate hearings to confirm Clarence Thomas to the United States Supreme Court.[5] To state bluntly my question to Gates and West: Isn't racism already a sign of our incapacity to love enough? Isn't love the cure for hatred? When love is won, what future is left for race? My own answer: none. Shouldn't we find another language in which to think about the peoples of "the race"?

This brings out an unresolved theoretical issue in *The Future of the Race* without diminishing the urgency of its current practical concerns, nor the apparently perennial nature of America's racial dilemma that generates these concerns. When, in the modern world's most powerful economic, political, and cultural organization, will "black" and "white" become only signposts from the past, indicators of archeological sites showing how far the country has come? When will Frederick Douglass's and Martin Luther King, Jr.'s dreams be more fully realized? Perhaps love and hope require much more; since both are constantly threatened by hate and despair, perhaps we still require specific policies and laws that guarantee for all citizens a minimal level of decency and social worth befitting a civilized society.

Yet even outside the philosophical, theoretical, and practical questions that arise from West's concern with the ethics of the politics of race, Gates's more factual observations are poignant. If West is "a prisoner of hope," the sociological data presented by Gates points to the empirical bases of West's hope. Gates writes, "Race differences and class differentials have been ground together in this country in a crucible of misery and squalor, *in such a way that few of us know where one stops and the other begins.*"[6] I am one of the many who do not know anymore where race stops—or should stop.

Inquiring, like Douglass neither from the "ken of a statesman" nor "the vision of a prophet," one cannot but wonder whether the Negro's race (which, dialectically, is to also say the white's race, understood as identifiable by skin color) would come to *not* matter in America's understanding of its national identity. To entertain this wonder does not mean that one denies the reality or validity of existing racial identities, nor is it to confirm the "end-of-racism" dogma promoted by some conservatives who wish to attack policies of affirmative action or equal opportunity. Rather, my wonder should be seen for what it is: an exercise in hope, like practicing to live in service of a particular future. It is hope, I think, as Douglass dared to nurse in the power of the future to break the shackles of the present; it is the courage to seriously dream about a future where there could be love and care enough for everyone.

PHILOSOPHY OF THE "BLACK" EXPERIENCE

Meanwhile, one cannot but be baffled by the stubborn consistency of anti-African and antiblack racial experience in the modern times. W. E. B. Du Bois, who called his autobiography the "biography of a race," wrote that in the modern imagination to be considered racially black is to be equated to a problem. He recounts movingly his own coming-to-race-consciousness:

> Being a problem is a strange experience. . . . It is in the early days of a rollicking boyhood that the revelation first burst upon [me] . . . when the shadow swept across me. I was a little thing, away up in the hills of New England, where the dark Housatonic winds between Hoosac and Taghkanic to the sea. In a wee wooden schoolhouse, something put it into the boys' and girls' heads to buy gorgeous visiting cards—ten cents a package—and exchange. The exchange was merry, till one girl, a tall newcomer, refused my card—refused it peremptorily, with a glance. Then it

dawned on me with a certain suddenness that I was different
from the others' or like, mayhap, in heart and life and longing,
but shut out from their world by a vast veil. I had thereafter no
desire to tear down that veil, to creep through; I held all beyond
it in common contempt, and lived above it in a region of blue sky
and great wandering shadows. That sky was bluest when I could
beat my mates at examination-time, or beat them at a foot race,
or even beat their stringy heads.[7]

Some have read more than race in this narrative of a rejection, but race *is* the
prism that would structure Du Bois's autobiography—from the early days in
the United States to the last days in Nkrumah's Ghana. In an introduction to
another essay, Du Bois was more careful to explain: "My discussion of the
concept of race, and of the white and colored worlds, are not to be regarded
as digressions from the history of my life; rather my autobiography is a digres-
sive illustration and exemplification of what race has meant in the world in
the nineteenth and eighteenth centuries."[8] The racial life was typical of many
Americans, as Du Bois does not fail to note even of his closest childhood
friends, whose "strife" was not as, as he put it, "fiercely sunny" as his:

Their youth shrunk into tasteless sycophancy, or into silent
hatred of the pale world about them and mocking distrust of
everything white; or wasted itself in a bitter cry, Why did God
make me an outcast and a stranger in mine own house? The
shades of the prison-house closed round about us all: walls strait
and stubborn to the whitest, but relentlessly narrow, tall, and
unscalable to sons of night who might plod darkly on in resignation, or beat unavailing palms against the stone, or steadily, half
hopelessly, watch the streak of the blue above.[9]

The writings of James Baldwin, Langston Hughes, Richard Wright, Toni
Morrison, Alice Walker, Zora Neale Hurston, and so forth, give testimonies
to lives of countless black individuals and groups whose histories would
qualify for a title similar to the one chosen by Du Bois, the "biography of
a race."

In continental Africa, Chinua Achebe recounts what we might call his racial coming-of-age, a Du Boisian moment, you might say:

> I went to a good school modeled on British public schools. I read
> lots of English books there. I read *Treasure Island* and *Gulliver's
> Travels* and *Prisoner of Zenda*, and *Oliver Twist* and *Tom Brown's
> School Days* and such books in their dozens. But I also encoun-
> tered Ryder Haggard and John Buchan and the rest, and their
> "African" books.
>
> I did not see myself as an African to begin with. I took
> sides with the white men against the savages. In other words I
> went through my first level of schooling thinking I was of the
> party of the white man in his hair-raising adventures and narrow
> escapes. The white man was good and reasonable and intelligent
> and courageous. The savages arrayed against him were sinister
> and stupid or, at the most, cunning. I hated their guts.
>
> But a time came when I reached the appropriate age and
> realized that these writers has pulled a fast one on me! I was not
> on Marlowe's boat steaming up the Congo in *Heart of Darkness*.
> I was one of those strange beings jumping up and down on the
> river bank, making horrid faces. Or, if I insisted on the boat-ride,
> then I had to settle perhaps for that "improved specimen," as
> Conrad sarcastically calls him, more absurd than a dog in a pair
> of breeches trying to make out the witchcraft behind the ship's
> water-gauge."[10]

Achebe continued this reflection on race, life, and literature in an expanded,
controversial essay, "Racism in Conrad's *Heart of Darkness*."[11]

During the colonial period in Africa, even otherwise apolitical individuals were easily roused by blatant racial inequalities that were the order of the
day. In Congo, horrific racial acts were part of the normal processes of "paci-
fication" of the natives, and it is widely believed that Kurtz, the lead character in *Heart of Darkness*, was indeed "both a murderous head collector and an
intellectual, an emissary of science and progress." It was the same character—
a painter, a poet, and a journalist—who also wrote a seventeen-page report
to the International Society for the Suppression of Savage Customs, ending

with his scrawl in a shaky hand: "Exterminate all the brutes."[12] Adam Hochschild's recent biography of King Leopold II gives evidence that the character Kurtz was based on Leon Rom. Born in Mons in Belgium, Rom joined the Belgian army at age sixteen, and nine years later found himself a commissioner at Matadi, in charge of the king's notorious squad, the *Force Publique*. Rom's leadership of this brutal army and the cruelty he directly ordered to be visited on Africans disturbed his compatriots, prompting one of them to report to the king that Rom had "the reputation of having killed masses of peoples for petty reasons," and had from the spoils "rigged with human heads" his flower beds. Rom, the report noted, "kept a gallows permanently erected in front of the station." The inspiration for *Heart of Darkness*, it is known, is rooted in Conrad's travel to the Congo in 1890, at the time Rom was committing his racial crimes. Hochschild concluded that "the moral landscape of *Heart of Darkness* and the shadowy figure at its center are the creations not just of a novelist but of an open-eyed observer who caught the spirit of a time and a place with piercing accuracy."[13]

At Congo's independence, when African soldiers, through the instruments of the United Nations, worked to halt further destruction of the people in the emerging postcolonial era, a young Nigerian military engineer stationed in the Bukavu explained how the mood of nationalism that was sweeping through many parts of Africa at the time had inspired them to work to uplift the continent and the condition of the black race. This man, Olusegun Olasanjo, the current president of the Republic of Nigeria, recorded: "We were not satisfied with the second-class status that [the black race] had almost everywhere, including the continent of his birth. We believed then, just as I do now, that the black man everywhere had to struggle and indeed fight to break the shackles of oppression and exploitation, and lift himself above the sub-human level he had been kept for so long."[14]

Women as men, in Africa as in the Diaspora, have left records of their experiences of racial blackness. Who could forget Sojourner Truth's piercing questions:

> The man over there says women need to be helped into the carriages, and lifted over ditches, and to have the best place everywhere. Nobody ever helps me into carriages, and lifted over

ditches, or over mud-puddles, or gives me any best place! And ain't I a woman? Look at me! Look at my arm! I have sloughed, and planted, and gathered into barns, and no man could head me! And ain't I a woman? I could work as much and eat as much as a man—when I could get it—and bear the lash as well! And ain't I a woman? I have borne thirteen children and seen most of all sold off to slavery, and when I cried with my mother's grief, none but Jesus heard me! And ain't I a woman?[15]

More recently black women assert rights to reconstruct black women "her-stories," a critique of history that involves coming to terms with not just invisibility but also with explicitly destructive stereotypes: "We have . . . been outraged by the ways in which [history] has made us visible, when it has chosen to see us. History had constructed our sexuality and our femininity as deviating from those qualities with which white women, as the prize object of the western world, have been endowed. We have also been defined in less than human terms."[16]

In their diversity, blacks across place and time and gender speak of modes of modern existence in black—a mode of being characterized by highly specific encounters with antiblack racism, in intellectual and practical life. Authors, politicians, soldiers, and farmers—all evoke from their various lives and professions references that lead to stories of encounters with racism. The defining moments of this modern racial experience embed themselves in events that must include not only the racial dimensions of African colonization but also the uprooting of Africans from Africa to America into plantation slavery; in the struggles against social and political subordination in various locations; and in the partial achievements of freedom.

Could modern African philosophy possibly remain *African* if it ignores these universal racial dimensions of African and black history—the black bondage and black freedom? Like modern music, modern African philosophy must, I think, find ways to express the distinctly modern "black" sensibility and modes of experiences in Africa as out of it, in African and black languages and idioms. African and black music, for example, show a capacity both to "tell the story" of black lives as well as bear the dimensions of the extralinguistic which, in the case of African Americans, Paul Gilroy had called the "slave sublime." What, one must ask, in and of the philosophical traditions, are the philosophical equivalents of soukous, reggae, blues, or jazz? African and black philosophers, too, draw from the masters' *mitumba*, used or discarded instruments, from which they blow new songs of sorrows and freedom. Does it matter if their songs sound like something that had never before been heard?

There is no doubt that modern African and black philosophy, like the music, is born of struggle—in the discomforts of racial slavery, colonial and (post)colonial crises, and in a history of existential anguish that comes with experience of common racism. But these, precisely, are materials for philo- sophical reflection if philosophy, in general, originates and develops out of contexts in which serious questions arise about the adequacy of one's most cherished sense of self, one's beliefs about oneself and about the world— including beliefs about race and racial experiences. Race and the historical structures of racism are not simply about incidental facts of one's life, like height and eye color; they are significant features of our modern moral- identities, and involve issues that touch on personal relationships, the manner in which we regard ourselves and treat others, and the happiness and unhappiness that form the emotional contours of our practical lives. If philosophy's main task is to help one to ground one's beliefs and to justify them, if philosophy can critique and shed light on both legitimate and ille- gitimate structures that govern modern societies and histories, then this phi- losophy and its critical activities must concern itself with the fabric of our moral and social selves, including the moral structures of our racialized lives.

PHILOSOPHY AND THE "WHITE" EXPERIENCE

Many critics have questioned—in most cases with good reason—the validity of Charles Mill's suggestion that there exists a white racial social discourse that frames for exclusion blacks, as nonpersons, from what is therefore a white moral imagination.[17] But beyond reproach is Mill's observation that race and racialism powerfully operate to both allow and constrain morally consequential social behaviors in peoples. In the United

States, for example, race matters when it comes to the morally significant issues of how, when, and where a government intervenes to alleviate poverty, provide opportunities for education and jobs, or promote peace and enforce justice. Internationally, racial factors could hardly be left out of any significant discussions of major issues in modern diplomacy and war. Until recently the presumed identity of the United States as a "white" country, or of Europeans as a "white" people, was ideologically forged with the help of philosophers who provided often transcendental arguments for the construction of imaginary racial totalities. In the *Phenomenology and the Crisis of the Philosophy*, for example, Husserl speaks of Europeans as a race in a sublime, mystical, language:

> In the spiritual sense, it is clear that to Europe belong the English dominions, the United States, etc., but not, however, the Eskimos or Indians, or the Gypsies. Clearly, the title Europe designates the unity of a spiritual life and a creative activity—with all its aims, interests, cares, and troubles, with its plans, its establishments, its institutions. Therein individual human beings work in a variety of societies, on different levels, in families, stocks, nations, all intimately joined together in spirit and, as I said, in the unity of one spiritual image. This should stamp on persons, groups, and all their cultural accomplishments an all-unifying character.[18]

This mystical and spiritualized conception of race, complete with a divine mission—a mission whose fulfillment is as fixed as an "eternal pole," offers a blueprint of white racial boundaries, the contours of which defy common geographical sense. This is a conception of a white Europe that Husserl preferred to call a "philosophico-historical idea."[19] "The spiritual *telos* of European Man," he said, "in which is included the particular *telos* of separate nations and of individual human beings, lies in infinity; it is an infinite idea, toward which in secret the collective spiritual becoming, so to speak, strives. Just as in development it becomes a conscious *telos*, so too it becomes necessarily practical as a goal of the will, and thereby is introduced a new, a higher stage of development that is guided by norms, by normative ideas."[20]

From this Europe's "extraordinary teleology," and out of the racialized "spirit"—a spirit presumed "innate *only* in our Europe"[21]—is clearly demarcated the nonwhite Europeans: Africans, gypsies, Indians, and others. It seems, in fact, that *this* Europe constitutes itself through precisely the act of self-demarcation from those it considers racially Other and strange.

In answering the question "How is the spiritual image of Europe to be characterized?" Husserl reiterated what he had asserted earlier: Europe racially does not coincide with "Europe geographically, as it appears on maps, as though Europeans were to be in this way confined to the circle of those who live together in this territory."[22] Thus, in this racial, spiritual sense, Europe is wherever Europeans are, wherever they occupy space, or settle to reproduce white European forms of existence. But even in the physical dispersion, the presumed inner spiritual *unity* of Europeanness is thought to remain "consistent." The unitary consistency is possible because "no matter how inimical the European nations may be toward each other," writes Husserl, "still they have a special inner affinity of spirit that permeates all of them and transcends their national differences. It is a sort of fraternal relationship that gives us the consciousness of being at home in this circle." Like Pentheus's Other in Euripides's *Bacchae*, those outside of Europe's self-defined circle—Africans or, to stay with Husserl's example, Indians—are familiar ("sympathetically penetrable") yet must remain "strange to us."[23]

The practical effects of this Eurocentric and white philosophical teleology—or, depending on how you look at it, the historical intentions and practices to which this philosophy plays as an accompaniment—is not as hidden as Husserl's political mysticism and therefore easy to discern. When a philosophy is so clearly racially ideological, the material implications are transparent and detectable, especially to the eyes of those against which the ideology, like a double-barreled gun, is aimed. For centuries Africa and Asia bore the burden of Europe's racial self-image; it is as if the racial purity and consequence claimed for Europe were purchased by the impurity and inconsequence that Europe projects onto the brown-skinned peoples of the world.

In a 1985 study by Edem Kodjo, at the time secretary general of the

Husserl

Organization of African Unity, the cost of Europe's "penetration" of not just India but a full half of habitable earth was given physical measures:

> The map of the world such as it is today is the result of the bru-
> tal force of arms, the force that enabled European nations to
> spread out over half of the lands on earth. The races of European
> stock are today the masters of the immense territory that stretches
> from the Atlantic to Kimchaka (some twenty-seven million
> square kilometers); of the entire American territory (forty-two
> million square kilometers); of Australasia (eight million square
> kilometers); and the Antarctic (thirteen million square kilome-
> ters). This is the concretization of Europe overseas. . . . Out of the
> hundred and sixty million kilometers of the world's land, three-
> fifths belong to the Europeans. There is also the fact that the
> European powers still dominate in the other two-fifths where
> they control the destinies of other peoples through an unsus-
> pected system of political relations.[24]

It is this Europe that Husserl claims to be a racial unity; and his spiritual conception of this unity answers, *avant la lèttre*, Kodjo's rhetorical question: "Would it be unrealistic to talk about a Euroamerican 'transideological' world that combines the potentialities of the superpowers and the middle powers, on the sole basis of the racial factor?"[25]

In Husserl's understanding, however, race was more of a metaphysical fact than a political one; whiteness for him was a metaphysical "vague" form of "feeling," a feeling aesthetically informed by the transcendental imagina-tion, so that we know "even in its vagueness" that the racial idea is philo-sophically "correct"; race notion, he says, is the idea that "thoroughly . . . controls the changes in the European image, [giving to this image] a sense of direction and purpose." Furthermore, as an "emotional guide," this idea of race and whiteness announces itself not just presently but also as "antici-pated," which, by orienting actions, becomes "guaranteed as certainty."[26] Without doubt, this guarantee of unity is redeemed in Europe's dialectical relation to its assumed "opponents."

Albert Memmi was one of the first critics to illustrate that racism was part of colonialism throughout the world.[27] Race, symbolically, represented the salient relation uniting the colonialist and the colonized, as race was (1) the marker through which was thematized the supposedly unbridgeable gulf between the cultures of the colonialist and the colonized; and (2) the medium through which the established difference was exploited to the benefit of the colonialist. Given (1) and (2), race—and racism—became standards of facts. As if by reflex, "the colonialist stresses those things which keep him separate, rather than emphasizing that which might contribute to the foundation of joint community. In those differences, the colonized is always degraded and the colonialist finds justification for rejecting the subjects."[28] An argument cultivated in a colonial racial relation might go like this: Europeans conquered the world because their nature was predisposed to do so, while non-Europeans were colonized because their nature condemned them to be so.

The ahistorical conceptual gap between the white and the nonwhite, a gap made possible in the idea of race, also guaranteed that the European who adopts or adapts to a non-European culture is considered acting not "properly" European, but instead out of self-misunderstanding. At least this was what Husserl must have meant when he spoke of Indians and the relationship that ought to exist between Indian and European cultures. Although a multitude of peoples divided by class, religion, and language, Indians—Husserl thought—find only "home" and no strangeness among themselves (which enables "India" to appear as a totality, in a binary relation to Europe); then he characterized this relationship that exists between Europe and India, related by "fellowship and strangeness," as a "fellowship" sustained only in a one-way traffic of culture from Europe to India. While Indians "Europeanize" themselves, Europeans never "Indianize" themselves:

> Historical humanity does not always divide itself in the same way according to this category [of fellowship and strangeness]. We get a hint of that right in our own Europe. Therein lies something unique, which all other human groups, too, feel with regard to us, something that, apart from all considerations of expediency, becomes a motivation for them . . . constantly to Europeanize

themselves, whereas we, if we understand ourselves properly, will never, for example, Indianize ourselves.[29]

Postcolonial theorists of hybridity, or sociologists and historical theorists of the Black Atlantic, who pay attantion to and respect evidence from everyday experience, could hardly agree with Husserl's ahistorical view of a culturally and a racially pure, "proper," white Europe—whether in the geographical or cultural heart of Europe itself or in other parts of the world where Husserl thinks the racially chauvinistically defined European spirit had taken roots. Husserl was proclaiming in transcendental philosophy the colonial effects—and affects—that Meemi had politically and incisively theorized: Without room for ambiguity, the colonizer believes that "This place, the people here, the customs of this country are always inferior—by virtue of an inevitable and pre-established order."[30] Husserl's uncritical concept of Europe, especially in its relation to peoples he considered of non-European stock, I think, bears the mark of this pre-established order.

PROSPECTS FOR A NEW PHILOSOPHY OF AFRICA AND ITS DIASPORA

In the spring of 2000 the African Studies Center at the University of Pennsylvania organized a conference entitled "Transcending Traditions: African, African-American and Afro-Caribbean Studies in the 21st Century." Some of us accepted the invitation to participate in the conference because it appeared that few themes in black studies commanded at that time an equivalent level of provocation. The subject matter was clearly topical, for two weeks earlier there was a gathering at Rutgers' Center for African Studies around the theme "Reconfiguring African Studies," with subthemes such as: "Progressive Pedagogues: Teaching/Studying/ Rethinking Africa in American Universities," "Telling the Truth about Africa in America," or "Taking Risks: Innovative Approaches to Teaching about Africa." Also, farther south, and a few weeks before the Rutgers conference, the faculty of government and international relations at the Universidad Externado in Bogotá, Colombia, organized a conference whose topics bear on both the centuries-old and present-day African presence in Latin America: "Procesos de Paz en Africa; une experiencia para Colombia." These academic conferences came on the heels of more politically oriented assemblies of Africans and African-descended peoples in the United States, including the Washington Summit on Africa, an event that drew alike traditional and nontraditional African activists, from Randal Robinson to vote-hunters George W. Bush and Al Gore. Clearly, at the dawn of this century, "Africa" was on our minds. It seemed that we wished to envision, if we hadn't done so already, new meanings of, and for, Africa, meanings constructed and imbued with more progressive images for action and transformation. Would this not be one of the meanings of the University of Pennsylvania Africanists yearning for transcendence—transcendence of earlier meanings of Africa?

The idea of a transatlantic and transnational Africa or Africanity, linked by the politics and cultures of peoples of Africa and of African descent, is indeed a seductive one—it has always been. Current efforts to achieve such political and identity goals are reminiscent of the eighteenth and nineteenth centuries, when intellectuals and activists from Delaney and Garvey and Blyden to Du Bois and Nkrumah and Padmore sought to establish cultural and political institutions that would transform and transcend not just the imperial and colonial yoke choking the continent but also the limitations imposed by the systems of slavery and racism on black lives in Europe and the Americas.

Unlike the eighteenth and nineteenth centuries, however, current efforts are marked as much by black suffering as by hopes and opportunities available in a world that has become, beyond what could have been imagined two hundred or one hundred years ago, increasingly global, politically, economically, and culturally. The existence of these global opportunities for re/construction of personal and social identities are far-reaching and reflects itself, in the U.S. academia, by the number of departments devoted to Africana studies, and by the number of university presses and trade publishing houses devoting series either exclusively to Africana thought or, more generally, to studies of postcolonial conditions. Some of the most thematic articulation of these developments, in addition to Paul Gilroy's *The*

Black Atlantic, include Hazel Carby's *Cultures in Babylon: Black Britain and African America* and Paget Henry's *Caliban's Reason*, a work more regional in focus but most revealing about the ways in which the Caribbean in itself embodies both the conflicts and the opportunities for transnational identities. These books share points of views on Africa and the black experience that position the authors against what Manthia Diawara might have called African or African-American particularity. The books project a new temper that reimagines the "African" in a field richer than, and beyond, mere geographic reference to include Afro-Americans, Afro–Latin Americans, Afro-Caribbeans, and Afro-Europeans. Modern African identities, the authors would argue, are forged as hybrid, creole, multiple, and ever-changing. What needs to be transcended, from this perspective, is the kind of Afro-nationalism that prevents one from affirming the intrinsically mobile and dispersed reality of what it means to be culturally African and racially modern and black. *Cultures in Babylon* notes, for example, that the essays collected under the title

> span eighteen years of . . . transatlantic journeying from the United Kingdom to the United States. I arrived in America as a black Briton of Welsh and Jamaican parentage searching for an audience for *The Empire Strikes Back: Race and Racism in Seventies Britain*, written while I was a member of the Race and Politics group at the Centre for Contemporary Cultural studies in Birmingham, England. The response was not gratifying. The irrational rationale of publishing companies was patiently explained to this obviously ignorant European: the majority of African Americans were totally unaware of the existence of black communities in the UK; those who might be interested in such phenomenon would be African American; but African Americans did not constitute a sufficient reading public to warrant the publication of *Empire* in the USA.

"It is strange," Carby admits, "to write these words while being Chair of African American Studies at Yale University." She attributes this good fortune to Charles Davis, who was a "founding father" of the field of

African American studies, and whose vision of the field was "broad and international."[31]

The key to transcending particularistic traditions, therefore, requires cultivating broad and international perspectives in African and black studies. This is not merely academic; it is also political. A broad and international vision in the study of Africa, African America, Afro–Latin America, and the Afro-Caribbean, or the experiences of African and African-descended peoples in Europe, is crucial to counterbalancing the nativistic and nationalistic tendencies that prevent one from realizing the full scale of our modern experiences, hem in one's politics, and thwart the freedom to creatively construct more relevant Afro-identities. The question one must ask, however, is this: Does there exist now an adequately universal perspective capable of encompassing the hybrid, creolized, and dynamic character of the exilic African and black cultures—cultures without "home," cultures in Babylon?

Ironically, to successfully think globally and internationally requires one to think, quite consistently, locally. To have a broad or international view, in this case, could not mean to adopt a view from nowhere; it is rather an invitation to pay close attention to particulars, or a series of particulars. The idea of race and racism borne and suffered by Africans, for example, would be thought of not in terms of one category that captures all experiences of racism or racial identities, but rather in terms of race and racisms in the plural. It is also to pay attention to the always changing nature of racial experiences as well as African and Afro-identities. Pan-Africanism may be, as a commentator put it, "a cultural and political phenomenon that regards Africa, Africans, and African-descendants abroad as a unit";[32] but one must also recognize the different local historical contexts of, for instance, Nkrumah's statement that "independence of Ghana would be meaningless unless it was linked with the total liberation of the continent," and Garvey's first New York meeting of the then Jamaica-based Universal Negro Improvement Association, at which a "Declaration of Right of the Negro Peoples of the World" was adopted. The relative independence of the pan-Africanism of the Diaspora from the pan-Africanism of the continent is something that could hardly be ignored.

Think of a most recent example of this local differences, where Gilroy explained: "In opposition to both . . . nationalist or ethnically absolute approaches [to black experience], I want to develop a suggestion that cultural historians could take the Atlantic as one single, complex unit of analysis in their discussions of the modern world and use it to produce an explicitly transnational and intercultural perspective. . . . [S]hips were the living means by which the points within that Atlantic world were joined. They were mobile elements that stood for the shifting spaces in between the fixed places that they connected."[33] In relation to this quest for "one, single," even if "complex" point of view, consider the following observations by V. Y. Mudimbe: "A space is a construct. It is a theoretical articulation that claims to render present operations or, put simply, the reality of a place. . . . A space is, to say the least, a second order practice of life and human experience. This second degree organization, by its very being, considerably alters and transforms the primary logic in which it claims to root itself."[34] How does one construct new spaces and places without effecting, to use the cliché, "black on black" violence?

Cases from the past are instructive. When he explained his aspiration for Africa, Edward Wilmot Blyden said:

> Where now stand unbroken forests would spring up towns and villages, with their schools and churches . . . the natives would be taught the arts of civilization—that their energies would be properly directed . . . their prejudices would disappear . . . there would be rapid and important revulsion from the practices of heathenism, and a radical change in their social condition—the glorious principles of the Christian civilization would diffuse themselves throughout those benighted communities. Oh! that our people will take this matter into serious consideration, and think of the great privilege of kindling in the depths of the moral and spiritual gloom of Africa a glorious light—of causing the wilderness and the solitary place to be glad—the desert to bloom and blossom as the rose—and the whole land to be converted into a garden of the Lord.[35]

Blyden sees in Africa no villages and towns, only forests; the prejudices he saw were only African prejudices; and the glory and light that would descend on the new Africa are of only European origins. Martin Delaney, another influential cultural worker in and for Africa, also looked up only to Europe. "To England and France," he wrote, "we should look for sustenance, and the people of these two nations—as they would have everything to gain from such an adventure and eventual settlement of the EASTERN COAST OF AFRICA—the opening of an immense trade being the consequence."[36] Better than Blyden, Delaney suggests more explicitly reasons why England and France might have wished that Africa look up to them. The point, however, is not to inventory the easily verifiable costs to Africa of its various "trades" with European countries over five centuries—trades that are political, economic, and cultural. It is however useful to remind ourselves, cultural and intellectual workers that we are, of Wole Soyinka's counsel in his dated but still useful *Myth, Literature, and African World*: "There is nothing to choose . . . between the colonial mentality of an Ajayi Crowther, West Africa's first black bishop, who groveled before his white missionary superiors in a plea for patience and understanding of his 'backward, heathen, brutish' brothers, and the new black ideologues who are embarrassed by statements of self-apprehension by the new 'ideologically backward' Africans. Both suffer from externally induced fantasies of redemptive transformation in the image of alien masters. Both are victims of the doctrine of self-negation."[37] Whether therefore it is coming from a Mudimbe or a Soyinka, what one notices is not an argument for pernicious particularisms. It is rather the issue of determining whether the primary visions and ideologies that underwrite our global and transnational aspirations are truly less prejudicial and less antiblack than those previously proposed by European intellectuals who wanted us, children and devils that they thought we are, to look up to Europe's supposedly exclusive maturity and divinity.

How do we transcend the binaries—forest/schools, heathen/Christian, native/foreign, barbarism/civilization, prejudices/knowledge, moral and spiritual gloom/glorious enlightenment, desert/the garden of the Lord—all of which are synonyms for a primordial binary: Africa/Europe? This binary structures African and black identities in different ways, at different places.

In the Caribbean, Paget Henry explains,

> The process of racialization turned Africans into blacks, Indians
> into browns, and Europeans into whites. The process was most
> extreme between blacks and whites. In the origin narratives, sto-
> ries of conquest, civilizing missions, and other legitimizing dis-
> courses of European imperialism, the blackness of the Africans
> became their primary defining feature. In these narratives, color
> eclipsed culture. The latter became more visible as Africans were
> transformed into Negroes and niggers in the minds of
> Europeans. This racial violence shattered the cultural founda-
> tions of the African self, causing the latter to implode. Race
> became the primary signifier of Europeans and Africans and of
> the differences between them.[38]

As a result of this process of racialization of cultures, white and black
Caribbean identities became rigidly bounded, for the binary white/black
generates and sustains other purported qualitative differences: rational/irra-
tional, mind/body, spirit/ flesh, and so forth.

The historical effects of the myth and stereotype of the "wild" African,
and the scars left by this in the psyche of the Afro-Caribbean, African
American, Afro–Latin American,[39] or Afro-European cannot be overesti-
mated. Even our best minds are thrown into panic and anxiety at the point
of an inability to imagine positive identifications with Africa or things
African. James Baldwin, for example, never successfully overcame what he
liked to call his "African conundrum," an affliction that might for some
elicit just a little more than pity. In Baldwin's words:

> The most crucial time in my own development came when I was
> forced to recognize that I was a kind of bastard of the West;
> when I followed the line of my past I did not find myself in
> Europe, but in Africa. And this meant that in some subtle way,
> in a really profound way I brought to Shakespeare, Bach,
> Rembrandt, to the stones of Paris, to the cathedral at Chartres,
> and to the Empire State Building, a special attitude. These were
> not really my creations, they did not contain my history; I might

search in them in vain for ever for any reflection of myself; I was an interloper. At the same time I had no other heritage which I could possibly hope to use. I had certainly been unfitted for the jungle or the tribe.[40]

It might appear cruel to explain that this conundrum exists because one sees in Africa nothing but "jungles" and "tribes"—perhaps of gorillas rather than historical beings. The conundrum exists because Baldwin overlooked some of the largest sources of Europe's civilization. Speaking about these, the Reverend Dr. Palmer of New Orleans, more than a century before, had explained: "The enriching commerce which has built the splendid cities and marble palaces of England as well as America has been largely established upon the products of Southern soil; and the blooms upon Southern fields, gathered by black hands, have fed the spindles and looms of Manchester and Birmingham not less than that of Lawrence and Lowell."[41] In the same spirit, Thabo Mbeki, the president of South Africa, recently remarked that much is known—rarely talked about—of the economic benefits to the USA and to Europe from more than three centuries of their involvement in the African slave trade.[42] King Leopold II rendered Belgium monumental thanks to Congolese rubber and the brutality of forced and uncompensated African labor.[43] Eric Williams, Walter Rodney, and even some colonial officers such as the British Fredrick Lugard[44] incisively document the modern phenomenon of Europe's and America's self-enrichment on the back of African natural and human resources.

As a goal, in academically rethinking Africa, African America, Afro–Latin America, or Afro-Europe it makes sense, for obvious reasons, to refuse the invitation to render Africa and the reality of the "blackness" of its descendants even more invisible. For example, it is easy to say, today, that race is a "social construct"; but it is harder to remember a complementary truth: race is also *historically* constructed. It might take longer to dismantle the historical implications of the negative enframings of Africanity than it would take to aesthetically rearrange its black present. One cannot say with certainty how deep or shallow is the impact of centuries of denial of African humanity, under the fear of and perhaps contempt for the color black. But one can understand the value of building bridges of strength and resistance across the diversity of experiences of this strange modern relationship of Africa/Europe, white/black belonging and exclusion. Africanity could function as an idea encoding the reality of exile and migrancy, of identity as a work-in-process.

PHILOSOPHIZING THE UNIVERSAL AND THE PARTICULAR

A recent contribution in African philosophy promised to deliver a universal basis for African identity—a basis that would point the way to a common universal humanity rather than to our racial or cultural difference. Kwasi Wiredu's *Cultural Universals and Particulars* is a response to postmodern Western and African cultural relativists whose ardent commitment to racial and ethnic identity politics, he believes, leads to a forgetting that there are universals of humanity, and that there exist transracial and transcultural biological resources through which a universal humanity can be theoretically established and defended. For Wiredu: "In so far as it might be thought . . . that there is a necessary incompatibility between the perspectives of universalism and particularism, the standpoint of these essays is that the impression is illusory."[45] The collection of essays gathered as *Cultural Universals and Particulars* also specific in pointing out the bases upon which the apparent mutual exclusivity of "universalism" and "particularism" would be shown to be false. Wiredu asserts:

> Without [cultural] universals intercultural communication must be impossible. The case is developed first by deploying considerations about the nature of meaning presupposed by the very possibility of human communication. . . . Then . . . I continue the argument by specifying some cognitive and ethical universals. . . . There is an implicit biological orientation, the underlying idea being that the possibility of cultural universals is predicated on our common biological identity as a species of bipeds.[46]

By this orientation Wiredu presumes that cultural particulars are rarely in doubt, as there is hardly anyone who would seriously deny particularities of human cultures. It is more difficult to make the case for transcultural, universal laws of thought and conduct—hence the clear focus on combating relativistic and ethnocentric interpretations of humanity that deny a culture its—what wiredu assumed—*inherent* universality.

The best arguments, in the first part of the book, are devoted to theoretically isolating elements of cultures that are cross-culturally valid. For example, when Wiredu writes about biological foundations of systems of thought and conduct ("The Biological Foundation of Universal Norms"), he asserts that humans are "part of 'nature,'" by which he intends to reject the Cartesian dualistic theory of the person. Relying on an analysis of Akan languages, in particular two aphorisms, *Aboa onipa* ("Person, the animal") and *Akwada Nyame* ("Child as God"),[47] we are presented with the argument that the human being is an entity whose nature extends, in a continuum, from the animal (biologic) to "all the spirals of human potentialities" (God?). When he tries to show the universality of this Akan bio-spiritual wisdom, Wiredu relies, notably, on the philosophical works of Dewey and Hume, from which Wiredu draws the conclusion that the "law of non-contradiction" is a prime example of universal norm regulating the human mind.[48] But the crucial objective is that Wiredu wishes to show how this universal law of contradiction is also a biologically grounded fact for all humans. Relying on Dewey, this picture of genetic foundations of logic, which govern the law of contradiction, was drawn:

> Organic life is essentially an interaction with the environment in which there is a continual process of the expenditure of energy and its recovery. In the simpler organisms this interaction generally takes the form of direct contact, but in the more complex organisms, possessing distance receptors and endowed with special organs of motion, this process, which might be called one of trying to resolve a tension in the environment, takes on a serial character in which the earlier phases prepare the way for the later. Here talk of stimulus and response begins to make sense: A pattern develops of initial tension and exploratory activities for reintegration with the environment which modifies organic structures and conditions future interactions.

A series of successful and therefore stable adaptive "modifications," according to Dewey and now Wiredu, constitute "habit," and habits in this regard form the biological basis of organic learning. In the formation of habits, given "the time lag between tension and resolution, the exploratory activities, perforce, acquire the dimension of prevision, which together with the need to interact with kindred organisms—a cultural circumstance—gives rise to language and communication and thereby to the possibility of a logic of discourse."[49]

In order to supplement Dewey's genetic account of learning, Wiredu appeals to Hume's statement that "in all reasonings from experience"—in other words, in all logical judgments drawn on the basis of experience— "there is a step taken by the mind which is not supported by argument."[50] Wiredu is of the opinion that this preargument "foundation" of reasoning is no other than biologic; he says: "the trait of the human mind that is in question here is a natural, nay, biological one."[51] Drawing Hume and Dewey together to clinch his argument, Wiredu states that this biological human trait also naturally inheres to custom, and therefore cultures. According to him the biological trait "is found in custom, [in] that ingrained tendency of the mind, which alone moves us" to logical reasoning. In conclusion, the "present formulation is, in fact, best seen as a kind of definition of empirical reason. It expresses, at the level of the conscious cognition, an intellectual norm from which the evolutionary principle of custom provides a biological basis."[52]

This biosociology also informs Wiredu's thesis on cross-cultural communication. In "A Philosophical Perspective on the Concept of Human Communication," for example, he succinctly defines communication as "the transference of thought content from one person or group of persons to another."[53] He explains: "On the suggested view of mind, a thought content is an aspect of brain state. It is an empirical fact that patterns of brain processes can be set off by socially directed stimuli. . . . The transference of thought-content, from one person to another, then, is the inducement by the one in the other of some brain states through appropriate stimuli."[54] Such "stimuli" are, of course, conceptualized as possible by way of the Dewey-Hume cognitive naturalism. This is evident from the theory of "mind" that the above passage alluded to. Wiredu explains:

> By and large communication makes the mind. That, of course, is
> from a developmental point of view and is without prejudice to
> the fact that it is minds that make communication. Two basic
> factors are involved in communication, namely, conceptualiza-
> tion and articulation. The power to conceptualize is only a devel-
> opment/refinement of the capacity to react to stimuli in a
> law-like manner which is present in even amoebic forms of life.[55]

The connection between stimuli as both biocommunication and mind (interpretation of stimuli) therefore follows, according to Wiredu, rules both
instinctive and cultural. The instinctive rules form the basis of the qualities
universal to all human animals regardless of culture, while the cultural rules
form the basis of the local variations and particularities of cultures.

Wiredu thinks that "in so far as one can speak here of an analogue of
communication," the reality of universality at the level of instinct "take[s]
the form of instinctive gestures and noises, instinctually"—and therefore
universally—"standardized." Then, following Hume's demarche, he also
concludes that "the humble origins of the rules of conceptualization and
articulation which are distinctive of human communication"—in other
words, the functions of the "mind"—have to be derived from prior instinctive standards, so that human behavior is therefore governed by both
instinct and culture—the crux of Wiredu's thesis.

> Because of the element of instinct we can be sure of a certain
> species-distinctive uniformity in human actions and reactions.
> But because of the element of culture, that is, of habit, instruc-
> tion, and conscious thought, there will naturally be plenty of
> room for variation. The first consideration accounts for the pos-
> sibility of objectivity and universality in the standards of thought
> and action in our species, the second for various degrees of rela-
> tivity and subjectivity; the point, however, is that what unifies us
> is more fundamental than what differentiates us.[56]

The idea that the "universal" that provides for humans a "common"
humanity is stronger than the "particulars" that differentiate them is, then,
the central tenet in both Wiredu's anthropology and epistemology. In

addition, the political intent of *Cultural Universals and Particulars* is also clearly stated:

> While, on the one hand, there is unprecedented intensification of informational interaction among different cultures of the world, there is, on the other hand, increasing skepticism regarding the very foundation of such discourse; namely, the possibility of universal canons of thought and action. By a kind of (not necessarily explicit) self-critical echoing from the earlier intellectual self-aggrandize-ment of the West, some very articulate movements of thought therein—notably, but not only, postmodernism—are displaying extreme abstemiousness with respect to claims of universality.

Cultural Universals and Particulars seeks therefore to combat postmodern skepticism vis-à-vis traditional modern philosophy's claim to universality—even while Wiredu welcomes the reduced arrogance of a previously univer-salized Western particularity. The stake in favor of universalism and against particularism is unmistakable, and the real targets are both postmodern Western thinkers and the ex-colonized African or black intellectuals, espe-cially the latter group, who, "in seeking to redefine their self-identity," are insisting on "particulars—their own previously unrespected or neglected particularities—rather than universals."[57]

While it is pointless to reject the idea that humanity is shared across cultures (who could engage in such a denial?), the political positioning that Wiredu advances as an alternative to African or black philosophy's racial and cultural-nationalist claims to particularity (and I distinguish these African and black claims from the voguish and ironic protests of postmod-ernism against its own high modernity),[58] it is Wiredu's position on the black cultural nationalist claims that needs to be further examined. This examination could be initiated in two ways. First, I attempt an immanent critique of the sociobiology (or, more strictly, bioculturalism) that informs Wiredu's universalistic humanist politics; second, I inquire if African and black philosophy could develop or has already developed a more congenial and better historical relationship to postmodernism, one that would intrin-sically constitute an alternative to Wiredu's most stringent and, in my view, confusing biological requirements for any affirmation of the universal.

The basis upon which Wiredu predicated the possibility of a common and universal humanity is, in the end, biology. Because the human body is susceptible to environmental stimuli, it reacts to regulate its biological equilibrium along set patterns—patterns set most likely because the constituting behavior had proved successful as an adaptive mechanism in past circumstances. It is this pattern, the practical behavioral "memory" of human bodies, that, Wiredu claims, is regulated by instinct. While instinct thus grounds human biological universals, it is culture—habits and customs, regulated by cognitive learning—that accounts for the differences among humans. Some of the conceptual problems associated with this picture of the human being are as follows: What is "instinct"? We know that there are "bodies" and "instinctive" events—cathectical processes; but do we "know" (a) what (the universal) instinct *in itself* consists of?; and (b) if we think we know, is this not also knowledge that, we were told, is accessible to humans only through cultural habits and customs which, Wiredu also warned, differentiate?

To get the import of (a), one need not go further than retrace the steps in Wiredu's arguments back to their sources in Dewey and Hume, and especially Hume. When Hume speaks of that which makes judgments about conjunction or cause and effect in "experimental reasoning" possible, he provides no positive identification of a *thing* responsible for this particular "natural" mechanism. Hume's language is extremely vague: "What is the foundation of all conclusions from experience"? he asks, and then answeres: "In all reasoning from experience there is a *step* taken by the mind which is not supported by argument." What is this "step"? Is the word worth more than its value as a metaphoric expression? Does it point to a thing in natural or *biological* reality? The negative nature of the rest of Hume's defense of his statement does not help to answer these questions; he simply says that the "step"—whatever it is—is *not* supported by argument. What is it supported by, then? What is it that is supposedly "there" but cannot be positively accounted for in language—except to allude to it in the negative, as absence? Does Wiredu wish to force himself—and Hume—into some sort of negative theology or back to metaphysics?

Wiredu, on his own, does not illuminate the darkness of the "step" he points out as existing in Hume's thought. His later comments on Hume help matters along, but only to a point. By insisting that the so-called step not captured or supported by argument is a "biological one," Wiredu, drawing this time from Dewey, refers to it as instinct and "stimuli" of organic life. He explains:

> Organic life is essentially an interaction with the environment in which there is continual process of the expenditure of energy and its recovery. In the simpler organisms this interaction generally takes the form of direct contact, but in the more complex organism, possessing distance receptors and endowed with special organs of motion, this process, which might be called one of trying to resolve a tension with the environment, takes on a serial character in which earlier phases prepare the way for the later. Here talk of stimulus and response begins to make sense.

But then note where, precisely, "stimulus and response" starts to make sense: only when there "develops" a "pattern" regularizing a process of "reintegration," a process that simultaneously "modifies" past and "conditions" future organic structure of the animal, a modification and conditioning that constitutes what had earlier been called habit, the basis of learning. In this biocognitive schema, where does the supposedly universal biological "instinct" start and finish and the "habitual" cognitive processes of a particular culture begin and end? Or: should we also assume—as does, for example, Noam Chomsky—a nonbiological "universal grammar" common to all cultures? Wiredu does not pursue this point. And just as well, because it wouldn't help his case. Why?

Because—and this in regard to our question (b)—whether in Wiredu or Chomsky, arguing from biology or mathematical "nature" is not the best strategy for developing persuasive responses to the challenges posed by a politically ironic and epistemologically relativistic postmodernism, or African and black racial nationalism or transnational racial identity politics—a politics that, clearly, responds to historical situations of antiblack racism, capitalist exploitation, and experience of political marginalization. My disagreement with Wiredu's strategy could be summarized as follows:

there is no question that, biologically, the differences among humans are very little; but the same very little differences are always already political—or at least politicized. When Wiredu writes that "the possibility of cultural universals is predicated on our common biological identity as a species of bipeds," perhaps one needs to remind him that the Irish fight among themselves in the North not because some of them have six legs while others have two; the Tutsis and the Hutu kill each other not because some have iron legs while others have the real biological thing; and the Igbos sometimes fight with the Hausas not on account of skin color. Likewise, what causes "racial" conflict is not the color of skin per se, but the *interpretations* that seem to always precondition our perceptions of skin color. What matters, it seems to me, is not the green, blue, or brown eyes; the long or the short hair; the Oxford or the Cockney accent on the English language; and so forth, but the meanings—the social and cultural values—that we attach to these realities even at the moments of encountering them. They are these meanings and values, and how we negotiate them, as we must, not the "biological" facts behind or in front of them, that ultimately determine how we live and die—alas, biologically—with others.

Instead of an appeal to biology via an obscure metaphysical notion of "step" or even a patent appeal to biological genes, it seems to me that the best answer to a politically debilitating postmodern relativism and misguided black nationalism or African identity politics must be sought in a stronger commitment to *history*.[59] A commitment to modern history in general and to an open-textured understanding of black racial memory—not a biological racial essence—provides a sound basis for philosophical criticism of black history as well as a basis for an ethically informed economic and cultural critique of antiblack racism. This is a tradition of critique best exemplified in several existing traditions of African and African-American philosophy, including some of Wiredu's most recent essays (one of which bears the title "Decolonizing the Mind"). This is a form of critique that demasks and demystifies the false universalism of modern Western philosophy while protecting, on principled historical and ethical grounds, the claims we make for the legitimacy of politically and institutionally marginal kinds of philosophy that some of us have chosen to practice.

In recent times, Alain Locke's and Cornel West's works exemplify this tradition of historically informed black philosophical criticism. Each thinker workes from a strong historical sense of philosophy, and a strong philosophical sense of history, and provides creative responses to Euro-American postmodernism as well as black racial nationalism. Each exhibits toward these traditions an appropriation/resistance posture. Both in the early *Prophesy Deliverance!* and in the recent *Keeping Faith*, West, for example, describes himself as a "New World Modern African"—a label for an identity that would be possible not only for African Americans whose African ancestors were forcefully transplanted to the New World of America, but, to a large extent, modernized Africans in Africa (especially if one recognizes that there is also a New African World in Africa), as well as recent African immigrants and their "black" children scattered, thanks to the events of empire, throughout Europe and the United States. From the ambiguous resettlement of ex-slaves in Liberia through the voluntary return of Africans from Brazil to Nigeria's Lagos in the nineteenth century; from revolutionists Fanon's and Rodney's relocations to, respectively, Algeria and Tanzania in the twentieth century; or Du Bois's and Stokely Carmichael, aka Kwame Touré's self-exiles to, respectively, Ghana and Guinea; or West's current founding of "home" in Ethiopia: the identity of the modern African is marked by a history of movement and displacement. Peoples-on-the-move can best characterize an intrinsic quality of the modern African experience, even on the continent, in light of the colonial partitions and the subsequent geographical, cultural, and political dislocation of populations—and the re/formation of postcolonial identities into the Lusophone, the Francophone, or the Anglophone.[60] Africa, Europe, and the Americas have in modern times criss-crossed one another culturally, economically, and politically. The African inhabitants of any of these continents have not been insulated from the historical consequences of these transactions and they, the Africans, have in most cases been the willing agents of the movements, the cross-cultural exchanges, and the racial hybridization.

In the history of thought, major contributions to the development of modern African philosophy have been made not just by white European and American anthropologists but also by African Americans—from Langston Hughes and Alain Locke in the Harlem Renaissance to Du Bois and Padmore of pan-Africanism and, in our time, by academics Lucius Outlaw, Albert Mosley, and Leonard Harris. Historically and intellectually, therefore, there is a sense in which modern African philosophy was born out of questions concertedly posed by earlier generations of pan-Africanists, most of whom were active in the promotion of either Négritude or other "New Negro" ideologies. The cultural and intellectual history of African philosophy articulates the political and social histories of both Old World and New World "racial" Africans; it is an intellectual history out of which one could easily re/constitute a distinctively "black" modernity—or postmodernity.

By 1989 Cornel West had observed, within philosophy, the existence of "a widespread disenchantment with the traditional image of philosophy as a transcendental mode of inquiry, a tribunal of reason which grounds claims about Truth, Goodness, and Beauty," so that "the professional discipline of philosophy" was at the time "caught in an interregnum; mindful of the dead ends of analytical modes of philosophizing, it is yet unwilling to move into the frightening wilderness of pragmatism and historicism, and historiography." To the extent that this concern manifested itself as the "continental" versus "analytical" divides in European and American philosophies, it was also a concern shared by African and black philosophers, but by no means exclusively. The general climate of "disenchantment" in the establishment, however, very relevantly and fruitfully implicated the activities of Africans and blacks in terns of questions they—from Ghanaian William Amo in the eighteenth century to American Lucius Outlaw in the twentieth—had been raising all along about the philosophic traditions, regarding, in West's words, "the relation of knowledge and power, cognition and control, discourse and politics." African and black philosophers were interested in placing at the forefront debates about the "materiality of language—such as the ways in which styles of rationality and scientificality or identities and subjectivities are socially constructed and historically constituted."[61] These are debates whose relevance are far from exhausted.

In philosophy departments from Ethiopia to Ghana, Egypt to South Africa, transcendental idealism as well as the analytic traditions coexist, and neither is in danger of dying out, but these departments do take modern African and black experiences seriously as events to be interpreted and explained for purposes of African development and for a continued reproduction and promotion of various ideas about African or Afro-inspired humanities and cultures. The historical question of Africanity or blackness, more than any particular methodological or purely conceptual orientations, defines therefore what is and what is not "African" or "black" philosophy.

This concern with history makes it impossible to resist characterizing Afro-philosophical criticism as also a cultural criticism; philosophy becomes a philosophy of history, society, and culture, whereby—without neglecting other traditional philosophical issues—meanings of both Africa and black identities are debated by intellectuals, in response to the peculiar histories of black suffering and achievements in the modern world. Modern African philosophy, it seems to me, distinguishes itself by participating in putting forward creative solutions—or advancing better questions—to the perennial issues engaged in also by Western and other philosophical traditions and in explaining Africa and Africans to themselves at a particular historical moment. In an antiblack racist world, a philosophical practice committed to showing that African and black problems are also entirely human problems might appear to be a rebellious, disruptive practice. If, as it was once claimed (and is still claimed by a vocal minority) blacks do not think abstractly enough—a claim associated with a host of others, equally degrading—then, much as Hume argued centuries ago, "Negroes" could be said to be not capable of philosophical thought. The ideological nature of this form of philosophical racism cannot be said to have never tainted the current institutions and cultures of philosophy in Europe and in the United States, so that the very emergence of African or African-American philosophy in the hallowed confines of European and American academies must celebrate itself—as both a sign of recognition and principled rebellion.

Afro-philosophy's rebellious gestures often take the forms of symbolic and actual transgressions of traditional academic departmental boundaries. Richard Rorty, in remarks about one of his former students, characterized

Cornel West a few years ago as "a professor at Princeton [who] teaches in the Department of Religion rather than the Department of Philosophy," noting that "West's fellow philosophers usually regard him as Willamwitz-Möllendorf regarded the young Nietzsche, the author of *Birth of Tragedy*—as someone who has wandered so far outside his academic discipline that he no longer counts as a member of it."[62] The idiosyncratic nature of an individual philosopher's choices cannot be discounted in this example; but given other well-known cases, it is not out of place to imagine that while West's intellectual "wandering" put a distance between him and traditional academic philosophy departments, it brought him closer to the intellectual histories and political and social concerns of Africa and those of African-descended peoples in America and elsewhere. There lie the affirmative aspects of an otherwise intellectual and departmental rebellion.

Alain Locke might have been the first to establish this pattern of institutional black response to philosophy in the academy. At Howard University, where he educated many generations of African and African-American philosophers—and some of Africa's best modern political leaders, such as Nigeria's Nnamdi Azikiwe—Locke recognized that mastering the history of European philosophy was not enough to equip students for the task of understanding and explaining modern Africa or black cultures. As reported by Azikiwe, for example:

> My courses in philosophy [at Howard] were under Professor Locke. . . . He had just published *The New Negro* and he was sought after by many organizations to tell them the good news. His classroom lectures were usually dry but the substance was meaty. By delving into the various schools of philosophy I was convinced that although the western system was more systematic than the African, nevertheless African philosophy was practical in the sense that people did not waste time on frivolous arguments. Their philosophy was more pragmatic in that it was related to the practical problems of every day life which they solved by adapting themselves to the logic of reason and experience.[63]

The "everyday life" that required philosophically "pragmatic" engagements included the colonial, neocolonial, and racial experiences of Africans in Africa and blacks in the United States, and the "meaty" issues discussed by Locke must have included topics in black history, black values, black ethics, and black aesthetics.[64]

In the foreword to *The Negro and His Music*, Locke, writing in the third person, explained his own background and interests in words similar to those of his Nigerian student:

> [A]fter study at Harvard, Oxford and Berlin Universities, he has taught philosophy at Howard University since 1912, where he is professor of that subject. But avocationally, especially since editing *The New Negro* in 1925, he has been active as a literary and art critic and has become a spokesman and interpreter of the Negro's ever-increasing contribution to American culture and art. . . . [He is] more of a philosophical midwife to a generation of younger Negro poets, writers and artists than a professional philosopher.[65]

As in the case of West, is it ironic that a black philosopher who becomes interested in "Negro poets, writers and artists" might automatically start to feel himself or herself *less* than a "professional" philosopher? Which is greater: ancient philosophy's proverbial distrust of the arts, or—as we saw in chapters 2 and 3—modern philosophy's irrational prejudice against the Negro and the Negro experience?

NOTES

1. "The Future of the Negro," in *Negro Social and Political Thought, Representative Texts, 1850–1920*, ed. Howard Brotz, Part II, New York: Basic Books, 1996, p. 307.
2. See, for example, Michael Lind, *The Next American Nation*, New York: Free Press, 1995; Herbert Croly, *The Promise of American Life*, New York: Capricorn Books, 1964; Richard Rorty, *Achieving Our Country*, Cambridge, MA: Harvard University Press, 1998; and Orlando Patterson, *Rituals of Blood*, Washington, D.C.: Civitas/Counterpoint, 1998, and *The Ordeal of Integration*, Washington, D.C.: Civitas/Counterpoint, 1997.
3. Henry Louis Gates, Jr., and Cornel West, *The Future of the Race*, New York: Vintage Books, 1996, pp. xii, xvii, and xvi.
4. Douglass, "The Future of the Negro," p. 308.
5. Cornel West, *Race Matters*, Boston: Beacon Press, pp. 21–32.
6. Gates and West, *The Future of the Race*, p. xiii; my emphasis.

7. W. E. B. Du Bois, *Souls of Black Folk*, New York: Signet Classic, 1969, p. 44.

8. W. E. B. Du Bois, "Propaganda and War," in *W. E. B. Du Bois: A Reader*, ed. David Levering Lewis, New York: Henry Holt, pub date? p. 388.

9. W. E. B. Du Bois, *Souls of Black Folk*, p. 44.

10. Chinua Achebe, "African Literature as Restoration of Celebration," *Chinua Achebe: A Celebration*, Oxford: Heinemann, 1990, p. 7.

11. In Chinua Achebe, *Hopes and Impediments*, New York: Heinemann, 1984; see also his recent exploration of related themes, in an even more expanded form, in *Home and Exile* (New York: Oxford University Press, 1999).

12. Adam Hochschild, *King Leopold's Ghost : A Story Of Greed, Terror, and Heroism in Colonial Africa*, Boston: Houghton Mifflin, 1998, p. 212.

13. Ibid.

14. Olusegun Obasanjo, *Nzeogwu*, Ibadan: Spectrum Books, 1987, p. 2.

15. Sojourner Truth, "Ain't I a Woman?", in *Reflections: An Anthology of African American Philosophy*, ed. James A. Montmarquet and William H. Hardy, Belmont, CA: Wordsworth, 1999, p. 137. None of the current controversy about whether a white abolitionist helped Truth to polish this speech detracts from its rootedness in the racial experiences of this, and many, black women.

16. Hazel V. Carby, *Cultures in Babylon: Black Britain and African America*, London: Verso, 1999, pp. 67–68. The end of the passage cited included: "We cannot hope to reconstitute ourselves in all our absences, or to rectify the ill-conceived presences that invade herstory from history, but we do wish to bear witness to our own herstories. . . . What we will do is to offer ways in which the 'triple' oppression of gender, race and class can be understood, in its specificity, and also as it determines the lives of black women."

17. See Charles Mills, *The Racial Contract*, Ithaca, NY: Cornell University Press, 1998, and J. L. A. Garcia, "The Racial Contract Hypothesis," *Philosophia Africana* 14, 1 (May 2001). While I do not wish to defend Mills's thesis (it is doing well without me, thank you), I would like to point out that Garcia misreads it by taking the meaning of "contract" literally. There are universes of discourse—even moral discourse—and practice that easily draw boundaries of inclusion and exclusion, explicitly and sometimes only implicitly. Shall we conclude that such boundaries of moral sentiments do not exist, or that they never occur along racial lines?

18. Husserl, *Phenomenology and the Crisis of Philosophy*, trans. Quentin Lauer, New York: Harper, 1965, pp. 155–156.

19. Ibid., p. 149.

20. Ibid., p. 158.

21. Ibid., p. 155.

22. Ibid.

23. Ibid.

24. Edem Kodjo, *Africa Tomorrow*, trans. E. B. Khan, New York: Continuum, 1987, pp. 142–143.

25. Ibid.

26. Husserl, *Phenomenology*, p. 158.

27. Albert Memmi, *The Colonizer and the Colonized* [1957], trans. Howard Greenfeld, London: Earthscan, 1990. Recent related studies include Silvia Federici, *Enduring Western Civilization*, Westport, CT: Praeger, 1995; Etienne Balibar and Emmanuel Wallerstein, *Race, Nation, and Class*, London: Verso, 1991.

28. Memmi, *The Colonizer and the Colonized*, pp. 69–70; 71–72, passim.
29. Husserl, *Phenomenology*, p. 157.
30. Ibid., p. 68.
31. Carby, *Cultures in Babylon*, p. 1.
32. P. Olisanwuche Esedebe, *Pan-Africanism*, Washington, D.C.: Howard University Press, 1994, p. 5.
33. Paul Gilroy, *The Black Atlantic: Modernity and Double Consciousness*, Cambridge, MA: Harvard University Press, 1993, p. 16.
34. V. Y. Mudimbe, "Finale," in *The Surreptitious Speech*, ed. Mudimbe, Chicago: University of Chicago Press, 1992, p. 435.
35. Edward Wilmot Blyden, "The Call of Providence to the Descendants of Africa in America," in Brotz, *Negro Social and Political Thought*, pp. 112–139; p. 125.
36. Martin Delany, "Appendix A: Manner of Raising Funds" for "A Project for an Expedition of Adventure to the East Coast of Africa"; "The Condition, Elevation, Emigration, and Destiny of the Colored People of the United States," in Brotz, *Negro Social and Political Thought*, pp. 37–111; p. 99.
37. Wole Soyinka, *Myth, Literature, and the African World*, Cambridge: Cambridge University Press, 1972, p. xii.
38. Paget Henry, *Caliban's Reason: Introducing Afro-Caribbean Philosophy*, New York: Routledge, 2000, p. 11.
39. A recent study by the Minority Rights Group noted the well-documented impacts of the ideologies of *blanqueamiento* and *mestizaje*: "Latin American nations have long associated the loss or 'dilution' of African physical and cultural characteristics with the idea of 'progress'; hence Latin Americans have tended, both individually and collectively, to deny what is African in themselves and their culture. In numerous cases, too, countries in the region adopted policies specifically designed to achieve a physical and cultural whitening of the population" (*No Longer Invisible: Afro–Latin American Today*, London: Minority Rights Group, 1995, p. vii).
40. James Baldwin, *Notes of a Native Son*, New York: Beacon, 1964, p. 14.
41. Quoted by Blyden, "The Call of Providence," in Brotz, *Negro Social and Political Thought*, pp. 116–117, footnote.
42. Thabo Mbeki, "African Renaissance," *African Philosophy* 12, 1: 5–10.
43. See, for example, Hochschild, *King Leopold's Ghost*, New York: Houghton Mifflin, 1998.
44. Lord Lugard, *The Dual Mandate in Tropical Africa*, 5th ed., London: Archon Books, 1965.
45. Kwasi Wiredu, *Cultural Universals and Particulars*, Bloomington: Indiana University Press, 1996, p. 1.
46. Wiredu, *Cultural Universals and Particulars*, p. 1.
47. Ibid., p. 37.
48. "We need, more particularly, to reckon with norms of thought, for these have the importance of necessary conditions for the very possibility of a human community. The underlying reasoning is this: Without communication community is impossible, and without thought communication is impossible. But without some common norms of talk communication is impossible and without common norms of thought common norms of talk are unavailable" (p. 34). Further: "let us go back to the norm of non-contradiction. Of the basis of this principle we can be brief. Any universal liberties with it would be bound to be devastating to human society, for without it there would be no telling when a message is affirmed or denied, and the possibility of communication would be out of the question.

Worse, individual *human* survival would be in jeopardy, for if I cannot tell affirmation from denial in communication, neither can I tell the difference between my believing and not believing something. In other words my powers of thought, and with it my continued membership in the club of humans, would be at an end" (p. 37).

49. Ibid., p. 37.

50. For Hume's view on this issue see *Inquiry*, Bk. I, Part III, section 15, and Part I, section 5.

51. Wiredu, *Cultural Universals and Particulars*, p. 40.

52. Ibid., p. 40.

53. Ibid., p. 13.

54. Ibid., p. 20.

55. Ibid., p. 22.

56. Ibid.

57. Ibid., p. 1.

58. See Appiah's still useful article, "The Postcolonial and the Postmodern," in *In My Father's House* (New York: Oxford University Press, 1992), but in conjuction with Homi Bhabha's essay of the same title, "The Postcolonial and the Postmodern," in *The Location of Culture* (New York: Routledge, 1993).

59. In my book in progress tentatively called *A Mind of Our Own*, I advance a theory and philosophical model that I will call "modern afrohistorical reason." Until I return to that work, I will not criticize Wiredu's analytic epistemology any more.

60. Museveni, the president of Uganda, is known to have joked that he is neither Anglophone nor Francophone—because, he said, he had his own "phone." But the audience got the joke: many Ugandans suspect him of being a Tutsi, and therefore "really" a Rwandan; and the person who asked the question that evoked the joke is a foreign journalist who wanted the president to address the very comfortable relation between the governments in Kampala and Washington, D.C.

61. Cornel West, *American Evasion of Philosophy*, Madison: University of Wisconsin Press, 1989, pp. 3–4.

62. Richard Rorty, "The Professor and the Prophet," *Transition* 52 (1991): 70–78; 72.

63. Nnamdi Azikiwe, *My Odyssey*, New York: Praeger, 1970, p. 120.

64. This is a tradition continued today at Howard by philosophers such as the Nigerian Segun Gbadagesin, a symbolically not unremarkable trend in light of Locke's education of so many generations of Africans; this is pan-Africanism in practice and at its best.

65. A. Locke, *The Negro and His Music* [1936], Port Washington, NY: Kennikat Press, 1968, p. ii.

POSTSCRIPT:
TRANSCENDING RACE

As with the naming of some of my earlier books, this one had no certain title until the last moments of its composition. It started life under the name "Reason's Traces." I wished to write a historical survey of philosophical reason in modern Europe and modern Africa, with the aim of imagining what this reason might look like *apart from* its implication in racism and colonial and postcolonial capitalist modernity. I had pictured a sort of Kantian critique of modern and postcolonial reason, but one that circumvented ethnographic questions and the history of racial encounters as such and would not dwell directly on events connected with the modern geographic and political expansion of Europe. In short, I wished to study philosophic theories of reason in the Age of Enlightenment and in Africa's modernity, and thought I could succeed in the endeavor while protecting myself from a melancholic knowledge of history. In time, however, this original plan proved to be impossible, because I could not deny a prior philosophic commitment to an injunction which I considered—and still consider—perfectly reasonable, an injunction that cries out also from the work of Hegel: history is indispensable to the knowledge of philosophy.[1]

I retained the technical questions on problems of modern reason, or the reason of modernity, in the discussions of Hume and Kant. But I also turned omnivorous in my attitude to historical sources in the neighboring disciplines, especially those that address issues in African and black experiences of modernity. Cornel West once observed, about Rorty's work, that "though pregnant with rich possibilities," it remained "polemical [against other professional academics] and hence barren."[2] I suspect that polemics can sometimes ably fulfill Socratic functions, and that even the polemics addressed to an apparently closed academic club could have good societal effects; after all, the academy is itself a richly socially endowed and sometimes powerfully extended place. Instead of being "barren" and isolated from society, the best of the universities in the United States, in Europe, or in Africa are places where a larger society reproduces its effects, its history and its future, whether this be the history and future of its economy, politics, or culture. In return for the grooming services, state-supported grants and business and alumni endowments frequently and generously pour into the universities. The academy is far from a closed place, and often mirrors, warts and all, the society it serves.

To have wished to raise questions about the reason of philosophy in modern Europe and modern Africa "without the encumberance of race" was not the same as to have wished to deny current problems of race or philosophy; the formulation was meant simply to indicate a future-oriented character of an inquiry, and perhaps a wish that Western philosophy would be less encumbered by its history if, while engaging both the past and the present of race, it also focused more on participating in, and stirring up, arguments about the desirability and undesirability, the validity and invalidity of race as a commanding mechanism for fashioning future human and cultural identities. Examples abound that it is not necessary for humans to belong to a particular "race" in order to pursue and realize a socially meaningful sense of private or public humanity. The question to ask—a question whose consequences may not be merely theoretical—is whether wherever there are brownish- and pinkish-skinned Africans and Europeans and their descendants, there must also be "races." Are there ways to negotiate—in South Africa, Zimbabwe, or the United States, for example—black-white racial identities so that we can imagine a future in which race would have little or no social significance?

It wasn't until I came to the United States and England that I became black.[3] In Nigeria, I grew up believing that I belonged to the Igbo "tribe," so that when the Igbos had conflicts with other equally "tribal" groups—conflicts such as the one that led to the Biafra war of the 1960s—the language for articulating intergroup tensions and grievances was that of tribalism.

When we worked to overcome tribalism, we ideologically appealed to the national spirit: "One Nigeria!" As recently as 1993 when the vast majority of Nigerians, at home and in the Diaspora, protested the military intervention that annulled a presidential election in which Moshood Abiola had been a front-runner, the protests were framed in the language of national unity and tribal equity. It was significant to the protesters that Abiola, a Yoruba Muslim from a heavily Christian and animist culture of the south, built a winning national coalition that transcended ethnic, regional, and religious differences to encompass major and minor ethnic groups that inhabit the predominantly Muslim north, from marginal Yelwas to the powerful Hausa-Fulanis. In addition to hopes of ethnic, regional, and religious equity in national affairs, Abiola's emergence symbolized to many the coming to fruition of previous educational policies aimed at national integration. In the 1960s and the 1970s, powered by the oil boom, Nigeria pursued extensive policies of compulsory universal primary education that tracked students into multiethnic and religiously plural federal colleges and universities, culminating in a legal conscription of the graduates into a program of National Youth Service which required every graduate under thirty-three years of age to serve the nation for at least a year as a volunteer in an appropriate occupation at any region except that of one's birth. These primary and higher education policies had, among others, the goal of producing a detribalized modern citizenry, composed of individuals imbued with a national spirit who would think of themselves as Nigerians first, and only secondarily as having ethnic, religious, or regional allegiances.

This Nigerian program of national integration may sound to some as similar to the antiracist educational policies pursued in other countries and aimed at promoting racial integration. But Nigeria's "tribalism" is very different from the modern phenomenon of racism, just as the anthropologist's idea of "tribe" does not neatly overlap with the modern idea of "race."[4] People who unquestioningly consider themselves to be of the same race, for example, may at the same time never consider themselves to belong to the same tribe. This is the case with many Africans who would easily accept the proposition that all "real" Africans belong to one "black" race, but would never accept that all Africans are for that reason members of one tribe or ethnic group. Or Europeans and peoples of European descent who might characterize themselves as racially "white" or "Caucasian," but would never accept that all whites or Caucasians are for that reason members of one tribe.

The idea of tribe or ethnicity in Africa has little or nothing to do with the color of skin, eye, or hair. In Nigeria all the peoples who belong to the various tribes and ethnicities may be said to be considered racially "black" only because, as I and other Africans growing up in the modern world have discovered, one can be black—with those special and overdetermined meanings attaching to the label—without knowing or choosing it. With the exception of the very educated individuals who travel to South Africa, Europe, and the Americas, or who have read extensive literature produced by Africans and African-descended peoples in these parts of the world, Nigerians do not routinely identify themselves racially. In fact, the language of race and the vocabulary of racism as means of initiating and conducting intra- or intergroup conflicts are practically absent in most parts of contemporary Africa. With the exceptions of the Republic of South Africa, Zimbabwe, or Algeria, which have had large settlements of white populations, these observations apply to most of Africa's modern nations. Thus, despite travels in West and Central Africa where my status as "foreign" was always on display either through my physical features or inability to speak the local languages, it is outside of Africa that I learned the modern meanings of "blackness" as a racial identity.

One of the rituals I had to perform as a new graduate student at a university in New York City was the acquisition of the ubiquitous and all-American identification code, the Social Security number. The forms I was required to complete asked me to indicate which race I belonged to. I searched for "Igbo" but in vain. Instinctively, I turned over the form, looking for instructions as to a larger category under which the Nigerian Igbos might have been subsumed, but nothing prepared me for what I found: Nigerians are black all right, but not Algerians, who were categorized as white; the Sudanese are black, but not the Egyptians; and while the Zanzibarians of Tanzania are black, Libyans are white; and so forth. The table of racial classification made sense to me when I went back to my study and reread the dramatic passages at the beginning of Michel Foucault's *The Other of Things*. The opening pages of this book, you recall, began by describing a "certain Chinese encyclopedia," drawn from a story by Borges, in which it is reported that "animals are divided into: a) belonging to the Emperor, b) embalmed, c) tame, d) sucking pigs, e) sirens, f) fabulous, g) stray dogs, h) included in the present classification, i) frenzied, j) innumerable, k) drawn with a very fine camelhair brush, l) *et cetera*, m) having just broken the water pitcher, n) that from a long way off look like flies." For Foucault, "In the wonderment of this taxonomy the thing we apprehend in one great leap, the thing that, by means of the fable, is demonstrated as the exotic charm of another system of thought, is the limitation of our own, the stark impossibility of thinking *that*."[5] How can we think about the limits of our own systems of racial classifications—those structures of mind so naturalized and automatic that we usually don't even think about them at all? If we need not always have race, either in its present philosophical conceptions or in the current social and political positions that define various forms of racial identities and race relations, how did the idea itself of race, at least in our times, come to constitute itself—scientifically, socially, politically, and juridically?

For me the processes of learning the reality and the languages of race and racism have taken two different but related forms. On the one hand, as one whose interests and training are in philosophy, I sought through philosophical readings ways to understand race as I experienced it as part of modern culture. I believe that the discipline of philosophy could help one intellectually clarify some of the most subtle experiences of racial prejudices, as well as the more overt experiences of being an exotic object—the "black" who is also an immigrant. On the other hand, outside philosophy, there are fascinating studies of race in the fields of the biological sciences, historical sociology, and literature. It occurred to me, however, that a fruitful inquiry would not only seek to understand race through these academic disciplines, but also examine how the disciplines, in their various discourses, also played a part in the constitution and maintenance of the idea of race in modern political and cultural imagination. How did modern science, philosophy, in particular, participate in the invention and consolidation of the social, political, and juridical ideas of race? How could philosophy have shaped racial beliefs or historical practices of race in formal and everyday life?

The practical—as opposed to the merely theoretical—implications of this line of questioning become more obvious upon reading some of Orlando Patterson's works. In *Rituals of Blood*, for example, he noted, concerning the United States:

> In the midst of this nation of 265 million varied souls, there live some 34 million Afro-Americans, a mere 13 percent. And between them and the 208 million who are Euro-American, there is a strange dialectic, one that has its roots deep in the nation's past, one that—for all its historic savagery and prolonged perversities of repression and rape and lynching and economic exploitation and social rejection and abandonment, sometimes because of all that—links the two [groups] inextricably, obsessively, and, however paradoxical it may seem, transcendentally in a civilizational struggle that engenders the best in both groups, even as it brings out the worst in them, that creates even as it destroys, that ennobles even as it degrades.[6]

The flourish of the expression may come in the way, but one cannot but be startled at the idea that there could be an imaginary "dialectical" and "transcendental" quality to modern experiences of race either in the United States or elsewhere. It is the dialectical and transcendental aspects of our racial conceptions or racial experience that make racial discourse of interest to, and in, philosophy. Whether or not there is indeed a "civilizational struggle" between whites and blacks is a different matter[7]—and a matter that I consider debatable. I have therefore restricted myself in the current study to a more purely conceptual and philosophical interest: the idea that a *logical* form structures what is usually known as the white-black racial encounter. What is this logic? How does one philosophically explicate it?

My interests in the practical implications of the question are, however, obvious. Consider these historical observations: "The Afro-American lies at the heart of Euro-America's conception of itself as a 'race,' as a culture, as a people, and as a nation. 'Blackness' is the canvas against which 'whiteness' paints itself, the mirror in which the collective eye sees itself."[8] Thomas Jefferson's state of Virginia appears to give further credence to the argument: "Virginia, the Western world's first mass democracy since the fall of ancient Athens, was able to recreate this political miracle only in the context of the large contra-distinctive presence of slaves, who gave meaning to freedom by their own lack of freedom, and made unity among Euro-Americans possible by their very 'blackness.'"[9] Our inquiry—in chapter 2, for example—was into the conjunction of "blackness" and "slavery" in a major philosophical treatise of David Hume. The philosophical justification of this conjunction, in ways that priced the "dialectical" cost of either modern philosophical enlightenment or democracy and freedom as the enslavement of a "race" of black Africans, cannot be left to remain implicit. It is also of interest to read, as we partially do in chapters 5 and 6, the history of African and "black" responses to the peoples' modern racial experiences.[10]

Other scholars, in addition to Patterson, who thought through these themes in the contexts of historical sociology include Edmund Morgan, in *American Slavery, American Freedom: The Ordeal of Colonial Virginia*; Winthrop Jordan in *White over Black: American Attitudes toward the Negro, 1550–1812*; David Brion Davis in *The Problem of Slavery in Western Culture* and *The Problem of Slavery in the Age of Revolution 1770–1823*. There are also studies by Robert Ezra Park, *Race and Culture*; William J. Wilson, *Power, Race, and Privilege: Race Relations in Theoretical and Sociological Perspectives*. What philosophers contribute, I think, is a perspective grounded in the histories of philosophical thought in modern Europe and in Africa. Philosophy can re-mark the dialectical nature of the systems of thought that managed to articulate and sustain freedom in the modern world while degrading and expropriating in systematic ways the worldviews and cultures of individuals deemed "black," in ways that threaten to render black lives unworthy of modern freedom, responsibility, and social equality.

Of necessity, the philosophical traditions studied could not have been geographically and culturally clearly separated into "Western" and "African," or disciplinarily into philosophy and nonphilosophy. Modern African philosophy, for example, developed in dialogue with interpretations of Africans generated by non-Africans, largely in anthropology and historiogaphy.

From Négritude and critical ethnophilosophy to the schools of "professional" philosophy and critical race theory, African philosophy's interest in explaining Africa to Africans and to the world has been conducted multiculturally and across disciplinary boundaries. While philosophy should not be denied its wishes and pretensions to study in general "the human condition," it must be acknowledged that issues of most interest in human experience manifest themselves in particular historical and cultural situations. African philosophy is therefore a cultural philosophy as well as a philosophy of the modern culture—a modernity that has shown itself not to be beyond manifestations in "black" and "white."

Apart from these broad observations, however, it is wrong to expect that Western or so-called white philosophical traditions are always intrinsically racist (which is not the same as being "racialist"), or that key facets of modern African thought could not be racist. The truth is far more complex. There are strong forms of African and black responses—in the name of freedom and the dignity of the African—to the racial assaults of the modern age; but these critiques of antiblack racism in philosophy are hardly a monopoly of African philosophy. I have therefore tried to raise questions not just about philosophy's conceptual justification of race and racialism, and sometimes racism, but also its antiracist commitments. I do not believe that I was tempted to practice—as it is the vogue for some to sneer at the efforts by previously excluded women to refashion the traditions they inherit in the academy to bear witness to the history and the burden of that exclusion—resentment studies; or to practice antiphilosophy, only this time in Afro-pessimistic modes. I simply wished to contribute to ongoing conversations about the possibilities of a benevolently race-conscious critique of figures and texts in the history of philosophy, a critique through which contemporary philosophic traditions might both redeem their past misconceptions about race and Africa as well as contribute meaningfully to progressive and less mythical thinking on the subjects.

A benevolent race-conscious critique of modern European and African philosophic traditions does not deny that philosophy had been complicit in the formation and maintenance of the modern idea of race that fashions identities in Europe, America, and Africa; but it participates in the debates about means of achieving a possible postracial idea of humanity. A "postracial" philosophy of humanity therefore is not one to which race no longer matters; it does not deny that race is a factor that still plays potent and mostly damaging roles in the lives of individuals and groups historically oppressed for the sake of their race. A postracial philosophy also does not inattentively dream about a future when everyone should look alike in "gross morphology"—a utopian "natural" colorless compact. It is for us sufficient to indicate as postracial those moments, in thought and practice, where we acknowledge and work to overcome the explicit and the implicit racial social mechanisms operating to thwart opportunities for some and enhance opportunities for others. To transcend race in this modest sense of both recognition and sublation requires that disabling racial labels may no longer be forced upon individuals or groups. For although beneficial in formulating postinjury policies of redress for racially oppressed groups, racial profiling generated by racial labels does, in general, give to these groups no choice but to assume the burden of making their lives out of unattractive stereotypes—as guilty without a crime or as victims.[11] The discourse of racialism and the resulting practices of racism appear to exist predominantly to the benefit of those who claim racial superiority over others. To transcend race in the ways I think of it is therefore not an invitation to the oppressed to abandon resistance to racism, but rather a suggestion that this resistance must also be seen to include efforts to overcome the master narrative of race itself. It is to imagine a future when no one is forced into a position in which one must automatically bear the privileges or the costs of a racial tag.

NOTES

1. I am *not*, of course, referring to Hegel's Hegel, not even to Kojève's Hegel—the Hegel of "Man Is Self-Consciousness" (see Kojève, *Introduction to the Reading of Hegel*, ed. Allan Bloom, trans. James H. Nichols, Jr., Ithaca, NY: Cornell University Press, 1986). I find Jean Hyppolite's Hegel the most congenial (J. Hyppolite, *Figures de la pensée philosophique*, Paris: Presses Universitaires de France, 1971), but this is a topic for another occasion.

2. Cornel West, *The American Evasion of Philosophy: A Genealogy of Pragmatism*, Madison: University of Wisconsin Press, 1989. For Rorty's response see Rorty, "The Professor and the Prophet," in *Transition* 51(1991): 71–78.

3. Two qualifications, however, seem to be in order: first, it could be argued that race consciousness indirectly animated colonial constructions of "tribes" in many parts of modern Africa, so that "tribal" and ethnic identities such as Igbo, Tutsi, Wolof, Luo, Bantu, and so

forth were in large measure facilitated in their formations by race-conscious colonial authorities interested in promoting the benefits of their own many systems of "divide and rule." Speaking about the mechanisms of colonial rules in Africa (e.g., the "indirect rule"), Mamdani thinks that "tribes" were modes of containment of "native" populations by segregation, under cover of pre-existing or invented tribal groupings that were then severally placed under despotic native authorities (hence his description of colonial rule in many parts of Africa as "decentralized despotism"): "Defined and marked as a member of a tribe, the colonized African was more fully encapsulated in customarily governed relations than any predecessor or, for that matter, any contemporary in the colonized world. The more custom was enforced, the more the tribe was restructured and conserved as a more or less self-contained community—autonomous but not independent—as it never had been before. Encased by custom, frozen into so many tribes, each under the fist of its own Native Authority, the subject population was, as it were, containerized" (Mamoud Mamdani, *Citizen and Subject: Contemporary Africa and the Legacy of Late Colonialism*, Princeton, NJ: Princeton University Press, 1996, p. 51). The so-called native may therefore think of himself or herself as "tribed" but not "raced" only because the raciation was mediated by peculiar colonial modes of tribalization. Given the infrequency of direct contact with white colonial workers in a native authority setting, antiblack racism in an African "tribe" would be more institutionally mediated than directly experienced. Second, even so in the Nigerian example, direct experience of antiblack racism may not have been infrequent for an earlier, preindependence, generation. For example, the project of decolonization encompassed in many cities the desegregation of living quarters previously designated as government reserved areas (GRAs), where the "governments"—represented by administrators, international businessmen, and missionaries—were invariably white and European. The processes of nationalization at independence entailed the dismantling of systems of racial segregation that had prohibited Nigerians and other black Africans from owning houses in the GRAs. Accounts by older compatriots (e.g., Chinua Achebe) imply that in towns like Nsukka (where he lived and where I was raised) "native" inhabitants of a GRA might have at one time been invariably domestic servants to white expatriates.

4. In this respect, Thomas Sowell's *Preferential Policies: An International Perspective* (New York: W. Morrow, 1990), while illuminating in many of its cross-cultural analyses, fails to adequately address the peculiarity of racism in the United States, or the fact that affirmative action has been a successful policy to redress racial injuries (see also his *The Economics and Politics of Race: An International Perspective*, New York: W. Morrow, 1983).

5. Michel Foucault, *The Order of Things: An Archeology of Human Sciences*, New York: Vintage Books, 1970, p. xv.

6. Orlando Patterson, *Rituals of Blood: Consequences of Slavery in Two American Centuries*, Washington, D.C.: Civitas/Counterpoint, 1998, p. 240.

7. See, for example, Ali A. Mazrui, *Cultural Forces in World Politics* (London: J. Currey, 1990).

8. Patterson, *Rituals of Blood*, p. 240.

9. Ibid.

10. The success of D. A. Masolo's *African Philosophy in Search of Identity* is, indeed, predicated on the philosophical significance of modern Africans' search for a "racial" self.

11. For example, it cannot be denied that an ordinarily attractive stereotype such as that captured in the slogan "black is beautiful" nevertheless maintains indiscriminate regard for, and remains conceptually inadequate for specifying the details of a situation under which blackness is so affirmed. It is only white antiblack racism that gives such general and often

"blind" racial exhortations meaning and clarity. This particular exhortation is of a piece with white racial thinking prevalent in the general but confused belief which affirms but cannot qualify "white" claims to racial superiority.

Achebe, Chinua. "Colonialist Criticism." in Achebe, *Morning Yet on Creation Day: Essays.* Ibadan: Heinemann, 1977, pp. 3–18.

———. "Spelling Our Proper Name." In *Black Writers Redefine the Struggle: A Tribute to James Baldwin.* Amherst, MA: Institute for Advanced Study in the Humanities, University of Massachusetts, 1989.

———. *Things Fall Apart* [1958], New York: Doubleday, 1994.

Adickes, Rich. *Kant als Naturforscher,* 2 vols. Berlin: W. de Gruyter, 1924–1925.

Adorno, Theodor W., and Max Horkheimer. *The Dialectic of Enlightenment.* New York: Continuum, 1994.

Amadiume, Ifi. *Male Daughters, Female Husbands: Gender and Sex in African Society,* London: Zed Books, 1989.

Anonymous. *Personal Slavery Established, by the Suffrages of Custom and Right Reason. Being a Full Answer to the Gloomy and Visionary Reveries, of all the Fanatical and Enthusiastical Writers on the Subject.* Philadelphia, 1773.

Anselm, St. *Monologio.* Turino: Societá Editrice Internazionale, 1938.

———. *Proslogion.* Aberystwyth: Prisysgol Cymru, 1982.

Appiah, K. Anthony. *For Truth in Semantics.* Oxford: Basil Blackwell, 1986.

———. *In My Father's House: Africa in the Philosophy of Culture,* New York: Oxford University Press, 1992.

Appiah, K. Anthony, and A. Guttman. *Color Conscious: The Political Morality of Race.* Princeton, NJ: Princeton University Press, 1996.

Aquinas, Thomas. *Summa Contra Gentiles.* Torino, Roma: Casa Editrice Marietti, 1946.

Arendt, Hannah. *The Human Condition.* Chicago: University of Chicago Press, 1958.

———. *Kant's Political Philosophy.* Ed. Ronald Beiner, University of Chicago Press, 1982.

———. *The Origins of Totalitarianism.* New York: Harcourt Brace Jovanovich, 1973.

Ashcroft, Bill, Gareth Griffiths, and Helen Tiffin, eds. *The Postcolonial Studies Reader.* New York: Routledge, 1995.

Augstein, H. F. *Race: The Origins of an Idea, 1760–1850.* Bristol: Thoemmes Press, 1996.

Augustine, St. *Works of Augustine.* Edinburgh, 1934.

Bachelard, Suzanne. *Hommage à Jean Hyppolite.* Paris: Presses Universitaires de France, 1971.

Baier, Annette. *The Commons of the Mind.* Chicago: Open Court, 1997.

Balandier, Georges. *Ambiguous Africa*. Trans. Helen Weaver. London: Chatto and Windus, 1966.

Baldwin, James. *Notes of a Native Son*. New York: Beacon, 1964.

Balibar, Etienne. "Racism and Nationalism." In *Race, Nation, and Class: Ambiguous Identies*. Ed. Etienne Balibar and Immanuel Wallerstein. London: Verso, 1991.

Banton, Michael. *The Idea of Race*. Boulder, CO: Westview Press, 1977.

———. *Racial Consciousness*. New York: Longman, 1991.

Baran, Paul, and Paul M. Sweezy, *Monopoly Capital: An Essay on the American Economic and Social Order*. Harmondsworth: Penguin, 1966.

Barkan, Elazer. *The Retreat of Scientific Racism: Changing Concepts of Race in Britain and the United States between the World Wars*. Cambridge: Cambridge University Press, 1992.

Barzun, Jacques. *The French Race: Theories of Its Origin and Their Social and Political Implications, Prior to the Revolution*. New York: Columbia University Press, 1932.

Beattie, James. *An Essay on the Nature and Immutability of Truth, in Opposition to Sophistry and Skepticism* [1770]. Philadelphia: Solomon Wieatt, 1809.

Berlin, Sir Isaiah. *The Age of Enlightenment: The Eighteenth Century Philosophers* New York: Mentor Books, 1956.

———. *The Sense of Reality: Studies in Ideas and Their History*. Ed. Henry Hardy. New York: Farrar, Straus and Giroux, 1996.

Bhabha, Homi. *The Location of Culture*. New York: Routledge, 1994.

Blumenbach, Johann Friedrich. *On the Natural Variety of Mankind* [1775]. London: Longman, Green, 1865.

Bonaventure, St. *In Primum Librum Sententiarum*, in *Opera Omnia*, Vol. 1. Florence, 1882.

Boyle, Nicholas. *Goethe: The Poet and the Age, Vol. 1, The Poetics of Desire*. Oxford: Clarendon Press, 1991.

Bracken, Harry M. "Essence, Accident and Race," *Hermethena* (Dublin) (1973): 81–96

———. "Minds and Learning: The Chomskyian Revolution," *Metaphilosophy* 4 (July 1973).

———. "Philosophy and Racism," *Philosophia* (Israel) 8 (1978): 241–260.

Bricke, John. *Hume's Theory of Mind*. Edinburgh: Edinburgh University Press, 1980.

Brotz, Howard, ed. *Negro Social and Political Thought, 1850–1920*. New York: Basic Books, 1996.

Buffon, Georges Louis Leclerc, comte de. *Histoire naturelle générale et particuliere: avec la description du Cabinet du Roi*. 31 vols. Paris: Imprimerie Royale, 1758–1769.

Burcke, John. "The Wild Man's Pedigree." In *The Savage Within*, ed. Henrika Kuklick. New York: Cambridge University Press, 1991.

Canguilhem, George. *The Normal and the Pathological*. New York: Zone Books, 1989.

Carby, Hazel. *Cultures in Babylon: Black Britain and African American*. New York: Verso, 1999.

Cassirer, Ernst. *Kant's Life and Thought*. Trans. James Haden. New Haven, CT: Yale University Press, 1981.

———. *The Problem of Knowledge: Philosophy, Science and History since Hegel*. Trans. William H. Woglon and Charles W. Hendel. New Haven, CT: Yale University Press, 1950.

———. *Rousseau, Kant, and Goethe*. Trans. James Gutmann, Paul Oska Kristeller, and John Herman Randall, Jr. New York: Harper, 1963.

Caygill, Howard. *A Kant Dictionary*. Oxford: Blackwell, 1995.

Césaire, Aimé. *Aimé Césaire, the Collected Poetry*. Trans. and with an introduction and notes by Clayton Eshleman and Annette Smith. Berkeley: University of California Press, 1983.

———. *A voice for history/une voix pour l'histoire* [videorecording; 3 pts]. San Francisco, CA: California Newsreel, 1994.

———. *Discourse on Colonialism.* Trans. Joan Pinkham. New York: Monthly Review Press, 1973.

———. *Et les chiens se taisaient: tragédie: arrangement théâtral.* Paris: Présence Africaine, 1956.

———. *Ferrements.* Paris: Éditions du Seuil, 1960.

———. *Les Armes miraculeuses.* Paris: Gallimard, 1970.

———. *Non–Vicious Circle: Twenty Poems of Aimé Césaire.* Trans. and with an introduction and commentary by Gregson Davis. Stanford, CA: Stanford University Press, 1984.

———. *Soleil éclaté: mélanges offerts à Aimé Césaire à l'occasion de son soixante-dixième anniversaire par une équipe internationale d'artistes et de chercheurs.* Ed. Jacqueline Leiner. Tübingen: G. Narr, 1984.

———. *Tropiques.* Paris: Éditions Jean-Michel Place, 1978.

———. *Une Saison au Congo.* Paris: Éditions du Seuil, 1973.

———. *Une Tempête; d'après "La tempête" de Shakespeare. Adaptation pour un théâtre nègre.* Paris: Éditions du Seuil, 1969.

Chomsky, *Reflections on Language.* New York: Pantheon, 1975.

Cohen, William B. *The French Encounter with Africans.* Bloomington: Indiana University Press, 1980.

Columbus, Christopher. *Journals and Other Documents on the Life and Voyages of Christopher Columbus.* ed. S. E. Morison. New York: Doubleday, 1963.

Conrad, Joseph. *Heart of Darkness and The Secret Sharer.* New York: Signet Classics, 1983.

Copeland, Lewis. "The Negro as a Contrast Conception." In *Race Relations and the Race Problem: A Definition and an Analysis.* Ed. Edgar T. Thompson. New York: Greenwood Press, 1968, pp. 152–179.

Coppleston, Frederick. *A History of Philosophy*, Vol. 4. Westminster and Maryland: Newman Press, 1964.

Count, Earl W. *This Is Race: An Anthology Selected from the International Literature on the Races of Man.* New York: Henry Schuman, 1950.

Cox, Oliver. *Caste, Class and Race: A Study in Social Dynamics.* New York: Monthly Review Press, 1948.

Croly, Herbert. *The Promise of American Life.* New York: Capricorn Books, 1964.

Dathorne, O. R. *African Literature in the Twentieth Century.* Minneapolis: University of Minnesota Press, 1975.

Davis, David Brion. *The Problem of Slavery in the Age of Revolution, 1770–1823.* Ithaca, NY: Cornell University Press, 1975.

Derathé, Robert. *Rousseau et la science politique de son temps.* n.d.

Derrida, Jacques. *Of Grammatology.* Trans. Gayatri Spivak. Baltimore and London: Johns Hopkins University Press, 1976.

Descartes, René. *Discourse on Method.* Trans. Donald A. Cress. Indianapolis: Hacket, 1993.

———. *Meditations on First Philosophy* [1641]. Trans. Lawrence J. Lafleur. New York: Library of the Liberal Arts, Macmillan, 1951.

———. *Philosophical Letters.* Trans. Anthony Kenny. Oxford, 1970.

Diop, Alioune. Editorial, *Présence Africaine* 1 (November–December 1947): 1.

Douglass, Frederick. *My Bondage and My Freedom.* Ed. William L. Andrews. Urbana and Chicago: University of Illinois Press, 1987.

Eliade, Mircea. *The Sacred and the Profane*. Harvest Books, 1959.

Eribon, Didier. *Michel Foucault*. Trans. Betsy Wing. Cambridge, MA: Harvard University Press, 1991.

Estwick, Samuel. *Considerations of the Negro Cause, commonly so called, Adressed to the Right Honorable Lord Mansfield, Lord Chief Justice of the King's Bench, & C.* 3rd ed. London: J. Dodsley, 1772.

Euripides, *Bacchae*. Tran. Nicholas Rudall. Chicago: Ivan R. Dee, 1996.

Evans, Maurice. *Black and White in South East Africa*. London: Longman, Green, 1911.

Eze, Emmanuel Chukwudi, ed. *African Philosophy: An Anthology*. Masden, MA: Blackwell, 1998.

———. "The Color of Reason: The Idea of 'Race' in Kant's Anthropology." In *Anthropology and the German Enlightenment: Perspectives on Humanity*, ed. K. M. Faull. London: Buckness and Associated University Press, 1994, pp. 200–241.

———. "Out of Africa: Communication Theory and Cultural Hegemony." *Telos* 111 (Spring 1998): 139–164.

———. *Postcolonial African Philosophy: A Critical Reader*. Oxford: Blackwell, 1997.

———, ed. *Race and Enlightenment: A Reader*. Oxford: Blackwell, 1997.

Fabre, Michael. *From Harlem to Paris: Black American Writers in France, 1840-1980*. Chicago: University of Illinois Press, 1991.

Fanon, Frantz. *Black Skin, White Masks*. New York: Grove Press, 1967. [*Peau noire, masques blancs*. Paris: Éditions du Seuil, 1975.]

———. *Pour la révolution africaine: écrits politiques*. Paris: F. Maspero, 1969, reprinted 1978.

———. *Studies in a Dying Colonialism*. Introduction by Adolfo Gilly. Trans. Haakon Chevalier. New York: Monthly Review Press, 1965.

———. *The Wretched of the Earth*. Preface by Jean-Paul Sartre. Trans. Constance Farrington. New York: Grove Press, 1968. [*Les Damnés de la terre*. Paris: F. Maspero, 1968, reprinted 1978.]

Faull, Katherine, ed. *Anthropology and the German Enlightenment: Perspectives on Humanity*. London: Bucknell and Associated University Presses, 1995.

Federici, Silvia. *Enduring Western Civilization*. Westport, CT: Praeger, 1995.

Fisher, Kuno. *A Critique of Kant*. Trans. W. S. Hough. London: Swan, Sonnenschein, and Lowrey, 1888.

Flew, Anthony. *David Hume: Philosopher of Moral Science*. Oxford: Basil Blackwell, 1986.

Forte, Meyer. Preface to Bourdillon, ed., *Sacrifice*.

Foucault, Michel. *Discipline and Punish*. Trans. Alan Sheridan. New York: Vintage, 1979.

———. "Human Nature: Justice versus Power." In *Reflexive Waters: The Basic Concerns of Mankind*, ed. Fons Elders. London: Souvenir Press, 1974.

———. Introduction to George Canguilhem, *The Normal and the Pathological*. New York: Zone Books, 1991, pp. 7–24.

———. "Michel Foucault on Attica; An Interview." *Telos* 19 (Spring 1974): 154–161.

———. Notes to translation of Kant's *Anthropology*, mimeograph.

———. *The Order of Things: An Archeology of the Human Sciences*. New York: Vintage Books, 1973.

———. "Une Histoire restée muette," *La Quinzaine Littéraire* 8 (July 1, 1966).

Fox, Christopher, Roy Porter, Robert Wokler, eds. *Inventing Human Science: Eighteenth-Century Domains*. Berkeley: University of California Press, 1995.

Fox-Genovese, Elizabeth, and Eugene D. Genovese. *Fruits of Merchant Capital: Slavery and Bourgeois Property in the Rise and Expansion of Capitalism.* New York: Oxford University Press, 1983.

Franklin, John Hope, ed. *Color and Race.* Boston: Houghton Mifflin, 1968.

Freud, Sigmund. *The Standard Edition of the Complete Psychological Works of Sigmund Freud,* 23 vols. Trans. and ed. James Stratchey and Alan Tyson. London: Hogarth Press, 1927–1931.

Friedman, John Block. *The Monstrous Races in Medieval Art and Thought.* Cambridge, MA: Harvard University Press, 1981.

Garcia, J. L. A. "The Racial Contract Hypothesis," *Philosophia Africana,* vol. 4, no. 1 (May 2001).

Gates, Henry Louis, Jr., *Loose Canons.* New York: Oxford University Press, 1993.

———. ed. *"Race," Writing, and Difference.* Chicago: University Press of Chicago Press, 1986.

Gates, Henry Louis, Jr., and Cornel West, eds. *The Future of Race.* New York: Random House, 1996.

Gay, Peter. Preface to Cassirer, *Rousseau, Kant and Goethe.* Trans. James Gutmann, Paul Oskar Kristeller, and John Herman Randall, Jr. New York: Harper, 1963.

Gedan, Paul. "Physische Geographie." In Immanuel Kant, *Gesammelte Schriften.* 24 vols. Berlin: Königlich Preussische Akademie der Wissenschaften [der Deutschen Academie der Wissenschaften zur Berlin], 1900–1966.

Geertz, Clifford. *Available Light: Anthropological Reflections on Philosophical Topics.* Princeton, NJ: Princeton University Press, 2000.

Gellner, Ernest. *Nations and Nationalism.* Ithaca, NY: Cornell University Press, 1983.

Gilman, Sander. *On Blackness without Blacks: Essays on the Image of the Black in Germany.* Boston: G.K. Hall, 1982.

Gilroy, Paul. *The Black Atlantic: Modernity and Double Consciousness.* Cambridge, MA: Harvard University Press, 1993.

Goldberg, David Theo, ed. *Anatomy of Racism.* Minneapolis: University of Minnesota Press, 1990.

———. *Racist Culture: Philosophy and the Politics of Meaning.* Oxford: Blackwell, 1993.

Gorbineau, Comte de. *Essai sur l'inégalité des Races humaines.* Paris: [Firmin–Didot, 1853–1855] Belfond, 1967.

Grabbe, Christian Dietrich. *Duke Theodore of Gothland,* 1822.

Grass, Gunther. "Losses," *Granta* 42 (Winter 1992): 107.

Gregory, Stephen, and Roger Sanjek, eds. *Race.* New Brunswick, NJ: Rutgers University Press, 1994.

Harding, Sandra. "The Curious Coincidence between African and Feminist Moralities." In Eze, ed., *African Philosophy: An Anthology.* Masden, MA: Blackwell, 1998, chapter 41.

Hargrave, Francis. *An Argument in the Case of James Sommerset a Negro, lately determined by the Court of King's Bench: Wherein it is attempted to demonstrate the present Unlawfulness of domestic Slavery in England. To which is prefixed, a State of the Case.* London, 1772.

Hegel, G. W. F. *Lectures on the Philosophy of Religion.* Ed. Peter Hodgson. Berkeley: University of California Press, 1988.

———. *Lectures on Philosophy of World History.* Trans. H. B. Nisbet. Cambridge: Cambridge University Press, 1975.

———. *Phénoménologie de l'esprit*. 2 vols. Trans. Jean Hyppolite. Paris: Aubier Montagne, 1939.

Heidegger, Martin. *Basic Writings: Nine Key Essays, plus Introduction to Being and Time*. Ed. David Farell Krell. New York: Harper and Row, 1977.

———. *Being and Time*. Trans. J. Macquire and E. Robinson. New York: Harper and Row, 1962.

———. *Kant and the Problem of Metaphysics*. Trans. Richard Taft. Bloomington: Indiana University Press, 1990.

Henry, Paget. *Caliban's Reason: Introducing Afro-Caribbean Philosophy*. New York: Routledge, 2000.

Herder, Gottfried. *Letters on the Advancement of Humanity* (1793–1797), n.p.

Hobsbawn, Eric. *The Age of Revolution*. New York: New American Library, 1962.

Hochschild, Adam. *King Leopold's Ghost: A Story of Greed, Terror, and Heroism in Colonial Africa*. Boston: Houghton Mifflin, 1998.

Hountondji, Paulin. *African Philosophy: Myth and Reality*. Bloomington: Indiana University Press, 1996.

Huizinga, Johan. *The Waning of the Middle Ages: A Study of Life, Thought and Art in France and the Netherlands in the Dawn of the Renaissance*. New York: Doubleday, 1949.

Hume, David. *Essays Moral, Political, and Literary* [1777 ed.]. Ed. Eugene F. Miller. Indianapolis: Liberty Fund, 1987.

———. *On Human Nature and the Understanding*. Ed. Anthony Flew. New York: Collier Books, 1962.

———. *Letters of David Hume*. 2 vols. Ed. J. Y. T Greig. Oxford: Clarendon, 1932.

———. "Of National Character." In *Essays Moral, Political, and Literary [1777]*, ed. Eugene F. Miller. Indianapolis, Liberty Fund, 1987.

———. *The Philosophical Works*. Ed. T. H. Green and T. H. Grose. London, 1882.

———. *A Treatise of Human Nature: Being an Attempt to Introduce the Experimental Method of Reasoning into Moral Subjects*. Ed. L. A. Selby-Bigge. Oxford: Clarendon Press, 1978.

Husserl, Edmund. *Phenomenology and the Crisis of Philosophy*. Trans. Quentin Lauer. New York: Harper, 1965.

Hyppolite, Jean. *Figures de la pensée philosophique: Écrit de Jean Hyppolite (1931–1968)*. 2 vols. Paris: Presses Universitaires de France, 1971.

———. *Hegel et la pensée moderne: Séminaire sur Hegel dirigé par Jean Hyppolite au College de France (1967–1968)*. Ed. Jacques d'Hondt. Paris: Presses Universitaires de France, 1970.

———. *Hommage à Jean Hyppolite*. Paris: Presses Universitaires de France, 1971.

———. *Logique et existence: essai sur la logique de Hegel*. Paris: Presses Universitares de France, 1961.

Immerwahr, John. "Hume's Revised Racism," *Journal of History of Ideas* (1992): 3–23.

Irele, Abiola. *The African Experience in Literature and Ideology*. London: Heinemann Educational Books, 1981.

Jahneiz, Jahn. *Muntu*. New York: Grove Press, 1961.

James, C. L. R. *Black Jacobins*. New York: Vintage, 1963.

Jefferson, Thomas. *Notes on the State of Virginia*. Ed. William Peden. New York: Norton and Company, 1972.

Jospe, Alfred, ed. *Studies in Jewish Thought: An Anthology of German Jewish Scholarship.*
Detroit: Wayne State University Press, 1981.
———. *Tradition and Contemporary Experience: Essays on Jewish Thought and Life.* New York:
Schocken Books, 1970.
Julia, Didier. *La Question de l'homme et le fondement de la philosophie.* Paris: Aubier, 1964.
Julius, Anthony. *T. S. Eliot, Anti-Semitism and Literary Form.* New York: Cambridge
University Press, 1995.
Kames, Lord Henry Home. "Preliminary Discourse Concerning the Origin of Men and of
Language." In H. F. Augstein, *Race: The Origins of an Idea, 1760–1850.* Bristol:
Thoemmes Press, 1996, pp. 10–23.
Kant, Immanuel. *Anthropology from a Pragmatic Point of View.* Trans. Mary J. Gregor. The
Hague: Martinus Nijhoff, 1974. Trans. Victor Dowdell. Carbondale and
Edwardsville: Southern Illinois University Press, 1978.
———. *Critique of Judgment.* London: William Benton, 1952.
———. *Critique of Practical Reason.* Trans. Lewis White Beck. New York: Macmillan, 1993.
———. *Critique of Pure Reason.* Trans. Norman Kemp Smith. New York: St. Martin's Press,
1964.
———. *Entwurf und Ankündiung eines Collegii der physischen Geographie,* 1757.
———. *Gesammelte Schriften.* 24 vols. Berlin: Königlich Preussische Akademie der
Wissenschaften [Deutschen Academie der Wissenschaften zur Berlin], 1900–1966.
———. *Kant on History.* Ed. Lewis White Beck. New York: Macmillan, 1963.
———. *Kants philosophische Anthropologie. Nach handschriftlichen Vorlesungen.* Ed. Friedrich
Christian Starke. Leipzig, 1831.
———. *Lectures on Ethics* (1765–1766). Trans. Louis Infield, ed. Paul Menzer. London:
Methuen, 1930.
———. *Logic.* Trans. Robert S. Hartman and Wolfgang Schwarz. New York: Library of
Liberal Arts, Bobbs-Merrill, 1974.
———. *Observations on the Feeling of the Beautiful and the Sublime.* Trans. John T.
Goldthwait. Berkeley: University of California Press, 1960.
———. *Physische Geographie.* Zweiter Band, 1. Abs. 3 (IX 195); Kant-Ausgabe der
Philosophischen Bibliothek. Leipzig: n.p., 1920.
———. *Political Writings.* Ed. Hans Reiss, trans. H. B. Nisbet. Cambridge: Cambridge
University Press, 1970.
———. *Sämmtliche Werke.* Ed. G. Hartenstein. Leipzig: L. Voss, 1867.
Knox, Robert. *The Races of Men: A Fragment.* 2nd ed. London: Renshaw, 1850.
Kodjo, Edem. *Africa Tomorrow.* Trans. E. B. Khan. New York: Continuum, 1987.
Krüger, Gerhard. *Philosophie und Moral im kantischen Kritik.* Tübingen, 1931.
Lacan, Jacques. *The Seminar of Jacques Lacan, Book II.* Ed. Jacques-Alain Miller. New
York: W.W. Norton, 1995.
Lachterman, David. "Self-hood and self-consciousness: An Inquiry into Kantian Themes."
In *Essays in Honor of Jacob Klein.* Baltimore, MD: St. John's College Press, 1976, pp.
95–108.
Levinas, Emmanuel. "Intention, Ereignis und der Ander. Gesprach Zwischen Emmanuel
Levinas und Christoph von Wolzogen." *Humanismus der anderen Menschen.*
Hamburg: Felix Meiner, 1989.
Levinson, Stephen C., and Penelope Brown. "Immanuel Kant among the Tenejapans:
Anthropology as Empirical Philosophy," *Ethos* 22, 1 (March 1994): 3–41.

Lind, Michael. *The Next American Nation: The New Nationalism and the Fourth American Revolution*. New York: Free Press, 1995.

Linnaeus, Carl von. *Systema Naturae*. Editio decima tertia, Lipsiae. 1790. [*A general system of nature: through the three grand kingdoms of animals, vegetables and minerals*. Swansea: Voss and Morris for Lackington, Allen and Co., London, 1800–1801.]

Long, Edward. *Candid Reflections upon the Judgement Lately Awarded by the Court of King's Bench in the Westminster Hall on What Is Commonly Called the Negroe Cause*. London, 1772.

———. *History of Jamaica*. London, n.d.

Lovejoy, A. O. *Essays in the History of Ideas*. Baltimore, MD: Johns Hopkins University Press, 1965.

———. *The Great Chain of Being: A Study of the History of an Idea*. Cambridge, MA: Harvard University Press, 1936.

Lugard, Sir Fredrick. *The Dual Mandate in British Tropical Africa* [1922]. London: Archon Books, 1965.

———. "The Problem of Colour in Relation to the Idea of Equality," *Journal of Philosophical Studies* 1, 2 (April 1926).

Mamdani, Mamoud. *Citizen and Subject: Contemporary Africa and the Legacy of Late Colonialism*. Princeton, NJ: Princeton University Press, 1996.

Marcuse, Herbert. *Eros and Civilization: A Philosophical Inquiry into Freud*. Boston: Beacon Press, 1966.

———. *An Essay on Liberation*. Boston: Beacon Press, 1969.

———. *One-Dimensional Man*. London: Sphere Books, 1964.

Martin, Peter. *Schwarze Teufel, edle Mohren: Afrikaner in Bewus-tsein und Geschte der Deutschen*. Hamburg: Janus, 1993.

Marx, Karl. *Karl Marx: Selected Writings in Sociology and Social Philosophy*. Ed. T. B. Bottomore and Maximilian Rubel. Harmondsworth: Penguin, 1956.

May, J. A. *Kant's Concept of Geography and Its Relation to Recent Geographical Thought*. Toronto: University of Toronto Press, 1970.

Mbeki, Thabo. "African Renaissance," *African Philosophy* 12, 1: 5–10.

Memmi, Albert. *The Colonizer and the Colonized*. New York: Beacon Press, 1991.

Miller, Christopher. "Alioune Diop and the Unfinished Temple of Knowledge." In *The Surreptitious Speech*, ed. V. Y. Mudimbe. Chicago: University of Chicago Press, 1992; pp. 427–434.

———. *Theories of Africans*. Chicago: Chicago University Press, 1990.

Miller, James. *The Passion of Michel Foucault*. New York: Anchor, 1993.

Mills, Charles. *The Racial Contract: Blackness Visible: Essays on Philosophy and Race*. Ithaca, NY: Cornell University Press, 1998.

Mosse, George L. *Toward the Final Solution: A History of European Racism*. New York: Howard Fertig, 1978.

Mudimbe, V. Y. *The Idea of Africa*. Bloomington: Indiana University Press, 1994.

———. *The Invention of Africa*. Bloomington: Indiana University Press, 1988.

———, ed. *The Surreptitious Speech*. Chicago: University of Chicago Press, 1992.

Neugebauer, Christian. "The Racism of Kant and Hegel." In *Sage Philosophy: Indigenous Thinkers and Modern Debate on African Philosophy*, ed. Odera Oruka. New York: E.J. Brill, 1990, pp. 259–72.

Nisbet, Richard. *Slavery Not Forbidden by Scripture*. Philadelphia, 1773.

Norton, David Fate, ed. *The Cambridge Companion to Hume*. Cambridge: Cambridge University Press, 1993.

Nott, J. C., and G. R. Giddon. *Indigenous Races, or New Chapters of Ethnological Enquiry*. Philadelphia: Lippincott, 1857.

————. *Types of Mankind; or, Ethnological Researches*. Philadelphia: Lippincott, 1854.

Olschiki, Leonardo. "I 'Cantari dell' India' de Giuliano Dati," *La Bibliofilia* 40 (1938): 291–295.

Outlaw, Lucius. "African Philosophy: Deconstructive and Reconstructive Challenges." In *Contemporary Philosophy: A New Survey*, Vol. 5 of *African Philosophy*, ed. Guittorm Floistad. The Hague: Martinus Nijhoff, 1987.

————. *On Race and Philosophy*. New York: Routledge, 1996.

————. *Race, Ethnicity and Identity*, the Alfred P. Stiernotte Lectures in Philosophy, Quinipac College, Hamden, Conn., 1989.

Pagliaro, Harold, ed. *Racism in the Eighteenth Century*. Cleveland, OH: Press of Case Western Reserve University, 1973.

Palter, Robert. "Hume and Prejudice," *Hume Studies* 21, 1 (April 1995): 7-21.

Park, Robert E. "The Nature of Race Relations." In *Race Relations and the Race Problem: A Definition and an Analysis*, ed. Edgar T. Thompson. New York: Greenwood Press, 1968, pp. 3–45.

————. *Race and Culture*. Glencoe, IL: Free Press, 1950.

Park, Robert E., and Ernest W. Burgess. *Introduction to the Science of Sociology*. Chicago: University of Chicago Press, 1969.

Pascal, Blaise. *Pensées and Other Writings*. Trans. Honor Levi. New York: Oxford University Press, 1995.

Patterson, Orlando. *Ethnic Chauvinism: The Reactionary Impulse*. New York: Stein and Day, 1977.

————. *Freedom: Freedom in the Making of Western Culture*, Vol. 1. New York: Basic Books, 1991.

————. *The Ordeal of Integration: Progress and Resentment in America's "Racial" Crisis*. Washington, D.C.: Civitas/Counterpoint, 1997.

————. *Rituals of Blood: Consequences of Slavery in Two American Centuries*. Washington, D.C.: Civitas/Counterpoint, 1998.

Pelikan, J., ed. *Modern Religious Thought*. Boston: Little, Brown, 1990.

Penelhum, Terence. "Hume and Moral Psychology." *In The Cambridge Companion to Hume*, ed. David Fate Norton. Cambridge: Cambridge University Press, 1993, pp. 117–147.

Perham, Margery. Introduction to Sir Fredrick Lugard, *The Dual Mandate in British Tropical Africa*. 5th ed. London: Archon Books, 1965.

Pitte, Frederick van de. *Kant as Philosophical Anthropologist*. The Hague: Martinus Nijhoff, 1991.

Poliakov, Léon. *The Aryan Myth: A History of Racist and Nationalist Ideas in Europe*. London: Chatto, Heinemann, 1974.

Polo, Marco. *The Travels of Marco Polo*. Trans. R. E. Latham. New York: Penguin Classics, 1958.

Porter, Roy, and G. S. Rousseau. *The Ferment of Knowledge: Studies in the Historiography of Eighteenth-Century Science*. Cambridge: Cambridge University Press, 1980.

Popkin, Richard. "Hume's Racism," *Philosophical Forum* 9, 2–3 (1977/78): 211–226.

———. "The Philosophical Basis of Modern Racism." In *Racism in the Eighteenth Century*, ed. Harold Pagliaro. Cleveland, OH: Press of Case Western Reserve University, 1973, pp. 245–262.

Potter, Vincent, ed. *Readings in Epistemology: From Aquinas, Bacon, Galileo, Descartes, Locke, Berkeley, Hume, Kant*. New York: Fordham University Press, 1993.

Rabinow, Paul, ed. *The Foucault Reader*. New York: Pantheon, 1984.

Ramsay, James. *An Essay on the Treatment and Conversion of African Slaves*. Dublin, 1784.

Reich, Michael. "The Economics of Racism." In *Problems of Political Economy*, ed. David M. Gordon. Lexington, MA: Heath, 1971.

Ricoeur, Paul. *Freud and Philosophy*. New Haven, CT: Yale University Press, 1970.

Rorty, Richard. *Achieving Our Country: Leftist Thought in Twentieth-Century America*. Cambridge, MA: Harvard University Press, 1998.

———. *Essays on Heidegger and Others: Philosophical Papers Vol. 2*. New York: Cambridge University Press, 1991.

———. *Objectivity, Relativism, and Truth: Philosophical Papers Vol. 1*. New York: Cambridge University Press, 1991.

"The Professor and the Prophet," *Transition* 53 (1991): 71–78.

———. *Truth and Progress: Philosophical Papers*. New York: Cambridge University Press, 1998.

Rosenberg, Alexander. "Hume and the Philosophy of Science." In *The Cambridge Companion to Hume*, ed. David Fate Norton. Cambridge: Cambridge University Press, 1993, pp. 64–89.

Rousseau, Jean-Jacques. *The Confessions*. Trans. W. Conyngham Mallory. New York: Bretano, 1928. Trans. and ed. [1904], P. N. Furbank. London: David Campbell, 1992.

———. *Discourse on the Origin of Inequality*. Ed. Roger D. Masters and Christopher Kelly. Hanover, NH: University Press of New England, 1992.

———. *Essay on the Origin of Language*. Trans. John H. Moran and Alexander Gode. Chicago: University of Chicago Press, 1986.

———. *Of the Social Contract, or Principles of Political Right*. Trans. Charles Shrover. New York: Harper and Row, 1978.

Ryan, Patrick J. "Sailing beyond the Horizon," *America*, May 23, 1998.

Said, Edward. *Orientalism*. New York: Vintage Books, 1979.

Sartre, Jean-Paul. *Being and Nothingness*. Trans. Hazel Barnes. New York: Simon and Schuster, 1966.

———. *Black Orpheus*. Trans. S. W. Allen. Paris: Présence Africaine, 1963.

———. "Black Orpheus," *What Is Literature and Other Essays*, Cambridge, MA: Harvard University Press, 1988, pp. 291–330.

———. *Critique de la Raison Dialectique*. Paris: Gallimard, 1960.

———. *Existentialism and Human Emotions*. Secaucus, NJ: Philosophical Library, Carol Publishing Group, 1998.

———. "Orphée noir." In *Anthologie de la nouvelle poésie nègre et malgache de la langue française*, ed. Léopold Sédar Senghor. Paris: Presses Universitaires de France, 1948, 1969, pp. ix–xliv.

———. *What Is Literature and Other Essays*. Cambridge, MA: Harvard University Press, 1988.

Scheller, Max. *Formalism in Ethics and Non-Ethics of Value.* Trans. Manfred S. Frings and Roger Funk. Evanston, IL: Northwestern University Press, 1973.

Schultze, Fritz. *Kant und Darwin: Ein Beitrag zur Geschichte der Entwicklungslehre.* Jena: Hermann Dufft, 1875.

Senghor, Léopold Sédar. "African-Negro Aesthetics," *Diogene* 16 (Winter 1956): 23–38.

———. *Afrique africaine.* Lausanne: Clairefontaine, 1963.

———. *Anthologie de la nouvelle poésie nègre et malgache de langue française précédée de Orphée noir par Jean-Paul Sartre.* Paris: Presses Universitaires de France, 1977.

———. *The Collected Poetry.* Trans. and with an introduction by Melvin Dixon. Charlottesville: University Press of Virginia, 1991.

———. *Léopold Sédar Senghor; une étude de Armand Guibert. Avec un choix de poèmes et une chronologie bibliographique: Léopold Sédar Senghor et son temps.* Paris: P. Seghers, 1969.

———. *Les Fondements de l'Africanité ou Négritude et Arabité.* Paris: Présence Africaine, 1967.

———. *Liberté.* Vol. 1: *Négritude et humanisme*; Vol. 2: *Nation et voie africaine du socialism*; Vol. 3: *Négritude et civilisation de l'universel.* Paris: Seuil, 1964–1977.

———. "Negritude: A Humanism of the Twentieth Century." In *Postcolonial Discourse and Post-Colonial Theory: A Reader*, ed. Patrick Williams and Laura Chrisman. New York: Columbia University Press, 1994.

———. *Nocturnes.* Trans. John Reed and Olive Wake, with an introduction by Paulette J. Trout. New York: Third Press, 1971.

———. *On African Socialism.* Trans. and with an introduction by Mercer Cook. New York: Praeger, 1964.

———. *Pierre Teilhard de Chardin et le politique africaine.* Paris: Seuil, 1962.

———. *Poèmes.* Paris: Seuil, 1969, 1964.

———. *Pour une relecture africaine de Marx et d'Engels.* Dakar: Nouvelles Éditions africaines, 1976.

———. "The Psychology of the African Negro," *Diogene* 37 (Spring 1962): 1–15.

———. Serequeberhan, Tsenay. *African Philosophy: The Essential Readings.* New York: Paragon, 1991.

———. "Critique of Eurocentrism." In *Postcolonial African Philosophy*, ed. Emmanuel Eze. Oxford: Blackwell, 1996.

Sharp, Granville. *A Representation of the Injustice and the Dangerous Tendency of Tolerating Slavery; or of Admitting the Least Claim of Private Property in the Persons of Men, in England.* London: Benjamin White, 1779.

———. *The Law of Liberty, or, Royal Law, by which all mankind will certainly be judged. Earnestly recommended to the serious consideration of all slaveholders and slavedealers.* London: 1786.

Simmel, George. "The Sociological Significance of the 'Stranger.'" *Introduction to the Science of Sociology.* 3rd ed. Ed. Robert E. Park and Ernest W. Burgess. Chicago: University of Chicago Press, 1969, pp. 322–327.

Smeldley, Audrey. *Race in North America: Origin and Evolution of a Worldview.* Boulder, CO: Westview Press, 1993.

Soyinka, Wole. "The Fourth Stage through the Mysteries of Ogun to the Origin of Yoruba Tragedy." In *African Philosophy: A Reader*, ed. Emmanuel Eze. Oxford: Blackwell, 1998, pp. 438–446.

———. *Idanre and Other Poems.* New York: Hill and Wang, 1992.

——. *Myth, Literature, and the African World.* Cambridge: Cambridge University Press, 1972.

Spleth, Janice. *Léopold Sédar Senghor.* Boston: Twayne Publishers, 1985.

Starke, Friedrich Christian, ed. *Kants philosophische Anthropologie. Nach handschriftlichen Vorlesungen.* Leipzig, 1831.

Stover, Dietrich Johann Heinrich. *The life of Sir Charles Linnaeus: knight of the Swedish Order of the Polar Star, &c, &c. : to which is added a copious list of his works, and a biographical sketch of the life of his son.* London: E. Hobson for B. and J. White, 1794.

Stroud, Barry. *Hume.* London: Routledge and Kegan Paul, 1977.

Stumpf, Samuel Enoch. *Socrates to Sartre: A History of Philosophy.* 4th ed. New York: McGraw-Hill, 1988.

Suyin, Han. "Race Relations and the Third World," *Race: The Journal of the Institute of Race Relations,* 13, 1 (July 1971): 1–20.

Szasz, Thomas "The Sane Slave: A Historical Note on the Use of Medical Diagnosis as Justificatory Rhetoric," *American Journal of Psychotherapy* 25 (1971): 233–239.

Talmor, Ezra. *Descartes and Hume.* Oxford: Pergamon Press, 1980.

Tempels, Placide. *Bantu Philosophy.* Paris: Présence Africaine, 1959.

Thompson, Edgar T., ed. *Race Relations and the Race Problem: A Definition and an Analysis.* New York: Greenwood Press, 1968.

Thorndike, E. L. *Notes on Child Study. Its psychology and its relations to physiology, anthropology, sociology, sex, crime, religion, and education.* 2 vols. New York: Macmillan, 1903.

——. *Individuality.* Boston, 1911.

Todorov, Tzvetan. *On Human Diversity: Nationalism, Racism, and Exoticism in French Thought.* Cambridge, MA: Harvard University Press, 1993.

——. *Utur stubbotan rot: essaer till 200-arsminnet av Carl von Linnes dod.* Stockholm: Norstedt, 1978.

Truth, Sojourner. "Ain't I a Woman?" In *Reflections: An Anthology of African American Philosophy,* eds. James A. Montmarquel and William H. Hardy. Belmont, CA: Wordsworth, 1999.

Vaillant, Janet G. *Black, French, and African: A Life of Léopold Sédar Senghor.* Cambridge, MA: Harvard University Press, 1990.

Vico, Giambattista. *The New Science.* New York: Doubleday, 1961.

Vincent of Neauvais. *Speculum Naturale.* Douai, 1624.

Weber, Max. *From Max Weber: Essays in Sociology.* Ed. and trans. H. H. Gerth and C. Wright Mill. New York: Oxford University Press, 1958.

——. *The Protestant Ethic.* New York: Scribner's, 1958.

Wehrs, Donald R. "Colonialism, polyvocality, and Islam in l'aventure and Le devoir de violence," *MLN,* John Hopkins University Press, December 1992, volume 107.

West, Cornel. *The American Evasion of Philosophy: A Genealogy of Pragmatism.* Madison: University of Wisconsin Press, 1989.

——. *Keeping Faith: Philosophy and Race in America.* New York: Routledge, 1993.

——. *Prophesy Deliverance! An Afro-American Revolutionary Christianity.* Philadelphia: Westminster Press, 1989.

——. *Race Matters.* Boston: Beacon Press, 1993.

William, Howard Lloyd, ed. *Essays on Kant's Political Philosophy.* Chicago: University of Chicago Press, 1992.

Williams, Bernard. "Where Chomsky Stands," *New York Review of Books*, Nov. 11, 1976, pp. 43–45.

Williams, Forest. "Anthropology and the Critique of Aesthetic Judgement," *Kant Studien* 46 (1954–1955).

Williams, Patrick, and Laura Chrisman. *Postcolonial Discourse and Post-Colonial Theory: A Reader.* New York: Columbia University Press, 1994.

Wilson, William Julius. *The Declining Significance of Race: Blacks and the Changing American Institutions.* 2nd ed. Chicago: University of Chicago Press, 1978.

———. *Power, Racism, and Privilege: Race Relations in Theoretical and Sociohistorical Perspectives.* New York: Macmillan, 1973.

———. *The Truly Disadvantaged: The Inner City, the Underclass, and Public Policy.* Chicago: University of Chicago Press, 1987.

———. *When Work Disappears: The World of the New Urban Poor.* New York: Alfred Knopf, 1996.

Winthrop, Jordan. *White over Black: American Attitudes toward the Negro, 1550–1812.* Chapel Hill: University of North Carolina Press, 1968.

Wiredu, K. (J. E.). "How Not to Compare African Thought with Western Thought." In *African Philosophy: An Introduction*, ed. Richard Wright. 3rd ed. New York: University Press of America, 1984.

Wright, Richard, ed. *African Philosophy: An Introduction.* 3rd ed. New York: University Press of America, 1984.

Young, Robert J. C. *Colonial Desire: Hybridity in Theory, Culture and Race.* New York: Routledge, 1995.

Zahar, Renate. *Frantz Fanon: Colonialism and Alienation.* New York: Monthly Review Press, 1974.

INDEX